# Atlantic Nightmare

The longest continuous military campaign of World War

Richard Freeman

'I don't think it is even faintly realised the immense, impending revolution which the submarines will effect as offensive weapons of war.' – *Admiral Lord Fisher, 10 April 1904.*

This print edition is published by the author. Printed by KDP. Available from Amazon.com and other book stores. A Kindle version of this book is published by Endeavour Media Ltd.

ISBN: 9781792966729

Maps are based on those in *The Battle of the Atlantic,* HMSO 1946.

**Other books by Richard Freeman**

*The Great Edwardian Naval Feud*. Pen and Sword 2009.

*Admiral Insubordinate*. Endeavour Press 2013; Sharpe Books 2018.

*Unsinkable': Churchill and the First World War*. History Press 2013.

*Tempestuous Genius*. Endeavour Press 2015; Sharpe Books 2018.

# Contents

Ships' weights are given in gross tons.

Gross tonnages, cargo weights and tonnages sunk have been rounded for ease of reading.

Times, except in quotations, are given in twelve-hour format.

# Preface

No battle lasted longer than the 2075 days of the Battle of the Atlantic. Few battles are so apparently perplexing in their outcome. There was nothing in the dark days of September 1939 to February 1943 to suggest that the Allies could defeat the U-boat menace. Yet two months later the U-boats were tamed.

This book explores the tactics and strategy of the two sides and reveals how consistently admirals Raeder and Dönitz pursued ill-chosen strategies for the U-boat war. Central to their failure were their seven strategic errors. These are summarised at the end of the book. The analysis justifying this list is presented in the book itself.

A glossary of technical terms also appears at the end of the book.

# Part 1: Skirmishes

## 1 Convoy *SC-7*

### October 1940

The steam ship *Trevisa* was a mere 1800 tons. A negligible spot on the vast Atlantic Ocean. She had been built in Londonderry in 1915 and had peacefully ploughed the seas since then. On the night of 16 October 1940 she was just one of 35 merchant ships in Convoy *SC-7*. They had departed from Sydney, Nova Scotia, 11 days earlier. Six days out, the convoy had run into a fearsome gale. *Trevisa* was one of several ships that fell behind – an unprotected straggler.

The huge convoy covered five square miles of sea. At its centre were three columns of five ships. To either side were two columns of four ships. At the head of the centre column was Vice Admiral Lachlan Mackinnon, the convoy commodore. Mackinnon had already guided eleven convoys across the ocean before his command of the fateful *SC-7*. He had entered the navy in 1898 and seen action during the First World War, including at the Battle of Dogger Bank and the Battle of Jutland. His last post before retiring in 1939 as vice admiral had been as commander of the Second Battle Squadron. Along the way, he had been honoured by the Turkish Navy in 1911 and awarded the Legion of Honour by the French government in 1919. None of this had prepared him for what was now to come.

Mackinnon had taken up command of the convoy in the *Assyrian*, which was carrying 3700 tons of grain. (Convoy commodores usually selected one of the larger and faster ships to carry them in a particular convoy.) Strict radio silence meant that Mackinnon had to herd his 35-strong convoy by flags and aldis lamps. For this, he had with him his trusted team of five naval sailors. All his commands would be executed by his yeoman signaller and his two telegraphists. The flags themselves would be run up by his two young bunting tossers.

*Convoy SC-7 from HMS Vanity, October 1940*

'SC' stood for 'slow convoy'. The ships were weighed down by their bulk-cargoes of grain, coal, timber and steel. With favourable seas, 'slow' meant about eight knots. But *Trevisa*, with her 460 standards of timber, could not keep up. Her master, Robert Stonehouse, and his crew of 20 must have foreseen their fate as they slipped further and further behind. It came at 3.50 am. A single torpedo from *U-124* struck the struggling *Trevisa* aft. Stonehouse was unaware that Korvettenkapitän Georg-Wilhelm Schulz had fired on his vessel the previous evening. But Schulz – who would prove to be a U-boat ace – had doggedly tracked the *Trevisa* through the night. This was his fourth sinking of the war. Another 15 would follow.

The loss of the *Trevisa* was a small-scale event. Even the human cost was not as bad as it might have been. Stonehouse and 13 of his seamen were picked up by the corvette HMS *Bluebell* and taken safely back to Gourock in Scotland. But her sinking was part of a much greater tragedy. Convoy *SC-7* was no ordinary convoy. It was to prove to be one of the most deadly of the war.

One reason for the massacre of Convoy *SC-7* was its inadequate escort. The 1000-ton sloop HMS *Scarborough*, described by the war hero Captain Donald Macintyre as 'a lightly-armed warship designed for peacetime police work on distant foreign stations', was the sole escort for the first three-quarters of the convoy's passage. Her commander, Norman Dickinson, was a career naval officer; who had held that rank since 1936. The tragedy that was to come was no fault of his. Indeed he was to end the war much decorated and with the rank of captain. The odds, though, were overwhelmingly against the convoy from the moment it had set sail in so ill-protected a manner.

It was now 17 October. The convoy was nearly home. Dickinson was relieved to see the sloop HMS *Fowey* and the corvette HMS *Bluebell* taking up station alongside *Scarborough*. But even with this reinforcement the escort was still perilously thin. The escorts stood six miles apart. As Dickinson well knew, the gaps were more than wide enough for a U-boat to sneak through unseen.

Unknown to Dickinson, the ace U-boat commander Heinrich Bleichrodt in *U-48* had found the convoy on 16 October. Bleichrodt's prompt signal to Admiral Karl Dönitz in Lorient ensured that a wolf pack would soon be gathering ahead of the convoy. Meanwhile *U-48* went hunting alone. Bleichrodt's first victim was the 9500-ton tanker *Languedoc*. She was an easy target. A single torpedo slammed into her. Thinking that he had dealt with the tanker, Bleichrodt turned away to seek more prey. But, severely damaged as she was, *Languedoc* failed to sink. Her commander, John Thomson, called for assistance from *Bluebell*. Thomson and his 38 seamen boarded the corvette and four days later were safely landed at Gourock. It was left to *Bluebell* to sink *Languedoc* by gunfire.

Bleichrodt's second torpedo sank the 4000- ton *Scoresby*, loaded with 1700 fathoms of pit props, desperately needed for Britain's coal mines. Once more, the nearby *Bluebell* moved in to rescue the crew. A few hours later another straggler, the 3500-ton Greek-owned *Aenos,* was shelled and sunk by *U-38*. Her crew, drifting in open boats in the empty ocean, thought that their last hours had come. But they were to be amongst the luckiest of all the many victims of this horrendous convoy. Along came a fellow-straggler – the Canadian steamer *Eaglescliffe Hall* – and pulled the men from the water.

Mackinnon had had a busy day directing his escort vessels in their rescue work and keeping the convoy in formation. The attacks and sinkings were regrettable, but not out of line with what he had come to expect. But the convoy was nearing the dangerous Western Approaches – the U-boat's favourite hunting ground at this stage of the war. During the next three nights the wolf packs would be out, searching for their prey. And, however spread out convoys were in the vastness of the Atlantic, they were compelled to converge as they neared port. That made them easier targets for the U-boats to locate. At least, though, the convoy now had the additional protection of *Fowey* and *Bluebell*.

Mackinnon was relieved when dawn broke on 18 October. There were just three more sailing days to port and he had only lost three of his 35 vessels. Unknown to him, Dönitz had six U-boats within a day's sailing of the convoy. As darkness fell that evening, *U-48* was joined by *U-101* (ace commander Fritz Frauenheim), *U-46* (Engelbert Endrass), *U-123* (ace commander Karl-Heinz Moehle), *U-99* (ace commander Otto Kretschmer), *U-100* (ace commander Joachim Schepke) and *U-38* (ace commander Heinrich Liebe). It was one of the most formidable gatherings of U-boat commanders of the war. Not even the latest escort arrivals – the sloop HMS *Leith* and the corvette HMS

*Heartsease* – could make the slightest difference to the gruesome onslaught that was to come.

On the previous day *Scarborough* had made a vigorous attempt to chase and sink *U-48*. By the time she broke off from her unsuccessful hunt, she was well-separated from the convoy. It was not until 1.15 am on 18 October that she finally caught up with the merchant ships. Nineteen minutes later the sky was lit up by red Very lights from somewhere in the convoy. Almost immediately a signal reached Mackinnon to say that a ship had been hit. At 1.45 am Dickinson heard a loud explosion. He turned *Scarborough* 90 degrees to port to search across the convoy's rear for ships in peril. Dickinson expected to find two vessels but found only the 3500 ton *Carsbreck*, weighed down by her 6000 tons of iron ore. She was badly damaged but afloat. With more immediate crises to attend to, Dickinson returned to the convoy. It was not until 6.10 am that he decided that the limping 6 knot *Carsbreck* should be pulled out of the convoy. He ordered *Heartsease* to escort her back to port. Seven ships were sunk that night and four damaged. The hopelessness of Dickinson's situation in escorting such an inadequately protected convoy is clear from his report that night. The *Carsbreck* was the only vessel that he knew to have been hit. He heard unidentified explosions in the dark. He saw Very lights in the sky. But he knew no more than that.

When dawn brought a pause in the battle, Dickinson noted 'Sighted convoy'. He made no mention of how little there was of it or what condition it was in. At least, though, there would be no more attacks until dark. Shortly after midday he saw two rafts. *Scarborough* and *Bluebell* began a search and soon found the master and 18 seamen from the *Nora*, an Estonian cargo ship from another convoy, hit on 13 October by *U-103*.

During the day the convoy altered course, but to no avail. At 8.20 pm the first ship of the night was struck by a torpedo. Then the futility of Dickinson's situation returned as he watched the Very lights and heard the explosions. A typical section of his report runs:

> 22:05 - Sighted two horizontal red lights then some miles ahead. They burnt for about 15 seconds. Heard explosion ahead.

> 22:10 - Heard explosion ahead.

> 22:20 - Heard explosion ahead. Increased to 15 knots and sighted several ships.

> 22:37 - Heard two explosions ahead.

Then, suddenly:

> 22:40 - Sighted a "U" boat on surface straight ahead steaming fast on the same course. Distance 3000-4000 yards.

At last Dickinson could attack. *Scarborough's* guns went into action as she chased the glistening wake of the U-boat. But the boat speedily submerged. It was time for the asdic to take over. The U-boat was at a range of 3000-yards but the signal was clear. Dickinson ran in to within 800-yards. And then, mysteriously, the contact was lost. He called *Bluebell* to join the hunt and they searched for an hour. At this point Dickinson seems to have given up as a tanker exploded nearby and four torpedoed ships were in urgent need of help. He left *Bluebell* to pick up survivors from *Empire Miniver, Gunborg, Niritos* and *Beatus,* and returned to the convoy at 16 knots.

Ordinary Seaman Edward King was the only man to survive the attack on the 5000-ton *Fiscus*. He was lying dozing in his bunk when a violent explosion shook the ship and it took a heavy list to starboard. By the time King reached the deck the ship was rapidly taking on water. With no boats or rafts in sight he grabbed a rope attached to a loose packing case. The case had a life of its own as it carried him out to sea. King looked back to see a swirling mass of debris in the turbulent sea. Of his ship, there was not a trace. Two hours later, drifting aimlessly in the dark, he came across three Indian firemen, clinging to a refrigerator. They joined him to sit on top of the crate. The *Fiscus* had gone down at 23.55 hours on 18 October 1940. It was not until sometime on 21 October that the packing case floated towards a heavily loaded lifeboat. By this time the firemen were dead. An exhausted King was hauled on board to endure a further three days and nights on the open sea before being picked up by HMS *Clematis*.

When the enemy action recommenced at 0.28 am on 19 October Dickinson saw flashes on the horizon. Half-an-hour later he was able to identify the ship: *Blairspey*. The 4000-ton vessel, loaded with Grangemouth-bound timber, had been hit by a torpedo from *U-101*. She was damaged but afloat and was left to fall behind the convoy. There, she was torpedoed for a second time on the following day, this time by *U-100*. Neither attack succeeded in inflicting fatal damage. Taken in tow, *Blairspey* was beached on the Clyde five days later. She was back at sea in February 1942 and survived the war to retire in 1967.

By now the drama had switched to the commodore's ship. At around 1.22 am a torpedo from *U-101* had struck *Assyrian*. By 1.45 am she was reported to be slowly sinking. Admiral Mackinnon was amongst the last to leave the vessel. All he and his companions had for their survival was an improvised raft, which broke up on hitting the water. Later, the 58-year-old man was found clinging to a plank. By the time that he was hauled up onto the deck of *Scarborough* he was in a bad way. Pneumonia set in. Although Mackinnon survived, his health never returned to the point where he could sail again.

By 9.55 am on 20 October the battle was over. With relief, Dickinson recorded '09:55 - Sighted tug'. His last entries of that day – written in HMS *Scarborough* – record the winding down of the nightmare convoy:

> 14:30 - Sighted *Heartsease* escorting the damaged *Carsbreck*.
> Also sighted three other ships of convoy which I then
> proceeded to escort. The weather had been deteriorating all
> day and was now wind SE, force 8, overcast with rain squalls
> and low visibility.

16:10 - Distant rumbling explosion heard clearly between decks.

16:40 – Ditto.

22:15 - *Indian Star* joined me.

04:00 - Lost touch with ships in company in low visibility to Eastward of Altercarry [light].

*Scarborough* berthed at 8:30 am on 21 October alongside Princess Pier in Liverpool and disembarked the survivors. It was Trafalgar Day but there was no victory to celebrate.

The toll for 19 October was nine ships sunk and two damaged. This brought the total toll from *SC-7* to 20 out of 35 ships sunk. The catastrophe was a shock to the Admiralty. The Royal Navy had been confident that its greatest technological development of the First World War – asdic – would deliver the U-boats to the destroyers. But in the Battle of Convoy *SC-7* asdic had proved useless. Indeed, to put it more bluntly, the escorts had been useless. If this was the best that the Royal Navy could do, then the war was lost.

This book is the story of how the Allies rose from the nadir of the 16-19 October 1940 to defeat the U-boats three years later. It is a story of how the skills of resolute men and women, harnessed to dazzling technology and guided by brilliant strategy turned hapless escorting into precision hunting.

But first we must go back a little to ask how it was that the Royal Navy was so ill-prepared for war. What had gone wrong? For this we need to begin with the events of 28 June 1919.

# 2 Permission to build

## 1919 to 1939

### The Versailles Treaty 1919

On 28 June 1919 hundreds of dignitaries from around the world elbowed their way into the Hall of Mirrors at Versailles near Paris. The prime ministers and presidents of the victorious powers in the Great War fought their way to their places at the central table. In the chair was the 78-year-old Georges Clemenceau, the Prime Minister of France. Clemenceau had been on the sidelines in the war as Justice Minister until France was on the verge of collapse in November 1917. While those around him broke under the strain, he seized the premiership. As the man who had taken France to victory, he savoured the revenge of this day as he lived up to his nickname of 'the Tiger'.

Clemenceau called for silence in the packed hall, but the excited onlookers babbled on. At last the troublesome bystanders quietened.

'Bring in the Germans,' said Clemenceau in a demanding tone.

Two ushers, weighed down by silver chains, opened the great doors. By now the silence was one of fearful anticipation at the nature of the imminent historic act. Two men, heads pitiably bowed, were led in by four officers of the victorious powers: France, Great Britain, America and Italy. The wretched men were the German delegates: Dr Muller and Dr Bell. They were here to sign the Treaty of Versailles. They signed first. Then, one by one, the plenipotentiaries of the victorious powers signed. Before the signing was even finished, the windows of the great hall angrily vibrated as cannons in the gardens blasted out a victory salute and the Versailles fountains sprang into gushing life. The whole ceremony had taken a mere 23 minutes. The *Observer* newspaper correspondent described the event as 'curiously unimpressive' but nevertheless declared it to have been 'one of the greatest events in history'.

The Great War, as it was then known, was over. The German forces were reduced to a token. It was peace at last.

*The signing of the Treaty of Versailles in 1919. It sensibly banned Germany from possessing submarines.*

The Treaty of Versailles ran to 440 articles and several protocols. We shall confine ourselves to just two articles. First, Article 188, which required Germany to hand over all her submarines to the victorious allies and to destroy any boats still in construction. Then there were the severe limits placed on her surface fleet by Article 181. She was permitted to keep in commission six battleships of the *Deutschland* or *Lothringen* type, six light cruisers, twelve destroyers and twelve torpedo boats. All her other warships had to be placed in reserve or turned over to commercial operations. Since *Lothringen* was an obsolete pre-*Dreadnought* battleship, launched in 1904, the concessions within the Treaty amounted to very little. The German Navy was to be a navy too small to threaten anything more than an inland country with only a few paddle-steamers to defend itself.

But the limitations on Germany's capital ships were a sideshow compared to the one total prohibition: no submarines. By the end of the First World War the torpedo had become the principal means of naval attack. Germany's 351 U-boats had sunk over 5000 Allied merchant vessels. Now, in 1919, with no submarines, Germany was denied any possibility of exercising naval power beyond coastal patrols. From the British point of view the 'no submarines' restriction was her best guarantee of her security. Germany's U-boats had brought Britain to the verge of starvation in 1917. That was something the British were determined not to allow again.

In the light of this, what happened sixteen years later is astounding.

### The 1935 Anglo-German Naval Agreement

In November 1934 the German Ambassador in London, Leopold von Hoesch, presented the British Foreign Secretary with a brazen request. The German Führer, Herr Hitler, wished to enter into talks with the British government with a view to expanding the Germany Navy.

Samuel Hoare had only been in office as Foreign Secretary for 14 days when he received this request. Hoare was a man who trusted his own judgement. Casting aside the Versailles Treaty, he wrote to tell the German Ambassador that he had 'much pleasure' in confirming that Britain was willing to allow Germany to build warships.

The two countries immediately entered into conversations which led to the 1935 *Anglo-German Naval Agreement*. Germany was given permission to build a navy up to 35 per cent (by tonnage) of the size of the Royal Navy. The submarine clauses were more complicated, limiting German output to 45 per cent of the Commonwealth tonnage, but effectively the clauses gave Hitler permission to build to any limit he chose. All he had to do was to give notice and enter into 'friendly discussions' with Britain. No wonder that on the day of the signing, Hitler told Admiral Raeder that, 'Today is the happiest day of my life.'

*Sir Samuel Hoare MP, who blithely acceded to Hitler's desire to build submarines and warships.*

Winston Churchill, then a backbench Member of Parliament, made a powerful attack on the agreement in the Commons in July 1935. He homed in on Germany's desire to build submarines. He declared: 'If we are to assume … the hideous hypothesis of a war in which Britain and Germany would be on opposite sides … who in his senses would believe that the Germans, possessed of a great fleet of submarines … would abstain from the fullest use of that arm? Such a view seems to me to be the acme of gullibility.' But Churchill was in his wilderness years. No one paid the least attention to this yesterday's man.

The Battle of the Atlantic was born in this moment when the country ignored Churchill's astute warning.

### Raeder's fleet

The fleet that Germany was to build as a result of the agreement was the work of Admiral Erich Raeder. In proposing his massive shipbuilding programme to Hitler, he declared, 'The scale of a nation's world status is identical with the scale of its sea power.'

Born in 1876, the first influence on Raeder's life had been his father. As an authoritarian headmaster and a zealous church-goer, Hans Raeder dominated the household. He conducted family prayers, and sternly instilled 'the fear of God, love of truth, and cleanliness' into his three sons. Not surprisingly, the young Erich who joined the Imperial Navy in 1894 was a cold, austere and hard-working individual.

After his father, the next great influence on Raeder was Admiral Franz von Hipper. Raeder became Hipper's chief of staff when the latter took over command of the Imperial German Navy's scouting forces just before the First World War. Hipper was arguably the most talented sea-going admiral in that war. He was energetic, impulsive and hard-working, preferring life on his ship to the camaraderie of shore-based socialising. It was with Hipper at the Battle of Dogger Bank (1915) and the Battle of Jutland (1916) that Raeder honed his skills in big-ship work.

After the war, Raeder opposed the growing demand for democracy in Germany but nevertheless rose to be Commander-in-Chief of the Reichsmarine, the Weimar Republic's navy, in 1928. Although he despised the Republic, he clung to his post. When Hitler came to power in 1933 he kept Raeder at the head of the newly-named 'Kriegsmarine'.

And so began Germany's great fleet-building programme. Around the mid-1930s German war games concentrated on an attack on Poland. These revealed the importance of keeping French warships out of the Baltic Sea. For that,

Germany chose pocket battleships to draw off the French Navy into the Atlantic. Building work began on that basis. Three years later the gaming was still going on, but it now showed Britain to be a greater threat than France. It was too late to construct a navy powerful enough to take on the formidable Royal Navy. In any war with Britain, British merchant vessels would have to be the target. That meant building U-boats in great numbers. But few were built in those pre-war years. It is in Hitler that we find the explanation for this surprising omission.

Hitler, like Napoleon, never understood nor took much interest in naval warfare. Nor did he appreciate the importance of the seas to Britain. He clearly had little idea as to why he needed a navy or what type of navy that should be. But his crucial error (much to the advantage of the Allies) was his promise to Admiral Raeder that war with Britain would not start until 1944 at the earliest. This left Raeder free to build a huge navy over a long period, without the impediment of any imminent entanglements. His 'Z-Plan' proposed a 1944 navy of over 200 surface vessels. These were to include 10 battleships, 15 pocket battleships and four aircraft carriers.

But that long building period vanished when Hitler prepared for an early war. By 1938 it was clear that the Kriegsmarine had neither a surface fleet that could challenge the Royal Navy, nor a U-boat fleet that could sink the British merchant fleet. And, even if Hitler had delayed war until 1942, Raeder's navy would still have been only 35 per cent complete.

One man alone was undaunted at the prospect of a naval war without a large surface fleet: Karl Dönitz. But as a mere captain of submarines, no one asked him for his opinion. Battleships were the priority. U-boat building would have to make do with the crumbs.

In summary, Hitler's naval preparations for a war that he was determined on fighting were incoherent and chaotic. By choosing to go to war in 1939 rather than the 1944-46 that he had promised Raeder, his surface fleet was ill-prepared to take on the Royal Navy. Of the Z-Plan's great vessels, only four of the battleships were ever completed. Even so the struggle to build capital ships set back the U-boat programme. When war came on 3 September 1939, Rear Admiral Dönitz had just 57 sea-ready U-boats at his command. Of these, only 21 were ocean-going boats. And he was to lose nine of his boats by the end of the year.

*Grand Admiral Erich Raeder inspecting a shipbuilding yard in 1942.*

But the Reich was not the only country that had been neglecting its fleet.

*An ageing fleet*

The signing of the 1935 naval agreement stirred the indolent British Prime Minister Stanley Baldwin into belated action. In 1932 he had famously and fatalistically said, 'The bomber will always get through.' Now awakened to the threat across the English Channel, he announced a policy U-turn. The country was going to rearm in response to Germany's rapid build-up of its forces. Both money and time were short, so the government's rearming was to concentrate on air defence. Britain, said Baldwin, 'is an easy target for cross-Channel air raids'. There was now a belated rush to rearm in the face of shortages of every imaginable war material. The government initiated a hasty plan to build factories, to make or acquire machine tools and to train workers. The first call on these resources was the Royal Air Force. Even Baldwin's government accepted that, before anything else, Britain had to retain air superiority over its skies. Something had to give, and that was escort ship construction. Meanwhile the early war budgets prioritised a 55-division army and a large air force. In addition, resources were needed to build 1.5 million tons of merchant shipping a year.

Once war came the destroyer shortage was to prove to be the Royal Navy's weakest point. But the navy as a whole had been badly neglected between the wars. In the year following the 1935 Treaty Britain had only 15 capital ships yet had not one new one under construction. On the other hand, in the first year of the First World War Britain had had 68 capital ships and was building a further 12. Destroyer numbers showed a similar neglect: there had been 322 in 1914-1915 but by 1936 there were only 169.

The government came to its senses in 1936 when the decision was made to return to the 'Two Power Standard' that had been abandoned after the First World War. Once more the Royal Navy was to be the equal of the combined navies of Germany and Japan. Within a year Britain's shipbuilding yards had full order books. By 1939 the yards were working on nine battleships, six aircraft carriers, 25 cruisers, 43 destroyers and 19 submarines.

Nor must we forget the pre-war weakness of the other navy that was to play major role in the Atlantic battle: the Royal Canadian Navy. It started the war with only six destroyers and 3843 officers and men, but rapidly increased to 90,000 officers and men (of which just three per cent were regulars) and 400 warships.

# 3 War fever

## August 1939

### *U-boats to their war stations*

On 15 August 1939 the U-boat headquarters buzzed with activity as telephones rang, teleprinters clattered and messengers rushed from desk to desk. The U-boats were to be ordered to their war stations. The 6th Flotilla was recalled from firing practice; *U-57* was recalled from Pillau (now Baltiysk); and *U-47* from Neustadt. The 7th Flotilla was ordered to prepare for an emergency North Sea exercise.

This early deployment of the U-boats was critical to Dönitz's chances of success. Without Atlantic bases, every warship and U-boat had to sail from German bases in the North Sea and the Baltic Sea to run the gauntlet of the Channel or that of the passage past the North of Scotland. The first of these passages – the Channel – was cut off six days later when British warships began laying a mine barrage across the Strait of Dover. From then on, the only reasonably feasible passage from the German ports to the oceans was the long arc past the Shetland and Faroe Islands.

Dönitz prepared his mobilisation in the utmost secrecy. There were to be no signals to U-boats that might be intercepted. Instead he recalled those boats that were at exercise and gave his orders personally to each commander.

His initial deployment sent the eastern part of his fleet to the Baltic Sea in preparation for Hitler's attack on Poland. Five days later the North Sea and Atlantic boats were given their orders. Britain's access to the Atlantic was soon sprinkled with 21 U-boats ready for action.

Once at sea, Dönitz's commanders received their war orders. In comparison to what was to come they were surprisingly mild. Instead of an all-out sink-on-sight policy, troopships and merchant ships were to be stopped 'in accordance with prize regulations of the Hague Convention'. This meant that, at worst, a vessel could be detained for the duration of the war. Only vessels in convoy were to be 'attacked without warning', except for passenger vessels. These were to be allowed to proceed.

*Admiral Karl Dönitz, whose U-boat war was ill-supported by Raeder and Hitler.*

While Dönitz looked forward to the battle reports from his commanders, he brooded over the pathetic size of his U-boat fleet. The 21 boats that he had sent to the Atlantic represented 80 per cent of his ocean-going U-boats – a fact that underlined how unprepared the Kriegsmarine was for war. And even the fleet that he had was unready for war. As late as the day before the boats were to sail, the U-boat headquarters at Wilhelmshaven revealed that there were not enough torpedoes in stock. Dönitz acidly noted 'in spite of F.O. U/B's urging the matter for nearly four years'.

The Kriegsmarine had made its first strategic error. With too few U-boats to pose a war-winning threat to the Allies, the Allies were given precious time to build up their inadequate escort fleets.

## Britain's lifeline

Dönitz's target was British and Commonwealth merchant shipping. Britain had 17.9 million tons of merchant shipping plying the seas, while the Commonwealth provided an additional 3.1 million tons. The total of 21 million tons represented over 30 per cent of the world's merchant shipping and was Britain's lifeline. Together the ships brought in 55 million tons of food and raw materials each year.

But even before the first merchant ship was sunk, imports had to be cut in order to free shipping for waging war. By mid-August plans were in place to set aside 3 million tons of British merchant shipping for carrying troops, equipment and fuel for war purposes. From day one of the war, a shortage of shipping would be the most limiting factor in Britain's capacity to engage the German forces.

## The Fleet prepares for war

By August 1939 the British people sensed that war was almost certain. Febrile preparations could be seen up and down the land. On 8 August 1300 warplanes took to the skies to test Britain's air defence system. On the following day King George VI reviewed 133 ships of the Reserve Fleet at Weymouth Bay. These included the battleships *Ramillies* and *Revenge*, plus the aircraft carrier *Courageous*. The King inspected 1500 reservists and boarded a submarine, a destroyer and a trawler. The press was told that the review was primarily to enable the King to meet his officers, but the ships quickly departed after dark to their war stations. Two days later half of Britain spent a dark night in a test of the effectiveness of its blackout system.

So far, British moves had had a strongly precautionary air. Then, on 23 August, came the astounding news that Germany and Russia had signed a ten year non-aggression pact. This only made sense if Hitler was about to attack elsewhere. The British government responded by requisitioning 25 merchant vessels to convert to armed cruisers and 35 trawlers to fit with asdic for U-boat searching. The war against the U-boats had all but started.

On 1 September, German troops crossed over the Polish border.

# 4 Day of decision

## 3 September 1939

*'This country is at war with Germany'*

Two days later every Briton waited anxiously to know the outcome of Prime Minister Neville Chamberlain's ultimatum to Germany, demanding that Germany withdraw its troops from Poland. Was it peace, or was it war? Chamberlain spoke to the nation at 11.00 am that day. He was not a natural broadcaster, his manner being stiff and remote. He could never reach out to people in words. But the nation knew that this would be the most momentous broadcast in British history. Only the likes of lonely shepherds on the hillsides and miners deep below ground would not be hovering by a radio as the minutes ticked away to the fateful deadline.

'I am speaking to you from the Cabinet Room at 10 Downing Street,' said Chamberlain in his slow, clipped voice. He described how the German government had failed to reply to his ultimatum to withdraw its troops from Poland. Then followed the dreaded words, 'I have to tell you now that no such undertaking has been received, and that consequently this country is at war with Germany.'

Almost exactly an hour later, Dönitz issued the order to his U-boats to commence war:

HOSTILITIES WITH BRITAIN TO BE OPENED
FORTHWITH

Chamberlain's declaration of war would affect every listener to the core of their being. Death, disablement, separations, destruction would rain upon the people of Britain for the next six years. For some, the war years would be the most fulfilling of their lives. For others, they would be an experience from which they would never fully recover. But for one man, the war brought the

27

opportunity of a lifetime: Winston Churchill. He was about to dominate the life of the country like no other British politician had ever done before.

That afternoon, Chamberlain asked Churchill to come to his room in the House of Commons. For over two years the Prime Minister had rebuffed every warning that Churchill had made about the Nazi threat to peace. Now he graciously stooped to admit his adversary into the government as First Lord of the Admiralty, that is, the Cabinet Minister at the head of the Royal Navy. After his wilderness years, Churchill was finally in a position to play his part in dealing with the consequences of years of disarmament and abortive appeasement.

*Winston Churchill, Prime Minister from 10 May 1940, disembarking from HMS Ajax at Athens in December 1944.*

It was 6.00 pm when Churchill crossed the Admiralty threshold to take up the post that he had previously held from 1911 to 1915. In the First Lord's room he found his old wooden map case – surely a sign that the Royal Navy had changed less than it should have done in those inter-war years. Within minutes of Churchill's arrival, the wireless aerials on the top of Admiralty House were flashing 'Winston is back' to the fleet.

In all his ministerial posts, Churchill had been a pro-active minister. Where other ministers waited for briefs from their civil servants, Churchill goaded his staff into action. He led; he never followed. One of his first actions on returning to the Admiralty was to order the setting up of a map room. There, on a gigantic chart, he could follow the passages of all the fighting ships and the convoys. Day, and often night, he would be at the centre of the action. He was soon taking on additional staff to keep the map up to date.

### 'What now?'

The reaction in Germany that morning to Britain's declaration of war was one of stunned surprise. Although war with Britain had been mooted, there had always been a strong conviction that Britain would pull back at the last minute. This explains Hitler's extraordinary reaction to Chamberlain's ultimatum. He was with his Foreign Minister, Joachim von Ribbentrop, when his chief translator handed him a copy of the ultimatum at 9.00 am. Ribbentrop watched as the Führer read the message. He saw Hitler's face darken as he barked out, 'What now?'

In those two words we have the recurring theme of the story of the Battle of the Atlantic. Hitler had been certain that Britain would back down. Not for one moment had he imagined that he would find himself at war with Europe's greatest naval power and worse, a power which controlled all the seas that gave access to the Atlantic Ocean. It was a monumental miscalculation. And Hitler was not the only person to recognise the jeopardy that Germany now faced: the other was Grand Admiral Erich Raeder.

Like Hitler, Raeder received the news with incredulity. He was in the middle of his daily conference when a copy of the ultimatum was handed to him. Without saying a word he left the room along with his chief of staff. He did not reappear until an hour-and-a-half later. During that time he wrote a note, directed to no one in particular, but almost certainly addressed to posterity:

> On this day we are suddenly at war with Britain ... Yet the
> Führer has constantly asserted that we could count on there
> being no such war until approximately 1944!

All Raeder's plans for his great navy were based on that target date. Five years of further shipbuilding had been recklessly discarded by Hitler's precipitate war. Raeder was now to fight under most disadvantageous conditions. His two – still not commissioned – battleships faced the 12 of the Royal Navy. His seven cruisers and pocket battleships were to take on 18 British equivalents. He had no aircraft carriers, while Britain had seven at sea. As to destroyers, his 22 were outmatched by Britain's 184. He was even out-numbered in submarines, of which Germany had 57 and Britain 58. It says much for Raeder's confidence in his abilities that he did not resign that morning.

There was a third man for whom the news was unwelcome: Rear Admiral Karl Dönitz, commander of the U-boats. As an ex-First World War submarine commander, he was alert to the implications of war with Britain. On that fateful morning he was at his headquarters at Wilhelmshaven. (It was no more than a wooden hut, which may say something about Raeder's view of the U-boat service.) Like Raeder, Dönitz was in his daily conference when the message came over the teleprinter. Being lower in the hierarchy he only merited two words: 'Total Germany'. He stabbed the teleprint and threw it down onto the table, crying, 'Damnation! So it's war with Britain again.' He paused before adding, 'That it should happen to me a second time!'

However we look at the Germany of the 1930s and of Hitler's build-up of the Reich's forces, these three reactions are of one accord. No one had contemplated a naval war with Britain at such an early date. Nowhere in the naval high command was there any rejoicing at the chance to avenge the defeat of Jutland in 1916 or the surrender of the fleet at Scapa Flow in the Orkneys in

1918. The Kriegsmarine looked into the future and shuddered at what it foresaw.

*'Open hostilities against England'*

Dumbfounded as the high command was, it went into action. At 3.50 pm the U-boats at sea received their orders:

OPEN HOSTILITIES AGAINST ENGLAND
IMMEDIATELY, DO NOT WAIT TO BE ATTACKED
FIRST

Later in the afternoon the U-boat commanders received more precise orders. They were 'to make war on merchant shipping in accordance with operations order[s]'. Dönitz reminded them that they had to act 'in accordance with prize law'.

The same signal went to Hans Langsdorff and Paul Wenneker in command of the heavy cruisers *Graf Spee* and *Deutschland*, at sea and awaiting orders. On receipt of this signal, Wenneker wrote in his log: 'My immediate move is to a point 50 deg. North, 30 deg. West, so as to sit astride the shipping lane between America and Britain.'

But neither an escort vessel, nor a merchant ship was to be the first vessel to be sunk by the renascent Kriegsmarine.

# 5 An innocent victim

## 3 September 1939

Hitler had stumbled into a war with Britain. He was determined not to do the same with the United States. But his resolve to avoid upsetting the Americans was thwarted by a rogue U-boat commander on the first day of the war. Amongst the boats that Dönitz had sent out on patrol was *U-30*, commanded by Fritz-Julius Lemp. He had become a sea cadet aged 18 and had risen to the rank of Kapitänleutnant by 1937. At the outbreak of the war, Lemp had ten months' experience as a U-boat commander. It was not enough to save him from causing great embarrassment to the Reich.

Towards the end of August 1939 Lemp's boat was patrolling the north-south line from Iceland to Scotland, waiting for the peace or war signal. When the war order came on 3 September, he was in an excited state at the prospect of action. He eagerly set about looking for his first merchant vessel.

By 7.00 pm the sun had set. *U-30*, 60 miles south of Rockall, pitched on the gentle sea as Lemp peered into the gloom. By his side was Sub Lieutenant Hans-Peter Hinsch. It was Lemp who first made out a large dark form just visible in the lingering light. He had sighted the liner *Athenia*. She was carrying over 1400 passengers and crew from Liverpool to Canada. Amongst her passengers were 500 refugee Jews and over 300 United States citizens.

The *Athenia* was darkened and zigzagging. From this, Lemp concluded that she was a troopship or an armed merchant cruiser. The angry rattle of the action stations klaxon rang through *U-30* as Lemp gave the order to dive. The tanks filled and the boat glided silently beneath the waves.

Although he had told Hinsch that he would take a closer look at the suspect vessel, Lemp was thrilled to be at war and keen to show his prowess. He was in no mood to be cautious. For three hours he trailed the *Athenia* before giving orders to manoeuvre into position for an attack with *U-30's* forward tubes. The time was 7.39 pm. At 1600 yards *U-30* released a spread of three torpedoes. (A fourth remained stuck in its tube.) Two missed *Athenia* but the third sliced through her beam and smashed into her engine room. Lemp had fired the first shot of the war with Britain. It was a shot that Germany would soon regret.

*Fritz-Julius Lemp (wearing his Knight's Cross with Oak Leaves) in conversation with Dönitz in September 1940. The celebratory bunting was still being strung out to welcome the return of successful commanders.*

Lemp's elation did not last long. Within minutes his radio was picking up the distress calls from the stricken liner. His radio man passed him the transcribed signal: '*Athenia* torpedoed 56.42 north, 14.05 west.'

'What a mess! But why, why was she blacked out?' Lemp said to Hinsch.

An innocent victim

On the *Athenia,* the torpedo's explosion had had a devastating effect, way beyond its centre of impact in the engine room. The ten-year-old Margaret Hayworth was sitting with her mother and sister on the tourist deck at the moment of the explosion. The deck rose up in front of them as they were engulfed in smoke and fumes. The air was full of shorn wood and shards of metal, luggage and even human flesh. Mrs Heywood leapt out of her deckchair to lead her children away. But when she called to Margaret, her daughter did not move. She lay dead from a metal fragment that had penetrated her head.

Edith Lustig was taking a walk when the ship was hit. Passengers watched with horror as she was blown off the deck to disappear into the sea below.

The young Roy Barrington had his clothes ripped off by the blast. Two men, resting in deckchairs fell dead on the deck. A Mrs Turner was knocked unconscious by the blast. When she came to on the tourist deck she was lying amongst a mass of corpses.

The explosion had caused massive damage below. Two engine room men were in the propeller tunnels when the explosion came. They died in the blast of flying metal before the tunnels were filled with the rushing mass of tons of water.

At the time of the attack, the officer of the watch, Third Officer Colin Porteous, was searching the sea to starboard when a towering column of water rose up behind him. He felt the deck shudder under him. The *Athenia* momentarily heeled to starboard and then rolled back to list five degrees to port. Porteous had no need to ask what had happened. He pulled the lever that closed the watertight doors below. Even if they failed to save the ship, they would slow its sinking. Without a pause, he set the engine telegraph to Stop. Next came the call to David Don, Chief Radio Officer, to send out the SOS call. As the dots and dashes spread out on the 500 kilohertz distress frequency the ship reverberated to the sustained warning blast of its siren.

34

Most of the officers were at dinner when the torpedo struck. As soon as he heard the blast, Chief Officer Copland went to his station on the boat deck. The sight of ripped-up parts of the ship and the dead bodies were enough to tell him how serious the situation was. He knew it was vital to get the boats away before the ship's list made launching impossible.

The SOS was picked up by several nearby ships. The first ones to answer the call were the Norwegian tanker *Knute Nelson*, the Swedish motor yacht *Southern Cross* and the United States cargo vessel *City of Flint*. There were also three Royal Navy destroyers at hand: HMSs *Electra*, *Escort* and *Fame*. Lieutenant Commander Stuart Buss in *Electra* was the senior officer in the area so he took command of the rescue operation. His first action was to despatch *Fame* on a U-boat sweep. Amidst this profusion of aid, one ship refused the call of the stricken *Athenia*: the German liner *Bremen*.

The struggle for life now began. The *Athenia* was already listing sharply. Water was flooding in. Debris, dead bodies and the wounded created an air of panic. Children looking for parents, parents looking for children, and many passengers searching for lifebelts, all added to the terror. The mishap with the first lifeboat to load did not help. The No. 10 boat had been lowered prematurely over the listing side of the ship. The seamen had failed to hold the grab lines so the boat now dangled too far out to be boarded. The passengers were urged to jump but no one took the risk. Then one passenger – a Mr J R MacDonald – leapt across the perilous gap, landed in the boat, and threw the lines to the passengers on the deck.

Given the circumstances, the boats were loaded in an orderly fashion. There were moments of selflessness and incidents of cowardice. One woman, seeing a crowded boat, turned to another and said, 'You go ahead. Nobody loves me.' There was the man who is said to have dressed as a woman to get into a boat. There was the father who saw his daughter safely into a lifeboat, expecting to die with the ship. She died and he was saved.

An innocent victim

But getting into a boat was not the end of the ordeal for the passengers. It was night. They were at sea. It was cold. By the time most of the boats came alongside the rescue ships the rowers were numb with cold and, in some boats, passengers had already died. Then came the terrifying bosun's chair lift up onto the safety of a ship's deck. The lifeboats rocked on the waves and alternately slammed into the ships' beams or swung too far away for boarding. The petrified, the infirm and the injured had to be coaxed one by one into the chairs and hauled up, swaying into the darkness.

But they were the lucky ones. The fate of boat 5A was one of the greatest tragedies of the night. It was 4.00 am. The boats had been in the water for nearly nine hours. Everyone was cold, exhausted and in fear of their life. So when boat 5A drew alongside the tanker *Knute Nelson* it is understandable that it failed to hold back to allow boat 12 to finish discharging her passengers. Stewardess Mary MacLeod could hear shouts from *Nelson's* deck, warning the boat to stand clear. But in boat 5A many of the traumatised passengers could take no more. Those who cried, 'Stay out!' were outnumbered by the calls to move in. Able Seaman Dillon skilfully brought the boat astern of boat 12. Then came the disaster.

It was triggered by a seaman on the ship reporting a sinking lifeboat ahead of *Knute Nelson*. At first Captain Anderssen hesitated. But as the sighting was repeated he ordered full-ahead. The engines roared into life. *Knute Nelson's* propellers responded, thrashing the waves. Her 6000 tons edged ahead. All this time boat No. 5 had been securely tied to *Knute Nelson*. Under the strain of the ship's sudden move, the painter snapped and the boat floated free. Overhead someone on deck called for the engines to be stopped. By now the boat was being sucked ever closer towards the propellers. Dillon fought to fend off the boat with an oar. The passengers were screaming. The distance was shortening. At the last moment Dillon dropped the oar and dived into the sea. The stern of the boat was ripped off like tissue paper. Around ninety passengers were tipped into the swirling sea. Many went under the waves in an instant. Those who were able to, clung to the upturned remnant of the boat. They could see life-jacketed bodies in the sea around them. Some were already dead. Soon the *Knute Nelson* stopped and lines fell from her deck. A searchlight played on the waves. Meanwhile boat No. 9, which had been approached the *Knute Nelson*, pulled away in fear of suffering the same fate as No. 5.

*A boy survivor from the Athenia being taken off Knute Nelson.*

The last of the boats to reach a rescue ship was 14A. Loaded with 105 people she came alongside HMS *Electra* 10.00 am on 4 September. Chief Officer Copland was amongst these last survivors. As the rescue ships tallied up the living, Copland and Dr Sharman, a Glasgow doctor, realised that Mrs Griffiths, a patient, had almost certainly been left in *Athenia*. The ship was still afloat. She could still be boarded. Buss was reluctant to keep his heavily loaded destroyer stationary in a war zone. But Copland persuaded him to wait. Down went a boat to take Copland, Bosun Harvey and Able Seaman McLeod across to *Athenia*. The ship now had a list of 30 degrees. Her end was minutes away. The three men, ignoring the bodies, waded across the main deck and down a ladder to the hospital. It took the three of them to open the jammed door. Inside lay Mrs Griffiths, the water lapping at the level of her bed. They wrapped her in a sheet and laboured back to the deck. All around them water cascaded down floors, corridors and stairways, all at crazy angles. Mrs Griffiths was lowered into the boat. (Bosun Harvey was refused permission to go back to rescue his false teeth.) The boat pulled away. Minutes later *Athenia* disappeared.

One-hundred-and-twenty-eight passengers and crew lost their lives in the *Athenia* disaster. Her sinking was more than an embarrassment to the Reich. The rules of engagement for U-boats had been formulated to avoid just such a diplomatic disaster. But with the war one day old, no one was going to accept that the Kriegsmarine had a 'no liner' sinking policy. Dönitz was horrified, writing in the War Log on 4 September: 'The orders so far given were checked again after the sinking of the *Athenia*. It is inconceivable that they could be misinterpreted.'

Initially Raeder sidestepped the international row by denying that the *Athenia* had been sunk by a U-boat. But when Lemp returned to Wilhelmshaven on 27 September Raeder learnt the truth. He set in train a series of denials and obfuscations, including replacing the relevant page in *U-30*'s log. He also arranged for the German newspaper *Völkischer Beobachter* to carry the story under the headline: 'Churchill sank the Athenia'. He had done this, said Raeder, 'through the explosion of an infernal machine'. Hitler, though, knew the truth and was terrified of the possible repercussions. It would be so easy for another careless attack to bring America into the war. The order not to attack passenger ships was now to be *his* order, not Dönitz's. At 11.53 pm the U-boat commanders received their warning:

BY ORDER OF THE FÜHRER PASSENGER SHIPS UNTIL
FURTHER NOTICE WILL NOT BE ATTACKED, *EVEN IF
IN CONVOY*

Lemp did not suffer as a result of his wayward action. He received the Iron Cross 2$^{nd}$ class and in November 1940 was given command of *U-110* in which he conducted two patrols. His second patrol ended on 9 May 1941 when *U-110* was damaged by depth-charging. The sinking was to yield a rich harvest for the Allies as we shall in Chapter 17.

# 6 Early skirmishes

## September 1939

### The first merchant sinkings

In the first week of the war ten merchant ships were sunk. The first of these was the cargo ship *Bosnia* bringing 3200 tons of sulphur to Liverpool. *U-47* stopped her by gunfire on 5 September when she was off Cape Ortegal in the Bay of Biscay. Once the *Bosnia* had stopped, *U-47* sank her with a torpedo. One crew member died on the vessel and the remaining 32 took to the boats. These survivors were fortunate since the 9500-ton tanker *Eidanger* was not far behind. She picked up the survivors and disembarked them at Lisbon on the following day.

A few hours later the 5000-ton merchant ship *Royal Sceptre* was sighted by Herbert Schultze in *U-48*. She managed to send out a distress signal before being attacked by gunfire for 25 minutes when off Cape Finisterre. The U-boat ceased firing and sometime later resorted to a torpedo. By this stage the master was dead and nine seamen had been injured. The survivors took to the lifeboats. Two merchant ships answered the distress call and one, the 5500-ton *Browning* picked up the survivors. The *Browning* was outward-bound so landed the survivors in Brazil 21 days later. An American journalist who interviewed Schultze on his return from this patrol, described him as, 'a clean-cut fellow of thirty, hard as nails and full of that bluff self-confidence which you get, I suppose, when you gamble daily with your own life and the lives of others'. As to *U-48*, it was to prove to be the most successful U-boat of the war with 51 merchant ships (307,000 tons) sunk and one warship of 1000 tons sunk.

These stories are typical of the early part of the war. Both the *Bosnia* and the *Royal Sceptre* had been approached in daylight. Both ships had been initially attacked by gunfire. This gave their crews time to send out a distress call and to lower their boats. Later in the war, attacks would generally be by torpedo and at night. Torpedo sinkings were usually rapid, often making lifeboat escape impossible. And, whereas at the start of the war Hitler had ordered the U-boats to follow prize law, Dönitz later gave his commanders the impression that they were free to kill survivors in the sea and in boats.

Three days after the sinking of the *Royal Sceptre* there was a meeting of the Other Club, which Churchill and the politician-barrister F E Smith had founded in 1911. Over dinner, the U-boat menace was discussed. Lord Camrose, owner of the *Daily Telegraph,* amongst other newspapers, noted Churchill's forecast that the U-boat menace would grow rapidly in one year's time. He had based this forecast on the pattern of U-boat activity in the First World War. As it turned out, the U-Boat Arm grew much more slowly than Churchill had feared. Average monthly sinkings for 1939, 1940 and 1941 were 42, 47 and 42. The U-boat war did not become a vital threat to Britain until 1942.

## The return of the convoys

It was at his typically late hour of 9.30 pm that Churchill called his senior staff together to set the convoys into motion on 6 September 1939. The meeting was only a formality since the escorts and the commodores were already in place. By the end of the short discussion, all was agreed: the convoys would start on the following day. On Thursday 7 September 1939 Convoy *OA-1* left the River Thames for Liverpool, while Convoy *OB-1* left Liverpool for the Atlantic crossing. A radio message ordered all outward-bound ships in the English Channel and the Irish Sea to make for either Plymouth or Milford Haven to join a convoy. Meanwhile the coastal convoys to and from the Thames and the Firth of Forth began sailing. It was as if the convoy system of 1917-1918 had never stopped operating.

A week later the first inbound convoys left Freetown in Sierra Leone and Halifax, Nova Scotia. *HX-1* was the first of many convoys to be escorted by

41

the Royal Canadian Navy, which was as ready for convoy work as was the Royal Navy. HMCS *St Laurent* and HMCS *Saguenay* escorted 18 merchant ships for the western part of the passage to Liverpool. HMS *Berwick* and HMS *York* took over the escorting for the eastern side of the voyage. One British ship, the merchant ship *Kirnwood*, carrying a cargo of timber, put back. Of the remaining 17, all but one reached Liverpool on 30 September. The one casualty, the French *Vermont*, was sunk by *U-37*.

*An Atlantic convoy seen from a Sunderland flying boat.*

### Attacks without warning

On 7 September a high-level Kriegsmarine meeting had been called at Wilhelmshaven to discuss U-boat strategy. Around the table sat the Chief of the Naval War Staff, General Admiral Otto Schniewind; the Chief of the Operations Division, Admiral Kurt Frick; and Dönitz. It was at this meeting that the term 'wolf pack' was first used. The three men agreed that U-boats would work alone, hunting for independent sailings, 'until the convoy system was fully introduced'. ('Independent sailings' were merchant ships not in convoy because they were either too slow or too fast to be convoyed.) After that, 'U-Boats would work in packs'. In practice the number of U-boats was far too small to implement this plan. It would be nearly a year before Günther Prien led the first wolf pack attack on Convoy *HX-47*.

But wolf packs or no wolf packs, Dönitz was eager to inflict the maximum possible damage on Allied shipping. So far, Hitler's fear of annoying America had compelled the boats to stop independent sailings before sinking them. By the end of September Hitler was in bolder mood. He declared that 'merchant ships and troopships definitely established as being hostile' could be attacked without warning, as could ships sailing without lights. Any merchant ship that used a radio was to be stopped and attacked. This action was only to be expected since the *Second London Naval Treaty* of 1935 recognised that a merchant ship that was armed or that reported sightings of other vessels was effectively an auxiliary naval vessel. However Hitler still dared not permit the sinking of passenger ships. He was slowly edging his way into a more ferocious form of warfare. And Dönitz zealously supported him at every step. These were the early signs of what was to become a pitiless campaign against merchantmen and liners, with men and women as much targets as were the ships.

## Misplaced optimism

On 26 September Chamberlain reported to the Commons on the war situation. Buried in the middle of his lack lustre account was his judicious warning against 'over-optimism'. He was immediately followed by Churchill, who reported on the naval position. The First Lord of the Admiralty ignored his master's counsel and delivered a bizarrely sanguine account of the battle against the U-boats. After describing the 'very large number' of attacks that British ships had made on U-boats, he said that 'six or seven' had been destroyed. Buoyed up by this figure he more or less declared the U-boat menace to have been mastered. His confident mood was sustained by the diminishing rate of sinkings with first week losses of 65,000 tons; second week

46,000 tons; and third week 21,000 tons. 'In the last six days we have lost only 9,000 tons,' he concluded. These latter figures were accurate enough. But Churchill had been seriously misled by the Admiralty's claim of six or seven U-boats sunk: the true figure was two. With the benefit of hindsight we can appreciate that the war started slowly on both sides. Sinkings in the first few weeks were no basis for comforting extrapolations.

For the time being, this optimism continued to be justified by the figures: only eight convoyed ships were sunk in 1939, whereas 102 sailing independently went to the bottom.

These easy crossings of the early part of the war gave the Allies false hope that they had mastered convoy escorting. The truth was that the Kriegsmarine was unprepared for war. It would be some time before Dönitz had everything in place for serious war in the Atlantic.

### A shortage of destroyers

At the end of the First World War the Admiralty possessed 1354 warships, of which 407 were destroyers. The new war found the Admiralty with much the same burden of convoy work but only 184 destroyers. This shortage became real to Churchill when he visited the naval base at Scapa Flow in the Orkneys in early September. Admiral Charles Forbes, Commander-in-Chief of the Home Fleet, took him to sea in the battleship HMS *Nelson*. Churchill was surprised to find that the great ship was allowed to sail without any accompanying destroyers. Forbes politely explained that in normal circumstances a battleship would never be risked in this way, but such protection was now a luxury beyond the means of his fleet. Not even a First Lord on board was enough to justify an escort.

But at least the Admiralty staff had made out the ship construction orders. As soon as war was declared, orders for destroyers, cruisers and ancillary vessels sped from London to the shipyards of the United Kingdom. These vessels were to be on the front line of the near six-year-long Battle of the Atlantic.

## 'Catch and kill'

With the convoy system firmly re-established, Churchill came up with a surprising proposal on 12 September to introduce search units. These, he said, would hunt for U-boats and sink them – 'catch and kill' as he called it. 'The ideal Unit of Search would be one killer or two three-quarter killers, plus one aircraft-carrier, plus four ocean-going destroyers, plus two specially-constructed tankers of good speed,' he told the First Sea Lord, Admiral of the Fleet Sir Dudley Pound. This was an astonishing suggestion. Convoys had been instituted in the First World War precisely because searching for U-boats was a hopeless task. The escorts not only protected the merchant ships but also *brought the U-boats to the destroyers*. But the most astonishing thing is that the Admiralty had already set up hunter-killer groups. One of the first of these had been formed at Plymouth in the last days of August. On 3 September it sailed into the Atlantic. The results were to force an urgent re-think of Admiralty anti-U-boat warfare. Meanwhile, one of the first searches had a success that was to prove misleading.

## The first U-boat sinking

At this stage of the war there was nothing that Britain could do to stop Germany building U-boats, so destroying those at sea was imperative. It was to prove one of the greatest challenges of the war. One or two sinkings a month was to be a good figure until late 1941. So the first sinking of a U-boat was a matter for celebration. *U-39* had put to sea before the outbreak of war. It had been in commission for nearly a year but this was to be its first patrol. Its commander, Gerhard Glattes, had joined the Reichsmarine in 1927, moving into U-boats in 1936. On the twenty-seventh day of what had been an uneventful patrol he came across the carrier *Ark Royal* on anti-submarine patrol off Rockall Bank, north-west of Scotland. No U-boat commander could

45

have wished for a bigger target. Undetected, Glattes was able to move into his firing position. Away went three torpedoes. The tracks of the torpedoes were immediately spotted by the lookouts on *Ark Royal*. Over went the helm in an emergency turn as *Ark Royal* spun round to face *U-39*. The crew of *U-39* reported hearing the rewarding sound of the explosions but *Ark Royal* had not been hit. Possibly her narrowed profile saved her, but, according to one survivor, Erwin Prügel, the crew had been told that they were carrying some experimental torpedoes. These, he said, exploded while short of their target. *Ark Royal*'s destroyer screen now went into action. It was Bob Larner, the asdic operator on HMS *Foxhound,* who first picked up *U-39*'s asdic echo. *Foxhound's* commander, Philip Hadow, passed the sounding on to *Faulknor* and *Firedrake*. The slow and submerged *U-39* now had three 35 knot F-class destroyers homing in on its position.

All three destroyers dropped depth charges onto the U-boat. Within minutes it had suffered severe damage. Glattes was compelled to surface and surrender. Barely able to float, the waves washed over the U-boat as the men scrambled up from below. Boats were lowered from the three destroyers. Soon the submariners had been hauled aboard without any loss of life. The sinking was a humiliation for Glattes. This was his first patrol and he had failed to damage one of the Kriegsmarine's priority targets. Perhaps worse for him, his was the first U-boat to be sunk in the war. *U-39*'s crew were hauled off to be initially imprisoned in the Tower of London. Later they were all shipped to Canada. Dönitz had no knowledge of this first sinking since *U-39* was abandoned before being able to transmit her position. The other U-boats on the Atlantic patrol continued to report back to their base, but there was silence from Glattes. Dönitz's War Log recorded, 'the lack of response from *U-39* in spite of multiple requests to transmit location is cause for grave concern'.

But Glattes was not the only U-boat commander to fail Dönitz as the submariners learnt their trade. A few days after the sinking of *U-39* there was a more ominous event: the first sighting of a convoy by a U-boat. At 7.00 am on 15 September *U-31* was in the Bristol Channel when the sighting took place. Kapitänleutnant Johannes Habekost radioed to Dönitz 'Convoy in square 1253, main course 2400, speed 10 knots.' The convoy was lucky. Habekost had been a U-boat commander since 1936 but, like many commanders at that time, he was reluctant to take risks. He, and three neighbouring boats, failed to attack, provoking a furious outburst from Dönitz. 'I have dinned it into the C.O.s again and again that they must not let such chances go by,' he wrote in the War Log. It had been a discouraging week for the U-Boat Arm.

*Officers on the bridge of a destroyer searching for signs of an enemy presence.*

## Slow U-boat construction

So far, the sinkings were modest. Several factors accounted for this, including the inexperience of the U-boat commanders and the high number of malfunctioning torpedoes. But the principal reason was Dönitz's shortage of boats. On 8 September he warned Raeder that, without a rapid building programme, 'the branch in its present state will soon be practically non-existent'. Building more boats, he continued was 'the most important [task] for the future of U-boats'. He asked to be put in charge of U-boat production, but Raeder continued to keep tight control of shipbuilding. Much as he valued the U-boats, he prized his large ships even more.

After Raeder had failed to respond to Dönitz's pleas to enhance his authority over boat production, Dönitz turned to Hitler when he was making one of his rare visits to the U-boat headquarters at Wilhelmshaven in early September. The presence of Raeder and General Wilhelm Keitel, Chief of the Armed Forces High Command, gave Dönitz an ideal opportunity to press his case. He repeated his mantra of the U-Boat Arm being able to inflict 'decisive damage on England at her weakest point' but, he added, 'U-boat war can only be waged successfully if there are enough boats'. He needed 300 boats, he said. 'If this number of boats is available. I believe that the U-Boat Arm can achieve decisive success.' For now, though, Dönitz was a lone voice. Hitler's mind was on his land war, and Raeder was dreaming of capturing Norwegian bases for his capital ships. The U-boat war was a sideshow.

However, even a loan U-boat could be a danger when the circumstances were favourable as Korvettenkapitän Otto Schuhart in *U-39* was about to demonstrate.

# 7 The folly of the search units

## 17 September 1939

With the war only two weeks old, the Royal Navy had a lot to learn about U-boat warfare. One of these was the folly of the search units.

HMS *Courageous* – a First World War cruiser converted to a carrier – had been assigned to its search role before the war started. She arrived at Portland on 31 August and took on her two squadrons of twelve Fairey Swordfish planes. (Although generally considered to be obsolete, these flimsy biplanes were to play an important role as torpedo-carrying naval planes throughout the war.) On 3 September Captain William Makeig-Jones took *Courageous* to sea to begin her first patrol in the Western Approaches. With her were the four destroyers HMSs *Inglefield, Intrepid, Ivanhoe* and *Impulsive*. Two weeks later the patrol was working in the Atlantic Ocean, protecting the convoy routes in and out of Britain.

The disaster that was to unfold began when Makeig-Jones sent *Inglefield* and *Intrepid* away to assist a merchant ship that was threatened by a U-boat. *Courageous* now had just two destroyers to protect her.

Not far away *U-29* was out searching for a convoy. Dönitz had sent Schuhart to sea on 1 September with the 2$^{nd}$ U-boat Flotilla in anticipation of war. In two weeks Schuhart had sunk the 8000 ton tanker *Regent Tiger*, the 800 ton tug *Neptunia* and the 8000 ton tanker *British Influence*. These had all been unarmed and unescorted – easy prey.

During the afternoon of 17 September, Schuhart spotted a small search plane. He knew at once that it was hunting for U-boats. That was bad news. But the plane must have come from a carrier. That was good news. His own search was on.

At 6.00 pm Schuhart saw smoke on the horizon. Soon he had the mighty *Courageous* in his sight. Planes were circling overhead and two destroyers were nearby. 'At that time it looked like a hopeless operation,' he later wrote. 'Because of the aircraft, I could not surface and my underwater speed was less than 8 knots while the carrier could do 26. But we were told during our training to always stay close and that is exactly what I did.'

Suddenly Schuhart's luck changed. *Courageous* was about to launch some planes. She turned into the wind to aid their take-off. And there, right before Schuhart, was the full 786 feet of *Courageous's* beam. The time was 7.30 pm. It took Schuhart just ten minutes to manoeuvre *U-29* into a firing position. He was now only 3000 yards from the carrier. 'Fire!' Three torpedoes shot from *U-29*'s forward tubes. Two struck *Courageous* on her port bow.

*Courageous* immediately lost all electrical power. Paymaster Sub Lieutenant Ian Westmacott heard the explosions when he was at supper in the wardroom. He felt the ship lift as the crockery fell from the table. Then the lights went out. No orders came from the wrecked Tannoy. Westmacott raced up to the seaplane platform to find the decks seething with men waiting for orders. No one suspected that *Courageous* was in imminent danger of sinking. But within five minutes the 'Abandon ship' order came. Marine M Reidy recalled how the order was 'sent by word of mouth along the decks' passing from each man to his neighbour. By now the carrier was listing so badly that standing upright was difficult. Westmacott stripped off his clothing, jumped into the sea and swam towards the destroyers. Forty minutes later he was hauled up to safety.

Lieutenant Edgar Court-Hampton had a tougher escape. He had been resting on his bunk at the time of the explosions. When he reached the deck, the ship was listing badly. As he took off his clothes he slithered down the deck and crashed into a metal balcony. It was a hard smash, which left him badly bruised and with a dislocated thumb. He yanked the thumb back into line and dived into the oily sea. Court-Hampton swam around for 45 minutes before finding three seamen clinging to a plank. His officer-training came to the fore as he directed the men in swimming themselves and the plank towards a destroyer. Once alongside the vessel, he pushed the men up and then collapsed on the wrong side of the guardrail. Strong hands pulled him in. A hot bath and four whiskies restored Court-Hampton's strength. By 10.00 pm the destroyer was making for Plymouth with 300 men and 45 officers on board.

In addition to the destroyers, the Dutch liner *Veendam* and the British freighter *Collingworth* had come to the rescue. The *Veendam*, which had specialised in Caribbean cruises, had had her own drama when she was rammed at anchor in the Hudson river in 1928. It took the work of seven tugboats to bring her to the safety of a dry dock. Now she let down 14 of her lifeboats, which were soon filled with grateful survivors.

Despite the presence of the rescue vessels, 519 crew members went down with *Courageous*. One of these was Makeig-Jones. He had only assumed command of the carrier on 24 July. He made no attempt to leave his ship. The 18 year-old naval writer Tom Hughes was swimming away from *Courageous* when he caught his last sight of Makeig-Jones 'standing at the salute on the bridge as the vessel took her final plunge'.

When Schuhart looked through his periscope to see what damage he had done to *Courageous*, he saw that his boat was perilously near to a destroyer. He ordered a crash-dive, taking the boat down to 180 feet. His men had heard the explosions as the torpedoes hit *Courageous* but mistook them for depth charges. But these came soon enough as first one destroyer, then another, found the U-boat. For four hours the two destroyers dropped charges around *U-29*. Its pressure hull creaked and strained under the blasts as the men cowered in anticipation of the repeated attacks. But not one charge was able to inflict mortal damage. At 11.40 pm the destroyers had exhausted their depth charge supply. Now themselves vulnerable to U-boat attack, they quickly withdrew. Once Schuhart was sure that *U-29* was beyond danger, he surfaced and radioed to Dönitz: '*Courageous* destroyed. *U-29* homebound.'

The loss of *Courageous* was a shock to the nation and, coming so soon after the sinking of *Athenia*, was a formidable reminder of the sinister power of the U-boat. Churchill's reaction bode well for the navy. He learnt about the sinking when he stepped off a train at King's Cross on his return from a visit to Scapa Flow. He was surprised to find the First Sea Lord waiting on the platform. 'I have bad news for you, First Lord. The *Courageous* was sunk yesterday,' said Pound. Churchill calmly replied, 'We can't expect to carry on a war like this without those sort of things happening from time to time.'

*HMS Courageous sinking on 17 September 1939, so ending the folly of the search units.*

The Royal Navy could hardly have had a worse start to its war. Germany had not one single carrier. Britain had seven. But of what use was this advantage if the U-boats could so easily take one out? And what of the Admiralty's anti-U-boat strategy? Within two weeks of the start of the war the search units had proved worthless. It had been a bold idea: to actively go out and seek U-boats. But the idea was fallacious from the start. The principle of convoys was that the only way to destroy U-boats was to attract them to the destroyers. Searching was impracticable in the vastness of the Atlantic. But the lesson was quickly learned. The other three carriers that were still on hunter-killer patrol were withdrawn. For now the destroyers would have to work alone. But their work would be severely hampered by the Allies dearth of anti-submarine vessels.

The lack of destroyers was raised in the House of Commons on 20 September by Captain Frederick Bellenger MP. Bellenger had a creditable background from which to challenge the Admiralty since he had fought in the First World War and was still in the army reserve. So when he asked 'whether this ship was accompanied by its full complement of protecting destroyers' his question deserved to be taken seriously. But Churchill simply replied, 'Yes, Sir, she was accompanied by a full escort of destroyers.' If Churchill was aware that two of the destroyers were absent at the time of the attack, then his answer was disingenuous. What followed was worse: complacency. Mr Somerset de Chair MP, who had been mobilised on 24 August, asked Churchill how it had been possible for a U-boat 'to get within striking distance of the *Courageous*', given the Admiralty's repeated assurances that this was not possible. In reply Churchill once more said that he was satisfied with the Admiralty's means of 'coping with this peculiar form of menace'. His complacency was not to last. Indeed, after the war he admitted that 'the only thing that ever really frightened me during the war was the U-boat peril'.

While the destroyer shortage was a well-recognised problem for the convoy system, the Admiralty were still unaware of an equally serious deficiency: the limited capabilities of asdic. Introduced in the First World War, asdic continued to be developed between the wars. By 1939 the Admiralty were so confident of its effectiveness that they invited leading politicians to observe its use at sea. These demonstrations were held under unrealistic conditions. As a result many an observer went away convinced that the U-boats were no longer a threat to either warships or merchantmen. Churchill was one of the deceived. In June 1938 he had been invited by the then First Sea Lord, Admiral of the Fleet Ernle Chatfield, to see a demonstration of asdic at Portland. After sleeping aboard the flagship he boarded a destroyer to witness asdic in action. It was, he told Chatfield 'a marvellous system'. He had been duped into believing that, 'The submarine should be quite controllable in the outer seas and certainly in the Mediterranean.' The gravity of the deception of that demonstration was to reveal itself when asdic faced the skill and cunning of the U-boat commanders.

# 8 Testing the waters

## October to December 1939

### Raeder searches for new bases

During the last three months of 1939 Raeder was looking for ways to make the small U-boat fleet more effective. At the top of his list was his search for new bases. His existing North Sea bases at Hamburg, Bremerhaven and Wilhelmshaven, and his Baltic Sea bases at Danzig and Kiel were a long way from the Atlantic battleground. And all routes from them to the Atlantic hunting grounds were dominated by British warships.

Hitler tried to persuade Raeder to set up bases on the Belgian coast. Raeder quickly dismissed this suggestion. Instead he proposed to capture bases in Norway, and in particular to seize Trondheim. Such bases would have been a great improvement on his current situation, being nearer to the passage to Atlantic via the north of Scotland. Seizing the Norwegian ports also meant denying them to the Allies. But, behind these arguments, Raeder had an ulterior motive: Norway's fiords offered safe havens for his capital ships. As events were to prove, a large warship tucked deep into a fiord was almost immune from attacks by British planes.

Meanwhile Raeder had to satisfy himself with tentative moves to make better use of his small navy. By November he was seeking a means to harden the rules of engagement still further. To this end, he wanted the army to invade a neutral state, so widening the war. That, he said, would be the moment for the Kriegsmarine to announce a blockade of Britain. Under blockade terms, the U-boats would be able to sink both enemy and neutral vessels 'without warning', wrote Raeder in a memorandum. Göring was alarmed by Raeder's plans to upstage the Luftwaffe and immediately made plans of his own for intensifying the war. He declared that 'merchant ships in convoy might also be attacked from the air without warning'. How serious he was is hard to say since the Luftwaffe was more conspicuous by its absence than its presence in the Battle of the Atlantic. Nevertheless this episode is a good example of the pointless inter-service rivalry that so undermined the Reich's war effort.

Little more than a week later, Raeder was back in Hitler's Chancellery with fresh proposals for extending the U-boat attacks. This time he had passenger steamers in mind. Just 68 days had passed since the U-boats were prohibited from attacking these ships. Now Raeder wanted to sink them without warning on the grounds that they often carried troops. Hitler agreed to the proposal, provided that the target ships were known to have been converted for military use.

*Dönitz's tonnage strategy*

Given his shortage of U-boats, Dönitz showed remarkably little interest in strategies that would make the best use of them. Except on a very few occasions, he encouraged his commanders to sink tonnage. It mattered not what the tonnage was: wheat, timber, ores and oil all had the same priority. This attitude was advantageous to the Allies. Certain cargoes were of critical importance to Britain's survival and her capacity to wage war, oil being the principal example. Had Dönitz made a more concerted effort to concentrate on sinking tankers early in the war, the Battle of the Atlantic might well have brought British industry to a halt. An even more effective strategy would have been to prioritise sinking escort vessels, but Dönitz was addicted to totting up tonnage figures.

An immediate consequence of Dönitz's obsession with tonnage, was the need for more U-boats. In mid-October Dönitz made a roughly costed bid for new construction. He argued that U-boat building 'should take precedence over all other tasks and services' and set out his demand for the manpower needed: 29,000 men for boats and engine construction; 60,000 for torpedoes and mines; 5000 for instrument making; and 35,000 for unspecified work. In total, the U-Boat Arm was asking for 120,000 workers. But at this stage of the war, with no significant conquests to provide forced labour, German manpower was in short supply. Even more problematic for the U-Boat Arm was the fact that Hitler did not see the U-boats as war-winning machines: his faith was in the Luftwaffe and the Wehrmacht.

The tonnage war and the failure to prioritise sinking escort vessels were strategic error number two. But, occasionally, Dönitz went for a different sort of target: one that was more an arrogant demonstration of power than an act of strategy.

### 'We are in Scapa Flow!!!'

In his memoirs Dönitz claimed that an attack on Scapa Flow had been in his mind 'from the very outset'. The nudge into action came from Fregattenkapitän Victor Oehrn when he assured Dönitz that, 'I'm pretty sure we *could* find a way in.' Oehrn had been one of the first of the new generation of U-boat commanders to go into action, having gained experience in *U-14* during the Spanish Civil War. Now a staff officer in operations, he was in a position of influence. Dönitz listened and provisionally authorised the audacious attack.

By 11 September – less than two weeks into the war – Dönitz was studying aerial reconnaissance photographs of Scapa Flow. These seemed promising enough to request a more detailed survey. Dönitz asked Siegfried Knemeyer for high-quality photos of all the entrances to the Flow. This talented aviator and aeronautical engineer, who would soon make a name for himself for daring aerial reconnaissance, returned a few days later with just what Dönitz needed. The admiral pored over the pictures, studying Holm Sound with particular care. It had been blocked by two sunken ships. But Dönitz was sure that a narrow, shallow passage remained between the mainland and the tiny uninhabited island of Land Holm. He was convinced that he had found a back door into the Royal Navy's premier mooring.

After studying the tide tables, Dönitz decided on the night of 13-14 October for the attack, when the tidal flow would be slack around midnight. Manoeuvring a U-boat in the narrow passage was challenge enough without the hazard of a fast-running tide.

His commander was to be Günther Prien. Known as a fervent and ruthless Nazi, Prien had already shown his prowess by the time the war was only weeks old. With three merchant ships sunk on his first short patrol, he was a commander to be watched. Like Oehrn, he had learnt his trade in his country's duplicitous participation in the Spanish Civil War.

Prien was in high spirits as *U-47* slipped out of Kiel on 8 October for its long run north to Scapa Flow. The weather was clear and the sea calm so Prien had plenty of time to contemplate the hazards of his mission impossible. After an uneventful passage north, *U-47* surfaced at 7.00 pm off the Orkneys on 13 October. There was a fresh breeze blowing and not a ship in sight. The light was fading but Prien desperately needed the night to swallow up *U-47* as it approached the supposedly strongly guarded mooring.

Prien set a course for the entrance to Holm Sound, keeping as close to the mainland coast as he dare, for fear of being silhouetted against the skyline. Standing in the conning tower as *U-47* ran along the coast in the fading light he saw a man calmly riding a bicycle within yards of the boat. Then his boat was momentarily caught by the lights of a car on the mainland. Overhead the Northern Lights were flashing. Nothing suggested that he was now in a supposedly high-security war zone.

Prien's greatest fear was a collision with one of the submerged wrecks that were blocking his entrance to the Flow. At his first attempt, the channel seemed impassable, but he soon found a gap between the two ships below him. Minutes later *U-47* had passed into Kirk Flow. In jubilation, Prien wrote in the log, 'We are in Scapa Flow!!!' Before him lay the open water of the main Scapa mooring. He had achieved what the British Admiralty thought impossible.

It was now gone midnight. Despite the darkened sky there was enough light from the aurora borealis for Prien to see some of the smaller ships. Even so, at first neither he nor his lookouts picked out any of the four warships moored a few thousand yards ahead. Prien ran *U-47* in for some distance, anxiously searching for a target. Finding nothing, he turned away in disappointment. His triumphant penetration of the mooring had been in vain.

As the boat turned, a lookout spotted the low dark mass of a large ship. Prien stared through his glasses. He knew his enemy ships. This was a *Revenge* class battleship. Lurking behind her there was a less well-defined mass, which he took to be a battlecruiser. The time now was 0.58 am. Prien ordered the loading of the four forward tubes. One last look through the periscope. 'Fire! Three deadly torpedoes raced through the silent, dark sea to the sleeping *Royal Oak*. (One torpedo had stuck in its tube.) Two missed the target. The third slammed into *Royal Oak's* bows at 1.04 am. The ship shuddered from end to end but there was no explosion. Those seamen who were woken by the dull thump soon settled back to sleep in their hammocks.

Prien would not have been surprised at his lack of success. The torpedo firing mechanism in the early months of the war was notoriously unreliable. For all he knew, he might have scored three hits. It was time to try again. He turned *U-47* through 180 degrees and fired one torpedo from his stern tube. The men held their breath and waited. Nothing.

By now the forward tubes were reloaded. It was about 1.12 am when *U-47's* three functioning forward tubes despatched their second deadly consignment. By this time everyone in the boat was resigned to failure. But they were wrong. All three torpedoes hit their target. All three detonated. *Royal Oak* suffered a number of explosions as her armoured deck was ripped open. Her cordite, deep in the bowels of the ship, erupted in a towering ball of flame that rose high into the night sky. Within minutes *Royal Oak* was listing by 15 degrees.

*Royal Oak's* hatches were open on that warm evening. Soon water was pouring down the companion ways while hundreds of men fought for their lives in the darkness below. Thirteen minutes after Prien's torpedoes had struck, the great battleship sank beneath the gentle swell of the Flow.

*Royal Oak* went down with the loss of 833 officers and men out of a complement of 1234. Amongst those lost was Rear-Admiral Henry Blagrove, making him the first Royal Navy officer of flag rank to be killed in the Second World War. It is impossible not to wonder whether, as he met his end, Blagrove's mind flashed back to 24 January 1915. Then a lieutenant on HMS *Tiger*, he had helped despatch the armoured cruiser *Blücher* with her loss of around 700-1000 men at the Battle of Dogger Bank. He had also been present at the surrender of the German High Seas Fleet on 21 November 1918. Never could he have imagined that he would fall victim to that fleet's successor 21 years later.

*The crew of U-47 line-up on their return from sinking HMS Royal Oak at Scapa Flow in October 1939.*

Prien was awarded the Knight's Cross of the Iron Cross by Hitler – the first U-boat commander to receive it. He will return later in our story.

## The balance of the battle

By the end of the year the results of the U-boat war gave each side reasons to be satisfied and reasons to be worried. Considering how few ocean-going U-boats Dönitz had in late 1939, the average sinkings for October to December of 89,000 tons a month were a creditable performance for his commanders. But he reckoned that he needed to sink at least 700,000 tons a month to cripple Britain's trade.

The British Admiralty could draw satisfaction from the performance of its escorts: only eight convoyed ships were sunk in 1939, compared to the sinking of 102 sailing independent sailings. The convoy system seemed to be proving itself. But it did not look that way when Churchill told the War Council on 15 December that three tankers had just been lost. Losses, he told his colleagues, 'were assuming serious proportions'.

On the German side commanders were in despair at the repeated detonation failures of their torpedoes. Viktor Schütze in *U-25*, after having sunk one vessel of 6000 tons on 31 October, failed to sink anything else in the remaining three weeks of that patrol. On one occasion he fired four torpedoes at a stationary ship at short range, with no harm done to the vessel. Prien was to have the same problem when, around April 1940, he reported eight firings at motionless ships without a single detonation. At that time, though, it was not clear that the contact pistols were the cause of the mis-firings. Indeed, on no evidence at all, Dönitz satisfied himself that the failures were due to 'some special reason' connected with the Norwegian waters. (This is an odd remark since a Professor Cornelius had been appointed in November 1939 'to eliminate the faults in the pistols' and 'to ensure that the torpedoes will keep perfect depth'.)

# 9 Reclaiming the oceans

## August to December 1939

*Commerce raiding*

While the opening period of the U-boat war had been slowly evolving, Raeder had not forgotten his big ships. Their first great venture was to end calamitously.

Germany's failure to complete the Z-Plan before the war had begun had left Raeder with a ragged collection of capital ships. He had too few escorts to deploy them on any scale. Yet he had too many warships to simply not use them at all. In consequence, both Hitler and Raeder oscillated between advocating more aggressive use of the big ships and fearing to expose them to the greater forces of the Royal Navy. Nevertheless, as war approached, Raeder had laid his plans for a hazardous outing of the *Graf Spee* and the *Deutschland*.

Raeder had previously despatched their supply ship *Altmark* into the Atlantic on 2 August. She had crossed the ocean, called in at Port Arthur in Texas, and taken on 9400 tons of fuel oil. On 19 August she sailed off into the Atlantic. Shortly afterwards the two pocket battleships had sailed from their German bases. The *Deutschland* had taken up station in the North Atlantic and the *Graf Spee* in the South.

Raeder was well-aware of the danger of hazarding these precious vessels, unescorted on the high seas. He knew they could not survive a serious engagement with a substantial British force, so he placed his commanders under an unwelcome constraint. Enemy naval forces, 'even if inferior', he told them, 'were only to be engaged if it were to further the principal task of the war on merchant shipping'.

Hans Langsdorff, captain of the *Graf Spee* revealed how he interpreted Raeder's restrictive rules of engagement when he briefed his crew just before they left Germany. He told them that, 'There were to be no Falkland Islands nor Coronels for them.' (These were the two big-ship battles in the southern seas during the First World War. Coronel was a brilliant German victory; the Battle of the Falkland Islands was Admiral Fisher's revenge on Coronel. It was also the battle in which Admiral Maximilian von Spee met his death.) Langsdorff went on to explain to his men that he would not 'close large convoys' but stick to 'smaller ones which would be less heavily escorted'. This limited action was a humiliation for Langsdorff. It was not for such small fry that the *Graf Spee* and the *Deutschland* had been built.

The actions of the *Deutschland* in the next few months were small-scale and of no importance to our story. We shall therefore concentrate on the *Graf Spee,* whose fortunes and ultimate misfortune were to have significant consequences for the Battle of the Atlantic.

It was not until 26 September that Langsdorff received authorisation to attack Allied ships. Four days later he came across the British 5000-ton steamship *Clement* of the Booth Line. She was sailing 75 miles south-east of Pernambuco, Brazil, when a lookout sighted a distant warship. Captain Harris assumed this was HMS *Ajax*, rushed below and put on a smart white uniform. Back on the bridge he watched with interest as a plane approached. Then came the moment of horror as an Arado Ar 196 floatplane flew over the ship. The black crosses on the underside of its wings clearly identified it as a Luftwaffe plane. Harris knew the peril that his ship was now in. He ordered his radio operator to send out an SOS call while the boats were lowered. As the *Graf Spee* neared *Clement* she launched two torpedoes, both of which missed the steamer. Langsdorff turned to 11-inch shells. He was still firing these when Captain Harris was hauled up into the *Graf Spee* sometime later. Looking back at the still floating *Clement*, he remarked, 'She's a damned tough ship!'

In the case of the *Clement,* the spotter plane gave Harris early warning that the warship was German. But this was not Langsdorff's usual mode of attack:

he preferred deception. He would approach his victim end-on while flying a French ensign. Once he was near to his prey he displayed a large board with the words 'Do not use your wireless or you will be fired upon.'

Until the sinking of the *Clement* the British Admiralty had no idea that German surface raiders were at sea. But Captain Harris's prompt SOS ensured that the presence of the raiders was known worldwide. However, *Clement's* SOS gave no clue as to how many raiders there were, or in which oceans they intended to maraud.

The British Admiralty now faced perhaps the largest search operation that it had ever undertaken. Eight hunting groups were formed, any one of which being capable of destroying armoured ships of the Deutschland or Hipper class. The Royal Navy contingent included three battleships, two battlecruisers, fourteen cruisers and five aircraft carriers. The French contingent included an aircraft carrier, two battle-cruisers, and five cruisers.

Radio silence was to be maintained 'except when it was known that the presence of the hunting group had been disclosed'. The over-zealous application of this diktat was to delay the finding of the *Graf Spee*.

Although in theory the *Graf Spee* (and any other raiders) could be anywhere on the oceans, the Admiralty made the assumption that she would be found around the busiest parts of the trade routes. The hunting groups were warned not to be lured away from these areas. Additionally, the Admiralty ordered its commanders to seek out and destroy the German supply vessels. The raiders could not survive for long once they ran out of fuel oil, food and ammunition.

From here on we only need to follow the hunting group that was to find the *Graf Spee* – Group G, which was assigned to the south-east coast of America. This comprised HMSs *Exeter*, *Cumberland*, *Ajax* and *Achilles* under the command of Commodore Henry Harwood.

The *Graf Spee's* next victim was the 4600-ton cargo vessel *Newton Beech*, which was captured and sunk on 5 October. Her crew were all taken on board *Graf Spee* and later transferred to the *Altmark*. Like *Clement*, *Newton Beech* managed to send out a distress call, which was picked up by the British *Martand*. The *Martand* passed the signal on to *Cumberland*. And there it stayed. Radio silence ensured that the Admiralty had no knowledge of this sighting until 16 days later. By that time the information was worthless.

*Henry Harwood, who commanded the British squadron at the Battle of the River Plate, seen here as vice admiral at Alexandria in 1942.*

Two days after sinking the *Newton Beech*, *Graf Spee* attacked and sank the British cargo ship *Ashlea*. The 8000-ton *Huntsman* followed three days later. On 15 October the raider met the *Altmark* to refuel and to hand over her prisoners for transporting back to Germany.

It was now three weeks since the British Admiralty had had any information about the location of the *Graf Spee*. Then, on 22 October, news came from the Union Castle liner *Llanstephan Castle*. She had intercepted a signal from an unidentified ship under shell fire. This was presumably the 5300-ton *Trevanion* which had been stopped by gunfire. But still the hunting groups were nowhere near to encountering the *Graf Spee*. And so her unhindered raiding continued. Then, on 2 December, a sighting and a piece of intuition sealed her fate.

When Captain Stubbs of the cargo vessel *Doric Star* saw a distant warship he ordered his wireless operator, William Comber, to send out a distress signal. At the same time he asked the engine room for all possible speed: he intended to outrun his opponent – an improbable tactic given that the *Graf Spee's* top speed was 28 knots, against the 15 knots of the *Doric Star*. Langsdorff responded with a shell, which Stubbs disdainfully ignored. A second shell brought a rapid change of mind. Stubbs ordered 'Stop engines' and told his radio operator to report the attack. For all Stubbs's bravado, the *Graf Spee* was rapidly closing on the *Doric Star*. Stubbs knew that his ship would not survive the day but was determined to deny the *Graf Spee* the chance to sink her. He ordered his Chief Engineer to scuttle the vessel. The engineer had just gone off to execute the order when the radio operator reported an acknowledgement of his distress call. Stubbs called off the scuttling and began pitching the confidential papers, guns and ammunition overboard. This feverish action was still in progress when three German officers and thirty men, armed with revolvers, boarded the ship. There followed a meticulous search of the *Doric Star*, despite the fact that Stubbs had told the boarders that his cargo was wool. The boarders were right to be suspicious. The *Doric Star* was carrying eight tons of refrigerated meat, butter and cheese – just the sort of food that Langsdorff's men needed. But Langsdorff never discovered the nature of the cargo until the *Doric Star* was sinking. After an hour of shelling with 5.9-inch ammunition the *Doric Star* still refused to sink. Eventually she succumbed to a torpedo. By now the *Graf Spee* had sunk seven vessels. Two more were to go to the bottom: *Tairoa* on 3 December and *Streonshalh* on 7 December. Just before her last sinking, the *Graf Spee* rendezvoused with her supply ship. Most of her latest haul of prisoners were transferred to the *Altmark* and fuel was taken on board.

The smooth hand-over of prisoners and the refuelling were signs of the success of Raeder's plan. It looked as if he might have been right in putting his faith in the large ships. But radio was to prove the undoing of his scheme.

*Doric Star's* distress call was just what Harwood needed. The signal showed that the *Graf Spee* was on the east side of the Atlantic – not a rich picking ground. He reasoned that she would cross the Atlantic to raid in the busy sea lanes linking South America to the North Atlantic. He assumed that *Graf Spee* would steam at 15 knots and arrive in the River Plate area around 13 December. There, Langsdorff would find merchant ships laden with precious cargoes of wheat and frozen meat, so vital to feeding the British, and oil, so essential to the fighting ships. Harwood made his dispositions. With no immediate action in prospect, he sent off *Cumberland* to the Falkland Islands for a refit, with orders to remain at short notice to sail. Meanwhile, *Exeter*, *Achilles* and *Ajax* headed for Montevideo. The men on *Achilles* were in good heart, having just enjoyed three days' shore leave at Rio de Janeiro, where they had done their Christmas shopping and spent their small change in bars, casinos and dance halls.

### 'I think it is a pocket battleship'

At 5.20 am on 13 December Harwood's squadron was 340 miles from Montevideo in Uruguay. His ships were steaming line ahead, *Ajax* leading, followed by *Exeter* and the New Zealand vessel, *Achilles*. The sky was clear as the ships glided at 14 knots through the light sea. On board each ship, men exercised at action stations. Their mood was tense but excited as they prepared for the first large-ships clash of the war. It would later be known as the Battle of the River Plate.

It was *Exeter* that first saw the smoke on the horizon. She turned away from the line, raised speed and closed on the smudge. Within minutes Harwood had Captain Frederick Bell's signal: 'I think it is a pocket battleship.'

Harwood had already decided his dispositions of his three modest warships for their attack on the big beast with her 11-inch guns. He would spread out his vessels so as to force the *Graf Spee* to split her firing. *Ajax* and *Achilles* were to go to the north-north-west with orders to close in on the *Graf Spee*. Meanwhile *Exeter* turned to the west. This formation ensured that, as the battle progressed, the gap between the Allied ships would steadily widen, much to the disadvantage of *Graf Spee's* guns.

By now the two sides were closing at around 50 miles per hour.

The first shots of the battle came from the *Graf Spee* at 6.18 am when *Ajax* and *Achilles* were still 19,800 yards from the enemy. *Exeter* was slightly closer at 19,400 yards. One salvo fell 300 yards short of *Exeter*. For an opening salvo it was an ominously close shot.

Harwood replied two minutes later. He did so in an unusually un-naval fashion, shouting to his Gunnery Lieutenant, Richard Jennings, 'There's the fucking Scheer! Open fire at her!'

When *Exeter* replied with her four forward 8-inch guns, she had closed the range to 18,700 yards. A few minutes later she was in a position to bring her two rear guns into action as well.

Meanwhile *Achilles* and *Ajax* had begun firing.

Langsdorff decided that *Exeter* was the greater threat. He was soon concentrating all his six of his 11-inch guns onto the heavy cruiser.

The first damage to *Exeter* came from a shot that fell short, killing the men of the starboard torpedo station. There was also damage to the ship's communications. One casualty was the Sick Berth Chief Petty Officer, Charles Pope. At the moment of impact he had some bottles of morphine sulphate in his hands. The shell blast knocked him unconscious and the precious bottles smashed as he fell to the deck.

*Exeter* had fired eight salvoes when confirmation came of the accuracy of the *Graf Spee's* guns. An 11-inch shell tore into B-turret, instantly destroying it and its guns. The debris from the explosion ripped through the bridge. Only Captain Bell and two officers escaped injury. The bridge was unusable and the communications systems were wrecked, compelling Bell to fight on from the aft conning position.

But when he arrived aft, Bell found that its communications were gone as well. Now his orders to the wheel had to be passed verbally down a long line of sailors to the depths below.

There was to be no easy escape for *Exeter*. At 6.38 am two more 11-inch shells found her as she turned to fire her torpedoes. One shell destroyed the A-turret. The other, penetrating deep into the ship, set off a number of fires. It was the effects of these shells that Lieutenant Ron Atwill and his repair party found below: 'we went aft to the scene of the explosion. What a shambles met our eyes – suitcases and clothing everywhere (sodden with fuel oil and fire-fighting water by this time), steel kit lockers blown apart and twisted into grotesque shapes, even somehow rolled up into balls and piled against the bulkheads'.

Jennings, who now had burst eardrums, was on the roof of Y-turret, shouting orders through an open hatch. But in her hour of agony *Exeter* had dealt an even more deadly blow to the *Graf Spee*. An 8-inch shell had passed through two decks and wrecked the raw fuel processing system. Now *Graf Spee* was down to fuel for 16 hours' sailing. There could be no immediate return to base.

With *Exeter* stricken, Langsdorff turned his attention to *Ajax* and *Achilles*. Like *Exeter*, the first 11-inch shell to reach *Achilles* fell short, but its splinters left two killed and two wounded in the fire director control tower. There were injuries on the bridge too with the Chief Yeoman Signaller seriously wounded and Captain Parry with leg wounds.

By 6.40 am the battle had degenerated into a set of independent actions as each ship struggled with its communications losses. *Exeter* was more or less cut off from the rest of the squadron, while *Achilles* had lost radio contact with *Ajax*.

Nevertheless *Ajax* and *Achilles* kept up the attack, turning as the *Graf Spee* manoeuvred so as to keep all their guns bearing on her. Langsdorff's response was, by now, half-hearted as he relied increasingly on course alterations and smoke.

Harwood could see that the *Graf Spee* was wavering. The range was now 16,000 yards. He ordered *Ajax* and *Achilles* to close on the enemy. They turned westward as the engine rooms were ordered to provide all possible speed. It was now 7.10 am.

A few minutes later the *Graf Spee* turned towards *Exeter* as if Langsdorff sensed how vulnerable the heavy cruiser now was. But his move was thwarted by the closing *Ajax* and *Achilles*. Their steady firing was scoring hits, one of which started a fire amidships. Once more Langsdorff changed his target as he turned back to the two cruisers. He was now firing 11-inch shells at 11,000 yards. Salvos began to straddle *Ajax*.

Inevitably a shell finally found her. It destroyed her X-turret, jammed her Y-turret and did considerable other damage. *Ajax* responded with a batch of four torpedoes, but the *Graf Spee* turned away.

By 7.40 am Harwood was weighing up his options. Given the wrecked state of *Exeter* and the seriously damaged state of *Ajax*, it was unlikely that further daylight action would yield a decisive result. He decided to withdraw with the intention of moving in after dark. The three ships turned away. As they did so the *Graf Spee* had the last word as she lobbed a few final salvoes at the squadron. *Ajax* lost her main topmast and with it her wireless aerials. But

Lieutenant Richard Washbourn, Gunnery Officer in *Achilles*, was not pleased at the turn-away: '[I felt] baulked of my prey ... The last twenty minutes at really effective range had been most enjoyable,' he later told a friend.

The battle had lasted just under one-and-a-half hours. The *Graf Spee* headed to Montevideo to carry out emergency repairs. She had received 70 hits and had lost 36 men. Amongst her wounded was Langsdorff who had spent the whole battle on his open bridge.

When the *Graf Spee* went into battle she still had some prisoners on board, including men from *Doric Star*. Caged in the bowels of the ship, they had anxiously followed the sounds of the combat. There was a cheer at the first sound of distant guns, recalled Captain Stubbs, 'as we knew that our lads had spotted the Nazi battleship'. Then the *Graf Spee* began to roll drunkenly: 'There was a tremendous crash over our heads. She had opened fire.' And when the guns directly above the prisoners fired, 'It was like an earthquake.' They were told nothing about the battle but drew their own conclusions when the *Graf Spee* pulled into Montevideo the next day: 'That, we knew, meant a British victory.'

Churchill had followed the battle with great interest. He wrote to Pound to congratulate him on how well *Exeter* had been 'able to stand up to such a prolonged and severe battering'. He concluded that 'we ought not readily to accept the non-repair during the war of *Exeter*. She should be strengthened and strutted internally as far as possible . . . and come home.'

## The end of the Graf Spee

When dawn broke on 14 December *Graf Spee* was moored in Montevideo harbour. She was now subject to International Law regarding neutral ports. Under the Hague Convention of 1907, *Graf Spee* was permitted to carry out essential repairs to make her seaworthy but she was forbidden from sending radio messages. And, more importantly, Uruguay had complete discretion in deciding how long *Graf Spee* could remain at Montevideo.

In port, Langsdorff was under pressure both from the British and the Uruguayans. The British pressure included an elaborate deception plan to convince Langsdorff that a massive force lay waiting for him at the mouth of the River Plate. In fact the British reinforcements were only HMS *Cumberland* which had arrived from the Falkland Islands. The other reinforcements, including *Ark Royal* and *Renown,* would not arrive until the 19th. Meanwhile Captain Henry McCall, the Naval Attaché at the British Embassy in Buenos Aires, had his spies on board the yacht *Achernar* lying in the channel leading to the harbour. As to the Uruguayans they refused Langsdorff a stay of more than 72 hours.

Despite the prohibition on the use of wireless, Langsdorff consulted Berlin. Hitler, Raeder and Jodl ordered him to 'fight your way through to Buenos Aires if possible'. He was forbidden to accept internment in Uruguay. Somewhat in contradiction to this last order, the trio added: 'Attempt effective destruction, if ship is scuttled.'

In the end Langsdorff settled for scuttling. The report from Captain McCall's, spies describes the scene on the morning of Sunday 17 December:

> Late in the forenoon, however, some extra boat traffic was observed and then the wounded were brought ashore. Shortly after 14.00, boat-loads of men and personal effects were seen to be transferring to the *Tacoma* lying a short distance away across the harbour. At first endeavours were made to preserve secrecy. Canvas screens were rigged up over the gangway so that observers from outboard could not see what was being put into the boats, and the men going on board the *Tacoma* were at once sent below. Later in the afternoon, however, all efforts to preserve secrecy were abandoned and boats full of men were openly ferried across the harbour. By 17.00 over seven hundred men had been counted leaving.

At 6.17 pm the *Graf Spee* left her berth and sailed five miles downstream where she stopped. Boats were seen to leave the ship. Shortly afterwards the explosions began.

Two days later Langsdorff wrote a note in which he said: 'I am happy to pay with my life for any possible reflection on the honour of the flag.' He then shot himself.

*Graf Spee sinking, 17 December 1939.*

### The irrelevance of the surface raiders

In the first four months of the war the commerce raiders had sunk just under 60,000 gross tons of merchant vessels – a rate of 15,000 tons a month. The U-boats would soon be sinking shipping at over ten times that rate. Many accounts of this period focus on the drama of the big ships prowling the seas. Each tragic sinking has proved a spectacle to be told and retold. Each cruiser or pocket battleship is presented as a bringer of unimaginable terror. Yet, as the figures show, the surface raiders were an irrelevance. Raeder naturally justified them on the grounds of the number of Allied warships that were tied down by the raiders. (*Graf Spee* had over twenty vessels searching for her.) But fundamentally, the raiders were an anachronism. The Second World War was a war of tanks, planes and submarines. Glamorous surface ships, other than aircraft carriers, had little place in this new form of warfare. The creation of this irrelevant fleet was the Kriegsmarine's third strategic error in relation to the Atlantic battle.

To round off our assessment of the surface raiders we need to add in the sortie of the battleships *Scharnhorst* and *Gneisenau* in late November. The two ships were sent out on a patrol between Iceland and the Faroe Islands. *Scharnhorst* sank the armed merchant cruiser HMS *Rawalpindi* on 23 November, whose captain, Edward Kennedy, chose to go down fighting against an overwhelming opponent. (Edward Kennedy was the father of the journalist Ludovic Kennedy, who was then an officer on HMS *Tartar*.) Later they encountered the cruiser HMS *Newcastle*, part of a large British force assembled to block the path of the German ships to the Atlantic. The Germans turned tail and made for Wilhelmshaven. Admiral Wilhelm Marschall, who had commanded the patrol, came in for fierce criticism on his return. An angry Admiral Kurt Fricke, scrawled across Marschall's war diary 'Battleships are supposed to shoot, not lay smoke-screens.'

In a war which, so far, lacked big actions and significant victories, Churchill embraced *Exeter's* return to Britain in February 1940 as an opportunity for celebration. Addressing her crew he said:

> 'In this sombre dark winter . . . the brilliant action of the Plate . . . came like a flash of light and colour on the scene, carrying with it an encouragement to all who are fighting, to ourselves and to our allies.'

74

# 10 The promise of radar

## 1937 to 1939

On 4 September 1937 three men boarded an Anson K6260 at Martlesham air base in Suffolk. Leading the team was the physicist Edward Bowen, one of the great radar pioneers. Aged 24 in 1935, he had been spotted by the radar genius Robert Watson-Watt and taken into his Radar Development Team as a Junior Scientific Officer. Now, in 1937, he was in charge of the development of air-to-surface radar. Alongside Bowen were Keith Wood, a technical assistant, and Sergeant Naish, who would pilot the plane that was to make radar history. On board with them was a prototype of a 200 megahertz radar set. The one thing that was not on board was a radio – an omission that came close to ending their days.

The men in the Anson were to join an exercise in which HMS *Courageous*, with her destroyers, would deploy her aircraft. By the time Bowen's team reached the exercise area there was a heavy haze and wisps of fog swirled around the plane. Bowen and Wood were too busy looking at the radar screen to bother about the weather. It was 8.00 am exactly when a strong echo at five or six miles showed up on their screen. This was coming from the ships. All looked set for the exercise to go smoothly ahead. But when the three men glanced down at the ocean again, they saw signal lamps flashing wildly, followed by gunfire. Before they could take in what was happening, *Courageous'* 15 Swordfish were taking off and coming towards the Anson. Bowen and Wood were simultaneously paralysed by fear and ecstatic at their success: the Swordfish were showing up on the radar. Had the Swordfish shot down the Anson that day, no one would have known that it had just made the first air to surface sighting of planes taking off from a carrier. Bowen, Sergeant Naish and Wood returned safely to Martlesham, where they discovered the truth about their sortie. The exercise had been cancelled two hours before it was due to start. They had been duly informed: by radio.

*Edward Bowen, who directed the development of air-to-surface radar.*

This first demonstration needed much refinement before the same technology could be packed into reconnaissance planes and bombers. It was not until December 1939 that the radar researchers had something that could do the job. This radar, known as ASV Mk 1, used a 1.5 metre signal (200 MHz). Its range and definition were limited but, at last, planes were able to spot ships and their aircraft, even in bad weather. But spotting *Courageous* was one thing: could ASV Mk I really spot a U-boat? It was not long before Bowen had the answer.

One day towards the end of November 1939 Bowen was working at his desk when a phone call from the Admiralty was put through to him. He was amazed to hear Admiral James Somerville on the other end of the line – humble researchers were not used to receiving such calls. But Somerville was a man in a hurry – 'the usual channels' were too slow for him. His appeal to Bowen was blunt: the U-boats were taking a heavy toll on Allied shipping and boldly moving on the surface at night in the Channel and around Scapa Flow. Asdic was no use for detecting surfaced U-boats, he told Bowen. The navy had no idea how to tackle this elusive enemy. Could the Radar Development Team help? Bowen replied that he thought that airborne radar might be able to detect a submarine, but no one had ever tested the idea. Somerville leapt at this tenuous means of defeating the night-time U-boats and asked whether Bowen and his team would agree to a trial.

By this time Bowen was based at RAF St Athan in South Wales, along with about 14,000 RAF personnel. It was wartime. It was winter. The weather was bad. And Somerville was in a hurry: the trials were to start on 2 December. The first step was for the radar team and their equipment to be flown to Gosport Naval Base in a Hudson. Bowen took one look at the murky winter sky and decided to make his own way to Portsmouth, driving 'under black-out conditions'. He made good time and found a bed for the night just outside Portsmouth. Next morning Bowen was in Somerville's office at an early hour, but there was no sign of the Hudson. (It did not arrive until late morning.)

Somerville outlined the plan. He first revealed a complication that he had not been able to mention over a telephone line. Gosport may have been a major Royal Navy base, but there was a risk of U-boat attacks in the waters around the base. Bowen's target was to be an obsolete submarine – the *L27*. Elaborate precautions had to be taken to ensure that the Hudson's radar found the boat before a U-boat sank it. This severely limited the means by which the *L27* and the Hudson could communicate during the trial. Radio was out of the question.

Before taking off, Bowen was shown around *L27*, where he and the commander discussed the proposed trial runs. A glance at the radio equipment in the submarine was enough to undermine Bowen's faith in the boat. The transmitter was a First World War device and the receiver used DEQ valves – a type that were already obsolete in 1914, even though the boat had been built in 1918. It was perhaps no bad thing that Somerville had ruled out the use of radio, thought Bowen.

And so the trial began. *L27* was to follow an agreed set of straight line runs. (A huge but necessary risk in an area where zigzagging was mandatory.) At the end of each run the submarine would signal its next run by Aldis lamp to the Hudson. *L27* would give start and stop signals for its runs with red and green Very pistols.

All did not go according to plan.

The exercise was to be carried out with great secrecy, which meant that no other planes or vessels were aware of what was going on. Winter also played its part. *L27* was lying ready to make its first run. Along came a plane, much like the Hudson, but obscured by the murky conditions. The submarine signalled to the plane, and the plane responded with a stick of bombs. The 'Hudson' was actually a Junkers JU-88 which had somehow penetrated the air space of the naval base. *L27* dived and stayed down for about half-an-hour. On surfacing, another plane appeared. Not being sure whether it was the Hudson, *L27* sent up a flare. The plane – a Spitfire this time – turned and spat 10 mm cannon at the submarine. Back down went *L27*, still having had no contact with the Hudson. On coming up again *L27* finally saw the Hudson, and sent up a recognition flare. But it was a dud – and their last. Finally communication was established by Aldis lamp and the trial runs began. But what of the results – bought at – nearly – the cost of the lives of the *L27* crew?

The results were not promising. At a height of 3000 feet, the Hudson could detect the submarine at ranges of up to three miles. End-on, the range was a great deal less. Such a short range would require planes searching for U-boats to run up and down six mile-wide strips – an unthinkably heavy strain on resources. ASV Mk I did not look like the miracle that Somerville needed.

For reasons that Bowen does not make clear, the results of the trials on the second day were significantly different. Patrolling at 5-6000 feet, the radar picked up *L27 end on* at 5 to 6 miles. Although beam-on detection was not tested that day, it would have been about double the range for end-on. This was the sort of performance that Somerville had asked for.

That December day set in train the events that were to lead to triumph in the Battle of the Atlantic. ASV Mk I proved to be not very reliable and did not account for many sinkings – although it was most successful at forcing U-boats to submerge. But it gave Churchill and the Chiefs of Staff confidence in the potential of radar and ensured that its research was the highest of all research priorities. The final wartime air-to-surface radar – ASV Mk III – was to deliver the critical turning point in the Battle of the Atlantic.

Meanwhile winning the Battle of the Atlantic depended entirely on the destroyers and other escort vessels. Now these were to become the target of the Nazi war machine.

# 11 Gold from the Thames mud

## Late 1939

### *The loss of HMS Blanche*

On the morning of 13 November the destroyer HMS *Blanche* was in the Thames Estuary with HMS *Basilisk*, escorting the minelayer HMS *Adventure*. Since the start of the war *Blanche* had escorted several North Sea convoys and had carried out patrols in the Channel. Escorting *Adventure* should have been just another routine task. But unknown to Lieutenant Commander R M Aubrey, *Blanche* was steaming into a minefield laid the previous night by four German destroyers.

The sea was calm and there was little sense of the peril that lurked below. Then, at 5.26 am *Adventure* struck a mine, which ripped open a massive chunk of her hull directly under the bridge. The damage was extensive and 23 men had been killed. She immediately began to flood. *Basilisk* was soon taking off the injured while *Blanche* stood guard. Shortly after taking up her station, she too struck a mine.

'A terrific explosion shook the ship,' Able Seaman Hoyle told the *Daily Mirror*. 'I saw a man blown right past me over the side of the ship and into the water … the mast snapped and crashed down.' Water immediately poured into *Blanche*. Soon the quarterdeck was awash, but there was still no order to abandon ship. The uninjured began a battle to rescue trapped comrades from below. They fought their way through the tangled mess of wood and steel, searching the darkened bowels of the ship. In the galley they found the cook, too badly injured to move unaided, and brought him up. Some of the badly injured had to be tied to stretchers before they could be brought to the deck. On deck, each injured man was put into a lifejacket for fear the ship would go under. One sailor told the *Mirror*, 'I saw a man give an injured mate his lifebelt'. Meanwhile the tug *Fabia* had arrived and tow ropes were attached to

*Blanche*. But she was too far gone. She rolled over and sank at 9.50 am. Lieutenant Commander Aubrey, in the sea with the survivors, swam round offering words of encouragement. The tug, released from the abandoned towing, soon pulled most of the men from the water. The remainder were picked up by a trawler and a pleasure boat. With one man dead and twelve injured, the human casualties were lighter than for the still floating *Adventure*.

HMS *Blanche* was the first British destroyer to be sunk in the war. Such losses were to be expected. How she was sunk was another matter. She was sunk by a magnetic mine. Its defeat would be a matter of the greatest urgency.

## Magnetic mines

Magnetic mines make use of the fact that steel-hulled ships have a magnetic field. One part of this is the magnetism induced in the hull during construction – the hammering and riveting are responsible for this. But that component is too weak to be detected by a mine. Instead the mines make use of the fact that, as a ship moves through the Earth's magnetic field, it distorts that field. This distortion gives ships in the Northern hemisphere a vertical magnetism with the north pole downwards. It was this polarity that was detected by the mines.

The basic German magnetic mines were launched from a surface vessel into water 10 to 15 fathoms deep (60 to 90 feet). They then sank to the bottom, where they automatically activated their ship detection systems. Once self-primed, a mine would detonate when it detected the vertical magnetism of a passing ship. (This basic form was also manufactured in versions for releasing from torpedo tubes or for dropping by parachute from low-flying planes.)

By the time that HMS *Blanche* was struck, Germany had been using magnetic mines for over two months. The 9000-ton cargo ship *Magdapur* had been the first ship to be sunk in this way. This occurred off the Suffolk coast on 10 September 1939. The damage of the *City of Paris* liner eight days later and the *Phryné* another six days later led the Admiralty to suspect that some new weapon was in use. A committee was established to investigate the phenomenon and it correctly concluded that these sinkings were caused by magnetic mines, but they had no knowledge of their mechanism. When the War Cabinet met on 19 November it was with the knowledge that five ships had succumbed that very day to magnetic mines. Churchill declared them to be 'a grave menace which might well be Hitler's "Secret weapon".'

Nothing better emphasised the potential seriousness of these mines than the attack on the light cruiser HMS *Belfast* on 21 November. She had put to sea to take part in a gunnery exercise but while still passing down the Firth of Forth, she struck a mine. Unlike the sinking of *Blanche*, there was a total embargo on reporting the attack on the *Belfast*. The damage was massive, including bending her keel. She was not recommissioned until November 1942. The enormity of one mine silently dropped into the Firth of Forth being able to put a warship out of action for three years did not escape the Admiralty. Finding a means of dealing with this threat was the highest war priority for the next few weeks.

The Kriegsmarine knew that they had created a devastating weapon, which they were having no difficulty in laying in estuaries up and down the East coast of England. German destroyers successfully laid mines outside Newcastle, the Humber, Cromer and the Thames estuary in 11 mine-laying operations. These had gone undetected despite the fact that large ships were involved. The destroyer *Hermann Künne* was nearly 2500 tons and 410 feet in length. Its captain, Friedrich Kothe, twice took his ship into the Thames. It is no wonder that he recalled, 'It was enough to give one a nervous break-down.'

By late November Raeder was able to report to Hitler that his ships had laid 540 magnetic mines in the Humber and Thames estuaries. Hitler congratulated him on his 'commendable performance'. In a speech to his commanders-in-chief he claimed that 'our little Navy' had 'swept the North Sea clear of the British'. Perhaps Hitler really believed this. We can be sure that Raeder was more realistic. Either way, the two men were soon to receive compelling confirmation of the Royal Navy's continuing presence.

On 13 December Lieutenant Commander Edward Bickford was on patrol in the North Sea in the submarine HMS *Salmon* when he sighted some German warships. These were three cruisers escorting minelaying destroyers. The ships – *Nürnberg*, *Leipzig* and *Köln* – were close enough together for Bickford to fire just one spread of torpedoes. Lookouts on *Nürnberg* spotted two torpedo wakes coming towards the ship. Despite a hard to port turn, one torpedo hit her in the bow. The damage was not mortal. The bulkheads held. *Nürnberg* made for Kiel at 18 knots. There she remained until her repairs were completed in April 1940.

*Leipzig's* fate was far more serious. A torpedo hit her amidships, ripping up her armoured deck and gouging a hole in her keel. She too made port, but was never to sail as a warship again. After repairs she was demoted to a training vessel.

Perhaps it was the damage to *Nürnberg* and *Leipzig* that made Raeder turn to the idea of dropping the mines from planes. He asked Göring to provide suitable planes, but Göring refused to help. Undeterred, Raeder decided to use some of his coastal planes for the operation. It was a serious error that would quickly lead to the neutering of the magnetic mines.

On 20 November nine obsolescent Heinkel 59 float planes took off to deliver mines to the Thames estuary. These flimsy craft, built on wooden frames covered with plywood and fabric, would have been more at home in a museum than on a hazardous mission to an estuary protected with anti-aircraft batteries. It was around 9.00 pm when one of the Heinkels was sighted flying over the sea near Shoeburyness at the mouth of the Thames estuary. A parachute with an object like a kit bag hanging below it opened under the plane. As the parachute descended it swung towards the estuary mud and dropped its load in an exposed position. Within minutes the Admiralty received a report of the drop. By midnight Lieutenant Commander John Ouvry and Lieutenant Commander Roger Lewis from HMS *Vernon* (the Royal Navy's Torpedo Branch) were with Churchill at the Admiralty, ready to take advantage of this lucky find. An hour-and-a-half later they were driving to Southend to inspect the precious object.

*One of the two magnetic mines pulled from the Thames mud in November 1939.*

Ouvry and Lewis had no trouble in recognising the nature of the mine, but in the early hours of the morning it was too dark to effect a recovery. They left the scene and made their plans for the safe defusing of the device. These included arranging for a nearby army base to make a non-magnetic spanner to fit the nuts of the mine. Next day, Ouvry and Lewis, with Chief Petty Officer Baldwin and Able Seaman Vearncombe, returned as the tide was receding. They were surprised to see a second mine sticking out of mud. This gave them two chances to defuse the device. Ouvry and Baldwin were the more experienced men on the scene, so they went to defuse the first mine while Lewis and Able Seaman A L Vearncombe watched through binoculars. If Ouvry and Lewis made a lethal mistake, the other two would at least know what not to do. Their caution proved unnecessary. Soon the detonating system of the first mine had been removed. It was ready to reveal its secrets.

Churchill had been anxiously awaiting news of the operation at the Admiralty. He was elated when the call came through confirming that the job was done; Ouvry and Lewis were on their way back. The two men were tired from having been up all night and the stress of a hazardous defusing operation, but Churchill had not finished with them. He gathered over 80 officers at the Admiralty to hear Ouvry's and Lewis's report. The audience was, said, 'thrilled'.

HMS *Vernon* set to work to study the mine's mechanism. It was soon understood and work on counter-measures began. There were two means by which the mine could be defeated. First, the mines could be destroyed by minesweepers. Second, there might be some means to protect the ships.

Sweeping for magnetic mines was a major challenge for the Admiralty. For a start, magnetic mines sat on the bottom of the sea so existing methods of minesweeping were of no value – those depended on catching the mine by various means. It was Professor Bernard Haigh of Greenwich Naval College who first suggested a method of detonating the mines while they were still on the seabed. This involved dragging heavy cables along the seabed with a massive current passing through them. But it was the Canadian scientist Sir Charles Goodeve who turned this suggesting into a working device, which he called 'the Double-L Sweep'. It was sometime in 1939 when Goodeve put Haigh's idea to the test on the Canoe Lake at Portsmouth. This was rather a public place for testing a top secret device so Goodeve and his team arrived with a sufficient array of model yachts to disguise their intentions. Although there were sailors present to assist in towing the models across the lake, only Goodeve and two assistants knew what was the purpose of the exercise. Goodeve crouched over a voltmeter at the side of the lake and watched as the needle flickered into life. Each flicker was the equivalent of the detonation of a German mine on the lakebed.

A jubilant Goodeve returned to his office to find a Top Secret envelope on his desk. He opened it and read: 'You should discontinue any research on the lines you have indicated in your latest report. It is clear to me that the method you suggest will prove self-cancelling, and cannot work.'

By February 1940 Goodeve's Double-L sweeps were being undertaken by wooden minesweepers in coastal waters. By the end of June, 300 mines had been located and detonated.

Goodeve's sweeping technology came at a time when the magnetic mine was the greatest hazard of the war. The success of his method fully justified the large number of minesweepers that were keeping British coastal waters clear. But sweeping could never find all the mines, nor cope with the problem of the Germans re-laying mines after a British sweep. What Goodeve needed was a method of protecting the steel ships from the mines themselves.

Goodeve decided that the simplest way to protect ships was to reverse their vertical polarity. His first device used vertical cables, attached to the ship, through which ran a current with its North pole upwards. The current could be adjusted to cancel out the ship's magnetism. There was nothing wrong with this method in theory. But in practice there was neither the cabling nor the money to install it except on a few priority vessels.

Goodeve recalled a French suggestion for permanently reversing vertical polarity. This involved running a horizontal insulated cable up and down a vessel while a 1000 to 2000 amp current flowed through it. He first tested the method on single plates and succeeded in inducing the required field. Then he moved on to applying the method to *Vernon's* lighter. His tests showed that it now had a south-pointing field. It was too soon to cry 'Eureka!' since Goodeve could not be certain that the vibration of a ship's engines might degrade the new field. Experience later proved that the induced fields were durable. *And* the process had the advantage that it could be carried out by a ship's own crew.

But Goodeve had still not shown that his method worked on the type of steel used for destroyers. The Admiral Superintendent of the Dockyard refused to let him have any destroyers for testing. For that, he needed the support of Rear-Admiral Frederick Wake-Walker at the Admiralty, who was away at that time. Goodeve was too impatient to wait for the admiral to return. He decided to act for himself. From London, he arranged the sending of an official Admiralty telegram to the Admiral Superintendent, which read: 'Urgent. Please summon Commander Goodeve and find why he has not yet reported on the results of wiping destroyers'. Goodeve got his destroyers. And his demagnetising, known as degaussing, worked on them.

# 12 Was that it?

## January to March 1940

*Weak commanders and faulty torpedoes*

As the old year passed, the 'Phoney War' showed no sign of coming to an end. For Britain, the war remained wholly defensive. Chamberlain had no wish to provoke Hitler by bombing German cities. Meanwhile, the best part of the British Army was sitting in France waiting for the Wehrmacht to take the offensive. But, after four months of moderate U-boat warfare, the Kriegsmarine Operations Division was ready to take a more aggressive approach.

The change in tactics was initiated by Fregattenkapitän Heinz Assmann, a Kriegsmarine staff officer. In a document dated 1 January 1940 he condemned the existing U-boat policy as 'too conservative'. He argued that 'the war against English merchant shipping could be more effectively waged, if there were some change in the U-boat policy' and criticised present strategy because 'it provoked too many successful counter-measures on the part of the English'. It is unlikely that Dönitz was involved in the preparation of this report, which appeared to criticise his war strategy.

A clue to the apparent lack of a Dönitz connection lies in Assmann's main recommendation: more mining. He pointed out that the Royal Navy 'has no defence against ground [magnetic] mines and those are therefore largely effective at present'. He called for urgent action since 'the sooner the operations are carried out the less opposition may be expected'. Assmann's backing of mines is understandable since the magnetic mine had had spectacular success in sinking Allied vessels in shallow waters in the last few months. He was unaware that the British were developing counter-measures, so it was logical for the Kriegsmarine to make the best use of a weapon that was, for now, proving itself. But this argument would not have appealed to

Dönitz. From first to last he wanted his U-boats to be sinking ships directly. His faith in his boats and his commanders was unswerving. Nor was Raeder convinced by Assmann's argument. He attributed the limited success of the U-boats solely to the shortage of boats suitable for long-range operations. Consequently, said Raeder, the best results would be obtained in local waters. As justification, he pointed out that 37 ships had been sunk by torpedo in January. (In fact 46 had been torpedoed, and nine had been sunk by mine, so Raeder had a stronger case than he knew.)

However, Dönitz still lacked enough U-boats to wage serious war. Additionally, many of his commanders were inexperienced. When Korvettenkapitän Herbert Sohler of *U-46* returned to port in early January he was able to report only one sinking. Dönitz acknowledged that this was a 'small result' but said it was due to Sohler's poor firing skill: 'I have decided to give the boat a period of firing practice before her next patrol.' Whether Sohler ever received additional training is not known. Nevertheless he stayed in command of *U-46* until May 1940. Still having sunk only two vessels totalling 8000 tons, he was finally relieved of his command. His poor performance saved him from the inevitable end of almost all U-boat commanders, allowing him to live to the age of 82, dying in 1991. Was it, though, Dönitz rather than Sohler who showed slackness in his sending an ineffective commander out on two further patrols?

Not all U-boat commanders were inadequate. Dönitz received a fillip when Commander Ludwig Mathes reported in early January that *U-44* had sunk eight vessels totalling 31,000 tons on its first active service patrol. This was just the sort of news that Dönitz needed to justify his torpedo policy rather than Assmann's mining. Mathes's patrol was the most successful of the war to date. Just over a month later *U-44* struck a British mine in the North Sea while departing for its second patrol. Its sinking with all hands was bad news for

Dönitz. He was desperately short of U-boats and just as short of good commanders.

*KorvettenkapitänHerbert Sohler (left). One of many ineffective U-boat commanders. During his five patrols in U-46 he sank only two vessels, totalling 8000 tons.*

Sohler and all the other U-boat commanders were under Dönitz's direct control. But Dönitz's greatest headache in early 1940 was outside his control: torpedo failures.

One of the highest profile failures had occurred on 30 October 1939. Commander Wilhelm Zahn in *U-56* could hardly have chosen a more embarrassing situation in which to be the victim of torpedo failure. He was at sea to the west of the Orkneys when he came across HMSs *Nelson*, *Rodney* and *Hood*. He was unaware that on board *Nelson* were Churchill, Admiral Sir Charles Forbes and Pound. (Surely this was a questionable gathering in such a hazardous position.) It was 10.30 am when Zahn saw the three cruisers in his periscope. They were heading straight for him – a position from which he could not attack. To his surprise the three vessels turned about 30 degrees, so exposing their beams to his torpedoes. *Rodney* was in the lead, but Zahn decided to attack *Nelson* which came next in the line. At a range of just under 300 yards he could hardly miss. Three torpedoes sped towards *Nelson*. Zahn's firing was perfect. All three torpedoes smashed into *Nelson's* beam. Two failed to explode at all. The third exploded when not in contact with *Nelson*. Zahn was so upset by his failure to even damage *Nelson* that he delayed reporting the contact to Wilhelmshaven until the evening. By then it was too late for Dönitz to direct the nearby *U-58* to the scene.

Failures like this infuriated Dönitz. It wasn't so much the missed sinkings that dismayed him as their effect on the morale of his men. They risked their lives every time they went to sea; they lived in appalling conditions of dirt and discomfort; and they fed off an unappetising, boring diet. Their compensation came in their sinkings. Being denied these by dud torpedoes made their sacrifices harder to face.

Amongst the boats that had recently reported torpedo failures were *U-15, U-20, U-24, U-59* and *U-60*. Their reports led to a major conference at Wilhelmshaven on 17 January between the U-boat Arm and the Torpedo Experimental Command in search of a definitive answer to the torpedo problem. The U-boat Arm was convinced that the MZ (magnetic) firing mechanism was the cause of the trouble. This detected the magnetism of the target ship to determine the right moment to detonate the torpedo's explosive charge under the vessel. The MZ was a tricky device to use since variations in the Earth's magnetism necessitated 16 versions of the MZ mechanism. And, when used, adjustments had to be made according to the weight of the target.

But the Torpedo Experimental Command were unwilling to accept responsibility for the failures. They argued that the fault must lie with the commanders having miscalculated the size of their target ships. Nevertheless the MZ mechanism was withdrawn a few months later. From the summer of 1940 to the end of 1942 the U-boats used only impact detonators.

*Admiral of the Fleet Sir Dudley Pound on the bridge of SS Queen Mary.*

A few days after the conference, Dönitz confided to the War Log his firm opinion that the torpedo failures were 'the greatest difficulty with which the U-Boat Arm has had to contend with since the beginning of the war'. He calculated that four out of ten unsuccessful shots were caused by torpedo failures. Translating this into lost tonnage sunk, he arrived at a figure of a missed 300,000 tons.

Another factor that limited the successes of Dönitz's boats was the poor locations of their bases. It was bad enough having bases that had no direct access to the Atlantic. This problem was exacerbated by the icing-up of the

Baltic in January. Passages in and out between the North Sea and the Baltic were taking days. Each boat had to be towed out, accompanied by an ice-breaking escort. Despite this assistance, *U-48's* propellers were damaged by ice; *U-29* had ice damage to her bow caps; and *U-53's* protective ice shoe was smashed, forcing it to return for repairs.

## Developments in anti-submarine warfare

While Raeder and Dönitz were exploring ways to inflict the maximum possible damage on Allied merchant ships, the British Admiralty was honing its anti-submarine warfare techniques. Fregattenkapitän Paul Büchel of *U-32* paid the British an unintended tribute when he reported to Dönitz in early January. He had been on a minelaying expedition off the River Clyde but told Dönitz that he had been unable to penetrate the inner Clyde on account of 'fixed listening stations' and 'strong patrols'. Not that Dönitz was ever ready to accept reports that suggested a lack of audacity in his commanders. He acidly recorded: 'Until I hear the Commanding Officer's verbal report I shall not be satisfied that the first operation was really impossible.' (Dönitz's debriefs of returning commanders were forensic in their probing of every decision a commander had made and every opportunity for attack that he had missed.)

Meanwhile, the British Admiralty were still maintaining their misplaced confidence in asdic. It was with their full support that Churchill was able to tell the War Cabinet on 20 January 1940 that 'Our faithful asdic detector smells them out in the depths of the sea ... I do not doubt that we shall break their strength and break their purpose.'

Morale in the Admiralty was remarkably high in early 1940. Towards the end of January, Churchill was in the Free Trade Hall in Manchester with his wife and their daughter Mary to give a speech on the war. Alderman White, the Lord Mayor, introduced him to the vast audience of 2500. The First Lord graphically described the war at sea which, he said, had been 'at full pitch from the very first moment'. In combative mood he accused Hitler of having 'no respect for the laws and conventions of war ... Our merchant ships and the ships of almost every neutral sea-going country have been sunk at sight ... Even humble fishing-boats have been attacked ... their crews left to drown.' He drew applause when he said, 'the Navy has not failed the nation'. He then turned to the 'marked success' of the Royal Navy: 'German trade had been swept from the seas'. The navy had convoyed 7500 ships, of which only 15 had been sunk. In the first five months of the war the escorts had proved highly effective. Almost all the successful U-boat attacks had been against the independent sailings, of which 162 had been sunk. This optimism in the Admiralty continued as the figures came in for the stopping of German trade. In February six cargo ships had left Spain for Germany; only one reached its destination. When a second group of seven vessels set out on the same course, not one reached Germany. Six of them had scuttled. The Royal Navy blockade of Germany had denied her any trade links by sea.

## Kriegsmarine Enigma

In February 1940 Dönitz uncharacteristically ignored his own rules when he sent *U-33* off to lay mines in the Firth of Clyde. A sunk U-boat in shallow waters could easily be raised by the Allies. For this reason mine-layers left their Enigma machines behind when they sailed. But somehow *U-33* departed with its machine on board.

Signs that this would not be an easy patrol appeared even before departure when one hole was found in a torpedo tube and another in a copper pipe. The crew patched up the holes and departed on their mission. By Sunday 11 February Kapitänleutnant Hans-Wilhelm von Dresky had his boat sitting on the Clyde mud, ready for night time mine-laying.

Sometime after midnight von Dresky ordered his boat to surface. Four lookouts took up their stations in the dark. Within minutes the alarm sounded as a warship came into view. Von Dresky, thinking that the vessel was a cruiser putting to sea, ordered a dive while the ship passed by. But he was mistaken in his identification: the vessel was the minesweeper HMS *Gleaner* on patrol. At first von Dresky was lucky as *Gleaner* passed by and *U-33* and went off into the night. Later, at 2.50 am *Gleaner's* asdic began to ping. A lookout spotted something white – possibly the spray from *U-33's* periscope. Lieutenant Commander Hugh Price swung *Gleaner* round and homed-in on the source of the echoes. Depth charges were soon crashing around von Dresky's boat as it sank to the paltry depth of 118 feet, where it sat on the bottom. The boat survived this first attack and the second at 4.00 am. Then came the 5.00 am attack. By now *U-33* was immobilised on the seabed. There was no hope of creeping away. All von Dresky could do was to order the tanks to be blown to force the boat's rise. In the chaotic ascent, the boat burst through the surface. The hatch flew open and most of the men scrambled up the ladder and dived into the water. Back in the boat a rear-guard set the explosive charges. All the while, *Gleaner's* guns were hammering away at the U-boat. As the panic increased, von Dresky aborted his attempt to unscrew the Enigma machine. Instead, he handed out Enigma wheels to members of the crew for disposal when they were in the water. But one man, Friedrich Kumpf, forgot to discard his wheels. And he never even noticed the unknown British seaman who pulled them from his pockets as he boarded *Gleaner*. This was the first capture of the extra wheels that the U-boat Enigma used compared to the Wehrmacht version. They were soon in the hands of the Government Code and Cypher School at Bletchley Park. The intelligence that resulted from Bletchley Park's Enigma decrypts was known as 'Ultra' and became the most closely guarded secret of the war. (When Ultra messages went to commanders overseas, they were handed to a Special Liaison Unit at each command post. These officers allowed the commander to read the Ultra message before taking it from him and destroying it. No commander was allowed to copy or forward an Ultra-based message.)

In the case of *U-33,* the wheels had fallen into British hands by chance, but a more systematic approach was needed if Bletchley Park was to keep up its supply of Enigma decrypts. In June Admiral Charles Forbes belatedly issued instructions to destroyer commanders on the importance of retrieving code-books, papers and machines from U-boats before their crews had a chance to destroy them. His approach was ruthless. The sailors were to approach the enemy vessel with Lewis guns blazing and attempt to jam a dead body in the conning tower hatch and so thwart any attempt to submerge. Any U-boat man seen to be throwing materials into the sea was to be gunned down without warning. (Whether such attacks ever happened is unknown. But it might have been actions like these that led Dönitz to say that the Allies were shooting submariners in the water.)

There was, though, still a long way to go before Kriegsmarine Enigma could be read. It would not be until November 1940 that anything useful for convoy operations could be extracted from the mass of signals between the U-Boat Arm and its boats. At that point, John Godfrey, the Director of Naval Intelligence, issued additional instructions on the capture of Enigma machines. They were to be sent to him by hand of an officer 'by the quickest possible route'. He went on, 'It is important that the machine should not be touched or disturbed in any way, except as is necessary for its removal and packing.'

Bletchley Park's fame for decrypting Enigma and other Axis codes has over-shadowed another important operation in defeating the U-boats: the Submarine Tracking Room at the Admiralty. A decrypted message, by itself, often meant very little. Only when put alongside other intelligence did its meaning and importance become clear. In the case of tracking U-boats, this task fell to Rodger Winn, who directed the Submarine Tracking Room throughout the war. Winn was a lawyer and a civilian, but he had the mental skills to sift confusing, conflicting and partial data and turn it into meaningful intelligence for convoy and escort commanders. His team ran a 24-hour operation at Admiralty House, taking in Bletchley Park's decrypts amongst other intelligence on U-boat locations and movements. His unit also produced a monthly bulletin of less time-critical intelligence, giving technical updates on both U-boats and Allied anti-submarine warfare.

*Bletchley Park in 1938 when the first intelligence workers gathered there.*

## The close of the Phoney War

By April 1940 the Phoney War was drawing to an end. Since 1939 hostilities had been largely confined to the sea. On land the German and Allied armies faced each other with no sign of a move on either side. In the air, both sides were hesitant about initiating a bombing war. And even at sea the war was perfunctory with no more than ten or so U-boats on operational patrols at any one time. For each of the seven days of 17-22 March 1940, the War Log entry consists of just three words: 'Nothing to report.' The same three words record the U-boat war for the eight days of 24-31 March. Tonnage sunk was steadily decreasing from 135,000 tons in January to 51,000 tons in April. A combination of a shortage of U-boats and defective torpedoes had severely limited what Dönitz could expect to achieve. The Allies meanwhile were convinced that they had the U-boat menace under control. Churchill was comforted knowing that, although Britain had suffered a net loss of 200,000 tons of shipping in the first six months of the war, this was less that the 450,000 tons lost 'in the single deadly month of April 1917'.

In early April 1940 Prime Minister Neville Chamberlain was in equally buoyant mood when he spoke at a meeting of the National Union of Conservative and Unionist Associations. It was on this occasion that he famously declared that Hitler had 'missed the bus'. Central to his argument was that the first seven months of the war had given Britain time to 'tune up every arm … so enormously to add to our fighting strength that we can face the future with a calm and steady mind whatever it brings'.

Four days later the German invasion of Norway began. Thirty five days later the German panzers rolled into France. These two events were to give Germany anchorages in Norway and ready-made ports on the French Atlantic coast. As far as the Battle of the Atlantic was concerned, Hitler had not missed the bus: he had jumped into a racing car and left a complacent Chamberlain standing bemused in the pits.

*Map 1. Sinkings September 1939 to May 1940: o = Merchant ship; + = U-boat.*

# 13 A new war

## April to June 1940

### The land war begins

The uneasy calm of the Phoney War came to an end with the German invasions of Denmark and Norway in April, followed by the invasion of France in May, the evacuation at Dunkirk and the seizure of the French Atlantic ports. This chapter explores how these events impacted on the Battle of the Atlantic.

Raeder had first suggested seizing Norwegian ports in a proposal to Hitler in October 1939. At that time he was more concerned about preventing Britain from obtaining the bases than their advantages to the Kriegsmarine. He was alarmed at the thought of the British being in control of the entry to the Baltic, so blocking the exit of German vessels. But once Hitler became committed to occupying the Norwegian ports, Raeder feared that all the credit would go to the Wehrmacht and the Luftwaffe. He was determined that his ships would play their own decisive role, even though he privately wrote that to do so 'breaks all rules of naval warfare'. As a result, he committed a massive naval force to confront the even greater power of the British Home Fleet. This is not the place to recount the invasion of Norway which began on 9 April. Our interest here is solely in how the invasion impacted on the naval strength of the Kriegsmarine in general and the Battle of the Atlantic in particular.

The invasion was a triumph for the Wehrmacht. For Raeder it was a catastrophe. He lost a total of 57 vessels, including the light cruisers *Königsberg* and *Karlsruhe*, 10 destroyers and 6 U-boats. The worst aspect for Raeder was the loss of his prize new cruiser *Blücher*, particularly since he had opposed allowing her to take part in the battle. The decision, he said, had proved an 'unequivocal strategic mistake'. And what had the Kriegsmarine gained that was of use in the Battle of the Atlantic? No more than some safe havens for both its U-boats and capital ships, but still havens too far from the Atlantic to be useful.

The needless sacrifice of these 57 vessels was the Kriegsmarine's fourth strategic error.

*British warships under German air attack at Narvik in April 1940.*

The Allied naval loses were also serious. The Royal Navy's loss of two cruisers and the carrier *Glorious* were bearable. But the nine destroyers that had gone to the bottom were another matter. The convoys were already too lightly escorted. Britain was in no position to lose these precious escort vessels. Worst of all, though, was that Germany now had unfettered access to Swedish iron ore.

The invasion of Norway was quickly followed by the German invasion of France on 10 May. Sixteen days later British ships started taking men off the beaches at Dunkirk. Six destroyers were sunk near the beaches and another 19 damaged. This was a further blow that the Royal Navy could scarcely contain. But worse was to come.

On 11 June, with France still fighting for her life, Italy entered the war. This had grievous implications for the Atlantic war. The Italian Navy possessed 106 submarines and 52 destroyers. Although Britain had a strong command over the Strait of Gibraltar, it was possible that much of the Italian fleet would make its way into the Atlantic. It might even gain the use of Spanish ports.

France capitulated ten days later. The Atlantic ports were there for Germany's taking. In just over ten weeks Britain had moved from a position of strength in the Atlantic to a position of the utmost peril. Not since the Spanish Armada had appeared in the English Channel in 1588 had Britain found herself so defenceless in the face of a formidable foe.

### 'The spell was broken'

Even before the signing of the French Armistice, Hitler had ordered the capture of the French Atlantic ports of Brest, Lorient and St. Nazaire. It was not long before the French realised that their fleet in harbour was in danger. By 17 June the 83 warships in Brest were sailing for safe havens in Dakar, Casablanca and other French territories. Ships in other ports followed. Later, in July, Churchill begged the French Admiral François Darlan to turn some of these vessels over to the Allies. When he refused, Force H in Gibraltar attacked the moored French Fleet at Mers-el-Kébir to prevent it falling into French hands. One battleship was sunk, five other warships were damaged and nearly 1300 French sailors were killed.

Meanwhile, the French dockyard workers were feverously destroying Brest harbour. By the time the German naval commander Vice admiral Lothar von Arnauld de la Perière arrived there on 21 June to take command, there were no ships in the harbour and the oil stores were ablaze. The colossal damage wrought by the dockyard workers was clearly visible, with sunken vessels blocking the harbour, smashed cranes and burning buildings. There was not a single dock in a useable state.

The Germans had never expected France to fall so rapidly, nor to find themselves in such easy possession of the Atlantic ports. When the Luftwaffe had strewn mines in the seas outside the French ports in an attempt to prevent the escape of the French Fleet, the German commanders never thought that within days they would be bringing U-boats into those same ports. No record had been kept of the locations of the minefields so the Kriegsmarine was compelled to set up a massive mine-clearing exercise before they could use the harbours.

Dönitz was one of the few naval people who had shown confidence in the Wehrmacht's powers of conquest. As the Wehrmacht sped across France, he had a train standing ready at Wilhelmshaven, loaded with torpedoes and spares, ready to despatch to Lorient. His anticipation of the fall of the ports ensured that they were ready for the first U-boats to fuel, provision and take on torpedoes by 28 June. This was an unimaginable disaster for the Allies. The U-boats, which had taken days to reach the Atlantic from German ports, could now sail directly into the ocean.

The speed of the setting up of the new bases was impressive. The first U-boat docked at Lorient on 7 July. By early August the new bases were carrying out minor repairs to U-boats. By October, Brest, the largest of the bases, had 650 German workers and 2500 French. However, it was never an easy base to manage, having a reputation for espionage on U-boat movements and sabotage in the repair yards. For the French, a nut dropped inside a pipe, a loose seal, or severed cable was a worthwhile form of protest at their humiliating occupation.

One of the first U-boat commanders to sail from the Atlantic ports was the ace Victor Oehrn in *U-37*. He departed on 30 August and returned 14 days later having sunk seven ships totalling 24,500 tons. Dönitz later commented on *U-37's* success, saying, 'The spell is broken.' The acquisition of the Atlantic ports quickly boosted sinkings. From a monthly average of 120,000 tons in the first six months of the year the sinkings by U-boat in the Atlantic grew to 245,000 tons a month. In part, though, this increase was due to the British Admiralty holding destroyers in home waters to repel a widely anticipated invasion of Britain.

## Allied destroyer shortage

With Norway and France both in German hands, Dönitz was able to release U-boats that had supported the two invasions to return to the Atlantic. Churchill, who had become Prime Minister and Minister of Defence on 10 May, was alarmed at the prospect of facing a newly invigorated U-Boat Arm with his depleted stock of destroyers. Added to the U-boat menace, there was the unthinkable peril of the loss of his French ally. Britain's modest naval programme of the late 1930s had been based on the assumption that the British and French fleets would stand together in a war against Germany. Now Churchill feared that Hitler might turn the French fleet against the Royal Navy. Britain's command of the sea would speedily vanish. It was this fear that led Churchill to appeal to President Roosevelt for the despatch of 35 American destroyers to tide Britain over until her own construction programme was in full production. The need, Churchill told Roosevelt was 'a matter of life or death'.

But aid from America was not to be had for the asking. On 26 June Churchill received disappointing news from America. Without the least warning, the United States Attorney General had cancelled a British order for 20 motor torpedo boats. The reason, he said, was that 'sales to a belligerent of an armed vessel is illegal'. The implications were terrifying: there would be no destroyers either. For now, Britain had to fight the Atlantic battle alone and unsupported.

*Operation Sea Lion*

While Raeder failed to find a clear strategy for the new naval war, Hitler caused further confusion as he wavered over Operation Sea Lion – his plan to invade Britain. His vacillation held up all other German strategic decisions and compelled Britain to keep large forces in home waters, ready to repel the invaders.

The Wehrmacht was not keen to risk the leap across the Channel. For them, Sealion was a last resort. General Alfred Jodl, Hitler's Chief of Operations, preferred using sea and air power to blockade Britain and terrorise her population into submission. The Luftwaffe, he argued, '[could] bring Britain, militarily, to her knees'. Even so, the Wehrmacht made a geographic study of Britain and printed 7000 copies of a guidebook for officers. This gave information on roads, key targets such as oil refineries and vehicle manufacturing plants. The south east of England could be 'readily transversed', the writers noted. They also mentioned Britain's 'admirably well-developed network of roads'. Raeder, on the other hand, was busy identifying the ships that he would use for the operation and collecting information on the English coastline from the Wash down to the Isle of Wight.

Hitler was particularly secretive about Operation Sealion. From beginning to end he never revealed his true intentions and was happy to keep his admirals and generals guessing his next move. Whether he was ever really serious about the invasion, we shall never know. But he was serious enough to divert massive resources to barge-building and other preparations. These activities directly impacted on the Atlantic war. On 25 July 1940 Raeder warned Hitler of the damaging effect that Sea Lion was having on the German economy. He claimed that inland water and maritime transport were seriously disrupted, dockyards had had to put off other work, U-boat production was curtailed as was work on the *Tirpitz*. Raeder's position is understandable. He needed to concentrate his boats in the Atlantic and begin using the French Atlantic coast ports. He was in no mood for any further diversion of resources to support the Wehrmacht.

Raeder's forces were also depleted by the preparations to lay millions of mines across the Channel to protect the invasion fleet. Additionally he had to keep ready numerous boats to sweep the British minefields if the invasion went ahead. By 31 July he was able to tell Hitler that the Kriegsmarine's own minelaying could be completed within two weeks of the Luftwaffe first 'gaining air superiority'.

On 31 July, Hitler called a conference with Field Marshal Keitel, Chief of the Armed Forces High Command, Jodl and Raeder to review the invasion preparations. Raeder reported good progress on his naval arrangements. All would be ready by 15 September. Having demonstrated his practical commitment to the invasion, Raeder then gave a lengthy speech on the technical difficulties of the invasion. He described the Wehrmacht's plan to invade when there was no moon as 'hazardous'. He talked of the risks of manoeuvring 'slow, unwieldy transport units, concentrated in a small space, mixed with motor-boats ... and escorted by light units of the Navy'. The navy, he declared, needed 'a certain amount of light for navigational reasons'. He continued with a discourse on tides, of landing craft beached for 12 hours before the tide could take them off again ... On and on he went. He knew that he was in danger of saying that his navy was incapable of effecting an invasion. To counteract this impression he finished by declaring that 'the best time for the operation, all things considered, would be May 1941'. But for all Raeder's attempts to use technical objections to disguise his antagonism to the plan, the army left the meeting still committed to being ready to invade on 15 September. All that was needed was Hitler's order to proceed.

The order never came. It was time for the U-boats to show just how much havoc they could create from their new bases.

The real Battle of the Atlantic was only just beginning.

# Part 2: Triumph of the hunters

## 14 'The Terror of Tobermory'

### Mid-1940

*Vice Admiral Sir Gilbert Stephenson*

With the U-boats operating from the Atlantic ports and the prospect of invasion gradually receding, Britain's survival now depended on the escorts. In the early months of the war the escort crews had been taken for granted. In the stampede to requisition and convert trawlers and other vessels into patrol ships, and the rush to man them, little thought had been given as to how battle-ready the officers and men were. It was around March 1940 that Admiral Pound recognised the problem. He was taking men from offices, schools, commerce and elsewhere in ever increasing numbers. After a meagre training they found themselves facing treacherous seas and a ruthless enemy. If the war at sea was to be won, Pound's improvised escorts had to be turned into, at least, consummate defenders of the merchant ships which in the longer term had to become deadly victors over the U-boats. He had no doubts who was the man for this job.

The 62-year-old Vice Admiral Sir Gilbert Stephenson had an impeccable pedigree. None other than the great Admiral 'Jacky' Fisher had singled him out to be a destroyer commander at the age of 23 in 1901. His acquaintance with U-boats went back 20 years to his time as Director of the Anti-Submarine Division of the Admiralty after the First World War. In this new war he already had four months of service as a convoy commodore with the Atlantic convoys. He had followed this by the job of organising the anti-submarine patrols off the Norwegian coast in early 1940. But Pound knew that Stephenson was made for greater things. *He* was the ideal man to set up and run an escort working-up base. He received his orders to find a suitable harbour in Quiberon Bay off the French Atlantic coast.

Stephenson's first task was to find and requisition his own command ship. He soon located the *Philante*, a sumptuous 1600-ton yacht owned by Sir Thomas Sopwith, the aviation magnate. It offered one of the most luxurious billets of the war with, according to *Yachting Magazine*, an oak-panelled wardroom that could seat 50 people at dinner at one table; and officers' cabins that had private bathrooms, divan beds and the fittings of a West End hotel suite. With *Philante* requisitioned, Stephenson was all set to begin his search for a Quiberon Bay base. And then came the invasion of France. The free world had shrunk overnight, as had Stephenson's options. He had to let *Philante* go as Quiberon Bay became enemy territory.

Stephenson was now directed north to set up his base on the Isle of Mull in the Scottish Inner Hebrides. There, far away from passing enemy vessels, was a small town looking out onto a large sheltered cove. Its name was Tobermory, now ever to be associated with the 'Terror of Tobermory' – Stephenson himself.

Once again Stephenson had to find his own command vessel. This time he picked out the passenger ship *Western Isles* which was laid-up in the Kyles of Bute. Her modest past was put behind her as she became the flagship of the Anti-Submarine Training School. Thousands of officers and men would come to associate her with the life-changing encounter that they would experience under Stephenson.

But the war was full of surprises and setbacks. Stephenson's work on setting up the Anti-Submarine Training School came to an abrupt halt with an imperative signal from the Admiralty. He and HMS *Western Isles* were to proceed to the beach at Dunkirk. The 62-year-old admiral spent three days and three nights without sleep organising boats and pulling men from the sea. Much of the time he was in the water, aiding exhausted men and nonswimmers. There he goaded other officers into more vigorous – and often, more dangerous – action to save the men. Having proved what he could do when pushed beyond the normal limits of human endurance, he was now ready to make the same demands of the men who would man the escort vessels.

*SS Batavia, the sister ship of HMS Western Isles.*

The idea of the Tobermory work-up programme was simple; its ambition was monumental. The British shipyards were steadily turning out new escort vessels (or converted requisitions) while the recruitment offices were signing up civilians to man them. A typical escort vessel would have just ten per cent Royal Navy officers and men. The remaining crew would almost certainly have never been to sea before, even in a pleasure craft. Somehow these men had to be turned into fighting teams, sure of their own skills and confident in those of their fellows. The exigencies of war allowed just a week to ten days for this near miracle to be achieved.

The war had been going on for nearly a year by the time that Tobermory opened for business – just at the time when the Atlantic battle began to become deadly serious. There was a huge backlog of ships already at sea, manned by barely-trained crews and in desperate need of Stephenson's course. At this stage of the war the training was described as 'a refresher course of a week or ten days in new weapons and tactics to vessels of destroyer class and under, after long periods at sea'. Later, the course would become standard for newly commissioned vessels as well as those already at sea.

On an escort vessel's arrival at Tobermory, Stephenson spent the first evening with the its commander. He was a shrewd judge of the officer class and would quickly reach his own conclusions as to the training needs of the officers and men of a particular vessel, and the strengths and weaknesses of their commander. On the following day the commander was required to meet his officers for a discussion of the organisation of the ship – presumably Stephenson provided some framework for this. Meanwhile Stephenson's staff inspected the ship from stem to stern, from the masthead to the keel. The least deficiency – Stephenson only had one standard: perfection – was noted and orders were issued for its remedy. Later in the morning the whole complement would watch a film on escort work. For most of the audience this would be the first time that they had had any exposure to the idea that escort work was *team* work. To find and sink a U-boat, every skill – asdic, navigation, ship-handling, signalling, gunnery, depth charge handling – had to support all the other skills. One weak link was enough for a U-boat to escape. Or, worse, for a destroyer to be the victim of the attack.

The second day was not yet over. The men and officers were kept busy honing their basic skills such as gunnery and depth charge working. And, later in the war, radar was added to the list for day two. The third day was devoted to signalling … and so the course went on.

But the heart of the course was the *ship training*. The commander would be given a manoeuvre to carry out – perhaps attacking a U-boat with the guns or tracking Tobermory's one submarine. Stephenson and his staff would watch hawk-eyed to assess how well each man and each function worked to support the others.

Escort commanders were enabled to see the battle from both sides. One day they would be in the destroyer chasing the submarine; another day they would be down in the submarine trying to escape the escort vessel above. Lieutenant Commander James Allon recalled the submarine as being 'very old'. 'It leaked like a sieve once under the sea [and] the pressure made the small leaks spurt out in, to me, an alarming way.'

A good deal of the training took place in classes held on *Western Isles*. These covered topics such as aircraft recognition and signalling. The more complex training – especially the working together aspects – was done by *Western Isles* staff on board the visiting vessel.

No one who trained under Stephenson ever forgot him. Some wished they could. Cyril Stephens, a torpedoman was succinct in his assessment of Tobermory: 'it was murder'.

There was more than a touch of the autocrat about Stephenson. He boasted that 'I had a rule never to ask permission to do anything, never to ask for anything – take it and tell them to pay for it, do it and tell them I've done it!' Without authority, he took officers off the course if he thought them unfit for their escort role. When challenged about this after the war, he told his biographer, Richard Baker, that, 'In many cases I had to take officers out of ships, not because there was anything wrong with them, but just because they were worn out – they were exhausted.'

Signalman Jim Maddison spent two weeks training at Tobermory. He later described Stephenson as 'a real tyrant ... who had everybody from the skipper to the ABs [able seamen] and stokers on their toes for twenty-four hours a day'.

In part Stephenson's reputation derives from his extreme determination to shake-up officers and to prepare them to face the worst that action could bring. He delighted in 'emergencies'. He sprung these on commanders and other officers without any warning: 'Your ship's sinking,' he would shout. Or 'the engine room's on fire'. 'You're under a massive air attack.' He compounded these improvisations by waiting for the commander to respond to one emergency and then piling another emergency on top, and another ... There was method behind Stephenson's eccentric style as he sought to expose any lurking incompetence in the officers. He knew that the officers he released into service had to face the bewildering mêlée of a night-time U-boat attack in foul weather, with ships ablaze, star shell overhead, guns thundering, and confused signals from the convoy. It was better for him to expose a commander's weaknesses at Tobermory than to leave that task to the U-boat commanders.

Stephenson never tired of seeking out new ways to expose an escort's weaknesses. He would order one vessel to raid another at night without being detected. In one case, a British vessel removed a Lewis gun from a Canadian corvette. He reckoned that pranks of this kind were the best way to ram home to commanders the importance of look-outs and watch-keeping.

Stephenson could be hard, too. When a ship arrived with a particularly dozy crew, he ordered them to bring all the stores up on deck and then put them back below.

Whatever the truth behind some of the stories (Stephenson acknowledged some but denied others when in retirement) his system worked. When he left the service after the war, 560 ships sent the Admiralty signals of thanks for his services. However much Stephenson made his trainees suffer or however harshly he exposed their deficiencies, they appreciated what he had done for them. A French naval officer recalled that: 'The extreme conscientiousness with which he takes his responsibilities forbids him to send into action any ship that has not every chance of winning.'

It is hard to over-estimate the contribution that Stephenson made to winning the Battle of the Atlantic. On 20 October 1944 the one-thousandth escort vessel passed through his course. When the then First Sea Lord, Admiral of the Fleet Sir Andrew Cunningham, congratulated Stephenson on VE day in May 1945, he rightly noted that '*Western Isles* methods are known and admired through the allied nations'.

So as our story continues, we must bear in mind that much of the Allied success in the Battle of the Atlantic was due to the Terror of Tobermory

# 15 The rise of the wolf packs

## July to December 1940

*Convoy HX-72*

On 9 September 1940 Convoy *HX-72* departed from Halifax, Nova Scotia, bound for Liverpool. The 43 merchant ships were under the command of Commodore H H Rogers. The convoy's sole escort was the merchant cruiser HMS *Jervis Bay*, weakly-armed with guns of 19$^{th}$ century design. Her presence was a testament to the perilous depths to which the Royal Navy had sunk as a result of the destroyers lost and damaged in the Norway campaign and at Dunkirk.

Rogers knew from the start that he had a difficult convoy. As soon as the mass of ships formed into lines at Halifax he could see the poor station-keeping. He was also concerned about the discipline of some of the foreign ships that he had in his care.

The convoy's troubles began nine days into its passage. A strong westerly gale lashed at the heavily laden vessels, damaging ships and cargoes. The masters of some of the steamers broke wireless silence, so putting at risk every one of the 43 ships. Soon the convoy was stretched out and stragglers began to fall behind. When Rogers. surveyed his charges, nothing seemed right.

As the convoy worked its slow passage across the ocean on 20 September, *U-47* was nearby, acting as a weather-station. The tedium of a job that irked ace commander Günther Prien was broken when the convoy came into view. Within minutes, his sighting report had been received at Lorient, the War Log noting '*U-47* made contact with an inward-bound convoy' and, more ominously 'All boats in the vicinity were therefore ordered to attacking positions on the enemy's course which would give them a chance to contact the enemy in daylight.' With 23 sinkings to his credit Prien was not the sort of commander to shy away from battle but with no torpedoes on board all he could do was to shadow the convoy until other U-boats arrived.

Dönitz soon had a pack of U-boats racing to the scene, where they were to form a line ahead of the convoy. But before the line could form, Rogers altered course. (This was a routine course change. Rogers had no idea that he was in the presence of the enemy.) Now a full frontal attack by the pack was impossible. The boats split up to attack as best they could.

Otto Kretschmer positioned *U-99* to the rear of the convoy, where he found the straggling oil tanker *Invershannon*. A single torpedo tore into her forward cargo tank, killing 16 of her crew. The rest took to the boats. Kretschmer calmly wrote in his log, 'Vessel of some 6,500-tons sinks within 20 seconds. I now proceed head-on into the convoy.' The *Invershannon* was so far behind the convoy that it was an hour before Rogers heard about the sinking. When he did so, he ordered the masters to increase speed to 10.5 knots and turn to port. This manoeuvre failed to shake off *U-99*. Kretschmer was still there, on the trail of his next victim, the merchant ship *Baron Blythswood*. A single torpedo tore the ship in two. Forty seconds later she was under the waves. The sole survivor was rescued by *U-99* and put into a nearby lifeboat. Kretschmer next went for the 5000-ton *Elmbank* with its hold full of timber and metals. Neither Kretschmer's torpedo nor his shelling succeeded in sinking the tough ship, so the crew had time to take to the boats; only one man was lost. This brought an end to the first day of the battle, in which *U-99* was the lone assailant.

Rogers had presided over a disastrous 24 hours. We can only imagine what he made of the news on the following day when he received a radio message to tell him that his sole escort, *Jervis Bay,* was to be withdrawn to support another convoy. He was left with 40 ships under his care and not a single warship to protect them. Ahead of him were 20 hours of danger before he would pick up the Western Approaches escort for the perilous last stage of the passage.

The sea was calm with a moderate wind. Visibility was good, as the U-boats that were arriving were not slow to recognise. The convoy was now reduced to 7 knots as it zig-zagged its way unknowingly towards the latest U-boat arrivals.

It was 4.00 am on 21 September when *U-48* reached the scene. Its commander, Heinrich Bleichrodt, another U-boat ace, quickly found the straggling 4500 ton merchant ship *Blairangus* carrying 1800 fathoms of timber. She was sunk with one torpedo just before dawn. Seven of her crew of 34 were lost. By now Rogers was aware that his convoy was under a large-scale, merciless, attack. He ordered the ships in the starboard column to turn while making smoke. With the convoy on its new course of 102 degrees the rendezvous with the escort was just 80 miles away.

The sun had risen. Rogers relaxed a little since it was clear that the U-boats were sticking to night attacks. Meanwhile *U-47* and *U-48* kept out of sight as they shadowed his ships.

The convoy masters no doubt gave a hearty cheer as they saw the Western Approaches escort coming into view two hours early at 1.30 pm on 21 September. The U-boats made no move to attack as the full escort gathered. By the end of the day, five escort vessels were protecting the convoy: the sloop HMS *Lowestoft*, the destroyer HMS *Shikari*, and three corvettes. This was September. Stephenson had only opened Tobermory for business in July. Few escorts had much experience; even fewer had any training in working together. *Lowestoft*, *Shikari* and the corvettes *Calendula*, *Heartsease* and *La Malouine* were soon to show how ineffective a barely-trained escort group could be.

116

*Korvettenkapitän Heinrich Bleichrodt, an early participant in the wolf pack attacks on merchant shipping. His commands sank or damaged a total of 164,000 tons of shipping.*

Darkness fell at 7.00 pm. The convoy ceased zigzagging. Rogers increased its speed to 10.5 knots. Amidst these manoeuvres, Joachim Schepke in *U-100* sidled unnoticed into the heart of the convoy and fired a spread of three torpedoes. His first hit was the 7000-ton steamship *Canonesa*, carrying bacon, cheese, fish and ham to Liverpool. (She was sailing immediately behind the merchant ship *Tregarthen* in which Rogers was commanding.) *Canonesa* was hit in her engine room. The resulting explosion caused massive damage and her decks were soon under water. But there was only one casualty as the ship sank to the bottom. Schepke's second torpedo sank the 10,500-ton tanker

*Torinia* loaded with 14,000 tons of fuel oil for the navy. Five of her men were lost. The third torpedo failed to find a target.

This spate of losses in the presence of the newly-arrived escort was too much for the masters. The convoy began to break up as star shell lit up the sky above, explosions and fires advertised the unfolding disasters, and a cacophony of orders came from megaphones. The day ended as *U-48* damaged the merchant ship *Broompark*.

On the following day *U-100* was back, sinking the tanker *Frederick S Fales* and the merchant ships *Empire Airman* and *Scholar* in quick succession. As a farewell shot, *U-32* damaged the merchant ship *Collegian*. With all their torpedoes now gone, the U-boats departed.

The wolf pack attack on Convoy *HX-72* had sunk 11 ships with a gross tonnage of 73,000 tons. At no point did any of the escort ships make contact with any of the eight U-boats which attacked the convoy. Dönitz was demonstrating his new skill of coordinating a pack attack. All of the U-boat commanders had switched to surface attack at night. (In this position they could not be detected by asdic.) And some of them had gained the confidence to attack from the inside of the convoy. In September 1940 the Allies had no answer to these tactics. Individual escorts, stationed around a convoy and acting alone were no match for Dönitz's ferocious new methods. So great was the number of sinkings that the U-boat commanders later called this period 'The First Happy Time'.

Dönitz was delighted at the results of his wolf packs. Their success, he wrote, was due to:

> 1) early intelligence of the convoy far west when the escort was still weak
>
> 2) correct tactical procedure of boats as shadowers and operating over a wide area
>
> 3) favourable weather.

There was, though, an aspect that was to worry him from now until the end of the war. He had sent eight boats to attack Convoy *HX-72*. One (*U-99*) sank three ships. Another (*U-100*) sank seven ships. Of the six other boats, five made no sinkings, while *U-48* sank one ship of 4500 tons. The truth was that Dönitz had a large number of inexperienced and ineffective commanders. Kretschmer had been in U-boats since 1936; Schepke had started in 1935. Men of this experience were the backbone of the U-boat service. As the war progressed, the quality of recruits fell and training had to be curtailed. Dönitz was to fight a war with an ever diminishing stock of first class commanders. In contrast, the British Admiralty placed ever more emphasis on training as the war progressed. By 1943 the escort commanders would be more than a match for the U-boat commanders.

*Dönitz as commander*

In late 1940 Dönitz was the man who held Britain's future in his hands. The U-Boat Arm could not have had a more dedicated commander. He lived and breathed his boats. Never did he cease to believe that only *his* boats could defeat Britain.

No one could have been more zealous in his pursuit of having the best men and the best tactics. Every setback for his U-boats was matched by his careful analysis of what had gone wrong and why. Streams of papers, orders and instructions came from his pen as he sought to squeeze more from his limited resources.

Dönitz was aware that his U-boat command was a lonely one. Göring had no faith in anything but his planes. The Wehrmacht had little interest in the Kriegsmarine. As to Raeder, he preferred to work-up operations for his big ships. He was happy to leave Dönitz to run the unglamorous U-Boat Arm. And Hitler, who had very little understanding of sea power, largely ignored the admiral. Of the 74 directives that Hitler issued during the war, only two (both connected with the projected invasion of Britain) made any significant reference to naval operations.

*A U-boat at Lorient before the construction of the bunkers.*

This isolation suited Dönitz. It left him free to develop his own U-boat tactics, and, generally speaking, his strategy as well. Only when Hitler decided to withdraw boats from the Atlantic for operations in the Mediterranean and the Baltic later in the war, did Dönitz find his command restricted.

His isolation was also physical. From the fall of France to the St Nazaire raid in March 1942, his headquarters were at Lorient. There he followed an unchanging routine. He worked in the morning, lunched with his staff and then took a short rest. This was followed by a drive into the countryside with a few of his officers for a vigorous two hour walk with his dog. These walks gave Dönitz the opportunity to debate tactics and strategy with his officers. He was a good listener, eager to learn from his staff and happy to be challenged over his opinions and methods. His base lunches were a chance for open discussion rather than ritual occasions.

Equally important in his determination to hone his battle tactics, were his debriefs of commanders returning from patrols. They alone knew the realities of battle. At times, their successes would confirm Dönitz's methods. At other times, their failures would alert him to a shift in Allied tactics or technology. All this fed into his zealous brain.

Dönitz was fortunate in having officers who shared his absolute certainty that the U-boat was the decisive weapon in the war against Britain. They were united in his determination to sink the maximum possible tonnage, with or without the cooperation of the Luftwaffe, and irrespective of the delays in building up the U-boat fleet.

On a quiet night Dönitz would be in bed by 10.00 pm. But many a night was spent wide awake as he directed his wolf packs in their convoy battles.

Dönitz was a superb tactician. His strength lay in having the mind of an ex-U-boat commander. He could imagine the scene of a convoy battle and peer into the minds of the Allied escort commanders. He conducted his post-patrol debriefs with the acumen of a Sherlock Holmes. But that strength proved to be a weakness when the U-boat war needed a change of strategy in 1943.

There was, though, a profound structural weakness at the centre of Dönitz's operations. He and his small staff of enthusiastic young officers directed the U-boat war with next to no additional brain-power. Against him was the mighty structure built up by Churchill (as Minister of Defence) and Pound (as First Sea Lord). It was Churchill who chaired the chiefs of staff meetings. It was there that the reports of every possible type of research and analysis were discussed. It was there that the work of Bletchley Park, the Western Command and the Submarine Tracking Room were coordinated. Behind Admiral Sir Percy Noble, (later replaced by Max Horton) at Western Command there were hundreds of high-powered experts researching new technologies, analysing decrypts and conducting operational research. At no point in his War Diary did

Dönitz ever show any awareness of his pitifully small – and technically weak – entourage. He never rose above the level of a gifted sea commander.

### The ace commanders

The most important innovations in U-boat warfare came from the initiatives of the ace commanders. Of these, the most successful was Otto Kretschmer, who sank 46 ships totalling 273,000 tons as well as damaging five other ships. (This is all the more remarkable given how short his war was. He was captured in March 1941.) Kretschmer, born in 1912, was a fluent English speaker as a result of having studied in England when still a teenager. He joined the Reichsmarine in 1930, serving on surface vessels before he moved to U-boats in 1936. His first command was in *U-35* in 1937. By the time Kretschmer took command of the boat that made him famous – *U-99* – in April 1940, he was already regarded as an exceptional commander with eight sinkings to his credit.

Kretschmer had easily mastered the standard method of attacking from a submerged position with a fan of three or four torpedoes, launched simultaneously at the target vessel. Even with poor aiming, at least one torpedo was likely to find a target. But he despised this technique. His *U-99* carried fourteen torpedoes. Using the fan method he could at most sink four ships. Kretschmer argued that it would be more efficient to develop accurate aiming and use just one torpedo for each target vessel. To gain this level of accuracy, he attacked on the surface. His first use of this method was on his patrol from 25 July to 5 August 1940. With only 14 torpedoes he sank seven Allied ships totalling 58,000 tons. This was an impressive achievement in comparison with the performance of the U-boats to date. Other commanders soon took up Kretschmer's ideas. By the end of the war 31 ace commanders would sink 45,000 or more tons in one patrol. (Out of over 1400 U-boat commanders, the top 2.5 per cent accounted for 32 per cent of the tonnage sunk in the Atlantic.) Although Kretschmer held the record for the highest tonnage sunk, Günter

Hessler held the record for highest tonnage sunk in one patrol. He had sunk 87,000 tons in one patrol in 1941.

By September 1940 Dönitz was in buoyant mood at the successes of his boats and commanders. A visit by Hitler to the U-boat base at Wilhelmshaven was a good moment to impress the Führer with the U-Boat Arm's achievements. He forcefully presented the U-boat as *the* means to defeat Britain. For this he needed 300 boats, he said. Hitler ignored this demand as he continued his visit. Later, sitting round a large table in a packed officers' mess, Hitler startled his audience by saying, 'Field Marshal Göring and his Luftwaffe are going to chase the British fleet right round Britain!' This attitude helps to explain why Hitler did not better exploit the success of the wolf packs by accelerating the U-boat building programme. (Hitler had clearly forgotten what had happened at Dunkirk in 1940. He held back the Wehrmacht from attacking the fleeing Allies because Göring had promised that the Luftwaffe would 'wipe out the British on the beaches'.)

There were times, though, when Göring's planes made an effective contribution to the U-boat war. During late 1940 and early 1941 Allied merchant ships suffered greatly from attacks carried out by the Kampfgeschwader 40 (KG-40) based at Bordeaux in France and Stavanger in Norway. This medium and heavy bomber wing was the only significant unit replicating the U-boat activity from the air. Its sinkings to the end of 1940 were 108,000 tons at the cost of only one plane lost. In the first two months of 1941 the KG-40 planes sank 47 ships with only 15 planes on patrol. In total between August 1940 and February 1941, 340,000 tons of shipping were lost to KG-40 action.

One particular air-attack stands out: that on the liner *Empress of Britain*. She was operating as a troop ship in late 1940, taking men to and from the port of Suez at the southern end of the Suez Canal. On 26 October she was near to home as she passed the west coast of Ireland with 224 service people and a crew of 419 on board. Bomber pilot Fist Lieutenant Bernhard Jope was to prove a specialist in sinking large ships in a career that won him a Knight's Cross with Oak Leaves. On finding the *Empress* he made three strafing runs before dropping two 550 lb bombs. The initial damage was considerable but the vessel showed no signs of sinking. Soon, though, large fires took hold of the ship, forcing Captain Charles Sapsworth to order 'Abandon ship'. By 9.30 am only a skeleton crew remained onboard as the boats bobbed around it in the sea. Destroyers rescued the people in the boats as tugs arrived to tow the stricken liner to port. It was slow work – too slow. In the early hours of 28 October, Hans Jenisch in *U-32* arrived. He fired two torpedoes at the limping *Empress*. One failed to detonate. The other set off a mighty explosion, resulting in massive fires. The tugs slipped their lines, leaving the *Empress* to sink. This episode is striking for two reasons: not one person lost their life; and, for once, there was good U-boat/Luftwaffe coordination.

Admiral Raeder, though, was overjoyed at the success of the wolf pack tactics and placed little faith in the Luftwaffe. Sometime around the end of October he went to see Hitler with a simple message: it was the U-boats that would defeat Britain, not the Luftwaffe. All he needed was more boats. He reinforced this thesis when he wrote to Hitler on 14 November to plead: 'At the present rate of production, by 1941 we shall have thirty-seven finished U-boats less than planned. I must urgently request your help in the matter'. We can only speculate on what might have been the outcome had Raeder pressed harder for continued air support in the Atlantic battle.

*The bunkers are born*

By October 1940, Hitler was concerned about the vulnerability of the U-boat bases to Allied air attack. He and Dönitz met on 25 October and quickly agreed on the need to build the bomb-proof bunkers. A day or two later Dönitz and Dr Fritz Todt, Reich Minister for Armaments and Ammunition, had agreed the types and numbers of U-boat pens to be built. Hitler approved the plan on

23 December, so enabling the first of the 45,000 men to be employed on the project to start work. Only one in five was a German; French, Belgians, Dutch, Italians, Greeks, Spanish, Portuguese and Russians readily provided the rest of the labour, which was well-paid. The earliest bunkers to be completed were at Brest, which took in their first U-boats on 13 May 1942. They were to prove more durable than the boats they were to protect.

## End of the First Happy Time

The First Happy Time drew to a close around October 1940 with sinkings of 352,000 tons in that month. It would be seven months before the U-boats would reach that monthly figure again. The period had seen many personal triumphs for the U-boat commanders and their men. When in early November Kretschmer stepped onto the Lorient quayside after his fifth patrol in *U-99* he was greeted with the news that he was the recipient of a Knight's Cross with Oak Leaves. In his message to Kretschmer Hitler congratulated him on 'your heroic achievement in battle' and his sinking of 200,000 tons of shipping. (Kretschmer was one of only seven recipients of this award for extreme gallantry in 1940. In 1941 the award would go to Heinrich Liebe of *U-38*, Engelbert Endrass of *U-46*, Herbert Schultze of *U-48*, Viktor Schütze of *U-103* and Reinhard Suhren of *U-564*.) When Kretschmer received his award Dönitz asked him to nominate five other crew members for gallantry awards. Kretschmer responded that the request was 'unfair … All my crew deserve medals.'

Kretschmer received his award from Hitler's hands in the Berlin Chancellery. After the stiff formality of the investiture (rehearsed with the help of an adjutant) he was commanded to stay to lunch. He reluctantly took his allocated place on the Führer's right-hand side. All the talk was of the arrival that day of a Russian delegation led by Molotov. The meal, served with much pomp, was a poor reward for his having suffered the privations of U-boat life: no meat and no alcohol.

Behind the cold statistics of the First Happy Time lay the harsh reality of U-boat life. Many of Dönitz's men had now endured a year of U-boat warfare. Hundreds of patrols had been completed in the fearsome winter storms. Boats rose – their screws furiously beating thin air – as the mighty waves lifted and dropped them. It was as if the sea was determined to crush the men and to smash the boats. Men were thrown from bunks and hammocks. When standing, they were tossed around like tintacks in a can. In these storms the watches standing on the conning tower had to be anchored with steel chains to avoid being swept away. The boats plunged down into troughs while towering waves slammed down onto the exposed men. Sometimes even the chains were not enough to defy the sea, and men were swept overboard into the raging ferocious deep. As Cremer said, 'in such weather waging war stops'.

Only stoics with stable personalities were suited to U-boat life. Fuel, equipment and armaments took up almost all the space, compelling the men to live in the closest possible intimacy. There was no such thing as privacy beyond the commander's curtain around his tiny corner. Personal space had no meaning when bunks were shared. (Hot bunks came long before hot-desking.) Personal belongings beyond absolute essentials were unthinkable. A man's kitbag contained no more than a change of underclothes, a few handkerchiefs, a toothbrush and writing materials. In some boats the hardship and the proximity helped create a tight-knit comradeship – a pride born of common suffering.

The physical atmosphere was often stomach-churning. A U-boat was never rid of the stench of diesel, of the foul odour of cooking and old food, and of the sickening smell of unwashed bodies. Everything tasted of diesel and, when the fresh water plant failed, the universal flavour changed to salted diesel.

There were two lavatories on a U-boat but the men were so determined to maximise their sinkings that they invariably sacrificed one lavatory to use for additional food storage. Even unused bunks were filled with ammunition and spares.

It was a profoundly unhealthy life. When the men returned from a patrol they were so pale and listless that some refused home leave rather than present themselves to their families while looking so unmanly. Their first call was always the barber to hack off ragged beards and tangled hair. A further two or three weeks base recuperation were needed before their pallor and manly demeanour were restored.

At the end of the first year of the war the Kriegsmarine prepared a report on the U-Boat Arm's achievements. It described the operations as 'reasonably successful' and attributed that success largely to 'the slow build-up of the Allied convoy system'. It noted that the pressure of operations had resulted in U-boats spending no longer in port than was needed for repairs. The average boat had spent about half the year at sea. During this period there had been 61 operational boats, of which 28 had been lost, along with 79 officers, 273 petty officers, 412 men. Thirty-three officers, 114 petty officers and 280 men had been taken prisoner.

The report took a realistic view of the Atlantic battle, noting that 'neither the direct nor the indirect results of these successes constituted a turning point in the war against England'. Britain 'still did not lack shipping space'. As to the future, continued the report, the problem was not the 'numerically small' Allied escorts but 'rather enemy air cover, which had been surprisingly in evidence, and which might become dangerous'. It was a remarkably prescient observation.

But in November 1940 the U-Boat Arm was still the poor relation in the Reich's armoury. The Z-Plan had envisaged building up from 34 Atlantic boats in 1939 to 162 in 1947. That required an average production rate of about 17 U-boats a year. The planned output for 1940 was 18 boats. Yet by the end of that year 24 boats had been lost to enemy action and other causes. (The

127

Kriegsmarine's production targets were based on the assumption of losing only ten per cent of boats each year.)

If Hitler had accepted Raeder's faith in the U-boat's potential then he would have readily acceded to his request for urgent action. But Hitler, the man who had left the Battle of Britain half-fought, was now to leave the Battle of the Atlantic half-fought. Russia was calling.

### 'This is a thing to do _now_'

Just as Dönitz worried about the lack of new boats, Churchill fretted at his shortage of destroyers. The problem had become acute after the losses at Norway and Dunkirk followed by the need to keep destroyers in home waters, ready to repel the expected invasion. The convoys, meanwhile, were once more starved of support. For a second time Churchill wrote to President Roosevelt to beg for '50 or 60 of your oldest destroyers'. In his closing words he said, 'Mr President … this is a thing to do _now_'. Rarely can a British Prime Minister have bent the knee so low to save his country.

Churchill's appeal for destroyers was answered on 13 August when the Americans found a way round their internal legal problems which banned such sales. An exultant Roosevelt telegraphed to tell Churchill that he could have his destroyers and the motor torpedo boats. The first destroyers began to arrive at the end of September but it was months before they were ready for escort work. Meanwhile the U-boat's took their deadly toll with comparative ease. Two weeks after Churchill had received Roosevelt's telegram, Convoy _SC-7_ (which opened this book) saw the loss of 20 vessels. A few days later Convoy _HX-79_ brought the loss of 12 more merchant ships.

This particularly acute period of destroyer shortage lasted until the end of October, at which point Churchill concluded that the threat of invasion had passed. More than half of the vessels in home waters were released from their coastal patrolling for work in the Atlantic. This had an immediate impact on

U-boat operations as merchant sinkings fell from 352,000 tons in October to 146,000 in November.

*Figure 1 Sinkings 3 Sept 1939 to May 1940: o = Merchant ship; + = U-boat*

# 16 The return of the surface raiders

## Late 1940

### *Faith in the big ships*

In Raeder's view, the capture of the French Atlantic ports had created new opportunities for his capital ships. As early as July 1940 his staff were writing that 'the achievements of the U-boat and minelaying campaigns have done nothing to undermine the importance of the capital ship'. The authors drew the conclusion that 'the course of the war directly warrants a discussion about the *Rebirth of the Battleship*'. The use of the word 'discussion' was disingenuous since the memorandum went on to decisively declare that, 'The main protagonist in the war against the enemy's ocean communications is *the battleship itself.*' Once more the U-boat was to be pushed into the background.

There was, though, a lack of realism in the memorandum, even in relation to the existing ships. In late 1940 the Kriegsmarine had next to no capital ships ready to deploy. Both *Scharnhorst* and *Gneisenau* were undergoing repairs after their damage when supporting the invasion of Norway. The two new battleships – *Tirpitz* and *Bismarck* – were not yet completed. *Admiral Hipper's* sister ship, *Prinz Eugen* was fitting-out. And the *Lützow* was still minus her stern. That left just *Hipper* and *Admiral Scheer*. Nevertheless, Raeder decided to put his 'fleet' to sea. A new surface raiding campaign was to begin.

Raeder's orders to Admiral Theodor Krancke (*Scheer*) were to exploit 'operational surprise and other favourable circumstances'. In this way, he thought, they could circumvent the superior British naval power and, importantly, dislocate '*the enemy's supply and convoy system*'. It was a grand claim, but also a deluded one.

We shall first follow the *Scheer* raid.

The *Admiral Scheer* exited the Denmark Strait on 31 October. On 5 November the German intelligence service passed Krancke a decrypt of a British radio signal: Convoy *HX-84* from Halifax was passing to the south of *Scheer*. Krancke's Arado float plane was catapulted into the air at 9.40 am. Around midday Lieutenant Pietsch was back with his report of the convoy's location. Krancke set a course to intercept it. Two-and-a-half hours later, he saw smoke on the horizon. It was too soon to be a ship from the convoy. Whatever ship it was, she would surely report her sighting of such a large warship. Krancke had no choice. He raced towards the vessel, expecting some sort of hostile reception. All that he found was a mere banana boat, which meekly surrendered. And, to Krancke's relief, its crew had not signalled their sighting. By 4.00 pm the *Mopan* was sinking, her crew now being on board the *Admiral Scheer*.

Away to the south, the armed merchant cruiser *Jervis Bay* was escorting the 38 ships of the convoy. It was late afternoon when Captain Edward Fegen saw a large vessel on the horizon; he challenged it to identify itself several times but no answer came.

It was now 4.40 pm and the *Admiral Scheer* was four-and-a-half miles off the *Jervis Bay*. Krancke gave the order to open fire. As the first shells arched through the air, Fegen was briefly stupefied. For a moment he hesitated. To stay was insane. *Jervis Bay's* 6-inch guns were peashooters against *Scheer's* 11-inch armament. But if *Jervis Bay* engaged *Admiral Scheer* even for a brief period, the convoy would have a chance to scatter. So stay Fegen did. *Jervis Bay* took the great cruiser head-on. For 22 minutes she fired her futile shells at the gigantic warship. With his right-arm shattered Fegen was still on the bridge when it was shot away from underneath him. His VC said it all, 'for valour in challenging hopeless odds and giving his life to save the many ships it was his duty to protect'. Fegen's courage and sacrifice helped save the convoy. All but five of the merchant ships escaped.

*HMS Jervis Bay, the armed-merchant-cruiser, sunk by Admiral Scheer after 22 minutes of battle.*

*Scheer* continued raiding in the Atlantic before moving to the Indian Ocean in February 1941 where she sank two freighters and captured a tanker. Their distress calls were picked up by HMS *Glasgow*, based in Aden. Not long afterwards *Glasgow's* spotter aircraft found the *Admiral Scheer*, but she had disappeared by the time the carrier *Hermes* arrived on the scene along with four cruisers. *Admiral Scheer* was still able to raid at will. By the time she returned to Germany she had sunk 17 merchant ships, totalling 113,000 tons. This made her the Kriegsmarine's best performing surface vessel. But, to put this figure in context, during World War Two 34 U-boat commanders, each with crews of around 50 men, each sank over 100,000 tons of shipping. *Admiral Scheer* had a complement of around 1000 men. And *Scheer* never made another significant sortie. She was a very costly way of attempting to eliminate the Allied merchant fleet.

### The Admiral Hipper raid

*Admiral Hipper's* raiding ran in parallel with that of *Scheer*. She was ill-adapted for such a venture. She was a sprinter with a top speed of 32 knots – perfect for chasing destroyers or other escort vessels. But sprinters lack

132

endurance. She could manage 6800 miles at 20 knots, which was too little for serious ocean raiding. To go to sea she had to be accompanied by four tankers.

Captain Wilhelm Meisel's operation started badly in mid-December as the winter storms battered *Admiral Hipper*. After five days at sea Meisel was still stuck south-east of Greenland and with a failed starboard engine. To add to his woes, he was unable to locate his supply tanker *Friedrich Breme*. Eventually the *Hipper* reached the Atlantic and her raiding work began.

During the night of 24/25 December Meisel found the heavily-escorted troop convoy *WS-5A* on its way from Britain to Durban. He assumed that he had found a trade convoy. Fearing that there would be torpedo-armed destroyers with the convoy, he avoided a night attack. When dawn came he saw the cruiser HMS *Berwick* in his sights, with no other warships to be seen. Now knowing that he had a heavily escorted convoy ahead of him, Meisel called action stations and went in to attack. *Berwick*, which had closed up to pre-dawn action stations, replied immediately and summoned the other two cruisers to assist. The response from *Berwick*, *Bonaventure* and *Dunedin* resulted in a brief exchange of fire. Meisel then broke off and turned his attention to the convoy as a whole. By this time the convoy was scattering in a disorderly manner. In the mêlée that resulted *Hipper* only managed to damage one vessel: the liner *Empire Trooper*. Meisel could make no sense of the battlefield by this stage. He broke off the action and disappeared into the Atlantic. A muddled attempt by the escort carriers to find *Hipper* proved negative.

Both sides had made a poor showing. Meisel had once more demonstrated the unsuitability of lone capital ships for raiding. However, he was acting within the policy that Raeder had outlined to Hitler around this time: 'The main target is, as always, only the convoys and *not* the escort forces, which are always to be avoided unless very inferior in strength.'

133

As to the Allied side, a heavy escort had proved able to scare off a cruiser, but incapable of engaging her. It could be argued that the escort succeeded in its primary function: protecting the convoy. But to leave *Admiral Hipper* free to carry on raiding was a highly undesirable outcome. Also, *Hipper's* raid had resulted in severe damage to the heavy cruiser *Berwick*, which left her in dock until mid-1941.

On her way back to Brest, *Hipper* sank the 6000-ton cargo ship *Jumna*. While it is true Meisel was compelled to spend more time battling horrific storms than enemy ships, *Hipper* had hardly justified Raeder's confidence in her. The 50 merchant ships sunk by his U-boats in December underlined the lacklustre performance of his heavy cruiser.

*Ocean boarding vessels*

While Raeder was struggling to find a way of using his capital ships, the British Admiralty was developing its ocean boarding vessels as a means of enforcing the blockade of Germany. These were all requisitioned merchant ships for conversion to their new role. In all, there were to be 19 of these vessels, of which six were sunk. The intention was to use them primarily for intercepting foreign merchant ships that might be bound for German ports . In practice they often found themselves in much more perilous situations.

The fate of the HMS *Patroclus* (an ex-passenger ship) in November 1940 illustrates the fragility of the ocean boarding vessel concept in the age of U-boats. *Patroclus* received an SOS call from the unescorted *Casanare* bringing 1500 tons of bananas from the Cameroons to Britain. The 59-year-old Captain Gerald Wynter (who had retired from the navy in 1928) in *Patroclus* gave orders to make for the *Casanare*. Commander Martin, who was by his side on the bridge, cried out, 'If we go over there and stop we shall be sunk within half-an-hour, sir.' But Wynter refused to rescind the order.

The armed merchant cruiser HMS *Laurentic* also answered the call. As *Patroclus* and *Laurentic* reached the *Casanare*, a torpedo from *U-99* struck

*Laurentic* in her engine room. *Patroclus* began picking up survivors, leaving *U-99* free to attack again, which Kretschmer did. In all, *Patroclus* received three torpedo hits in the next 42 minutes. Most of the uninjured men managed to get into the boats but *Patroclus* was not taking on water so Commander Martin supervised the manning of the guns. After firing four rounds, *U-99* disappeared. Shortly afterwards another torpedo struck *Patroclus*. Still she did not sink. Martin and the few men left on board comforted themselves with rum and whisky and then settled down under blankets to await events. At 4.00 am yet another torpedo hit the ship. So far, all four torpedoes had hit in roughly the same place under the bridge. Then came the final torpedo, which struck the engine room. Martin and his companions slid down life-lines. He looked back to see *Patroclus* rolling over on her side before disappearing from sight.

It was a sad tale, which highlighted the futility of the ocean boarding vessel concept. The seas were too dangerous for lightly armed 11,000-ton ships to ply the oceans alone. As the great Admiral Lord Fisher said when he scrapped a mass of small ships in 1904, 'they could neither fight nor run away'.

Life on an ocean boarding vessel was a dangerous business. The crews of these armed vessels, which were masquerading as cargo vessels, were treated harshly if they were captured by the Germans. HMS *Crispin* was a typical case. Before the war she belonged to the Booth Steamship Company. On her requisitioning in 1940 she was fitted out with two 6-inch guns and various light AA weapons.

Convoy *OB-280* had left Liverpool on 31 January 1941. On 3 February at 10.00 pm *Crispin* was making a steady 10 knots. The watch was at action stations – they all knew that an attack would be without warning. And then it came. The ship was rocked by a huge explosion. There had been no U-boat sighting nor any chance for *Crispin* to use her weapons to protect the convoy. The torpedo had hit a bulkhead near the engine room. The lights went out and the ship stopped dead. A few men were killed by the blast. Those not too injured to move went on deck for the muster. The ship was rapidly taking on water and had a serious list. The call to abandon ship rang out. Able Seaman Woodley and Able Seaman Cross rushed to the 32 feet boat, standing ready to lower it. The fifty men who crammed themselves into the boat made the lowering a delicate task. But the two seamen let the boat into the water in perfect order. Then they slid down the lifelines to join their comrades. The men, three to an oar, pulled for their lives as they battled to heave away from the sinking *Crispin*. Their ordeal was soon over. At 6.00 am the destroyer HMS *Harvester* appeared. One-hundred-and-twenty-one men were hauled up from the boats. Twenty had died on *Crispin*.

*Fregattenkapitän Günter Hessler, who sank the ocean-boarding vessel HMS Crispin.*

The *Crispin* had been sunk by Günter Hessler in *U-107*, who also happened to be Dönitz's son-in-law. *Crispin* was his second sinking. He would go on to sink 19 boats by the time the war ended.

## Operation Berlin

The sorties of *Admiral Hipper* overlapped with another surface raiding operation, which once more raised the issue of how worthwhile these operations were. This time it was turn of the two battlecruisers *Scharnhorst* and *Gneisenau*. At over 30,000 tons and with a top speed of 31 knots, these were impressive and dangerous warships. When they exited Kiel on 22 January 1941 for Operation Berlin, Raeder had high hopes for these two of his finest capital ships.

Raeder had sent Admiral Günther Lütjens to sea in the expectation that *Scharnhorst* (Captain Kurt-Caesar Hoffmann) and *Gneisenau* (Admiral Wilhelm Marschall) would prove that 'the most effective weapon in ocean warfare is the battleship itself'. However, with so few capital ships at his disposal Raeder needed to avoid losing either of his battlecruisers. Consequently he hobbled Lütjens with his order to avoid combat 'on equal terms'. Lütjens was to engage in tip-and-run tactics. There would be no big-gun battles.

The consequences of Raeder's stricture to not engage on equal terms soon became apparent. On 8 February *Scharnhorst* and *Gneisenau* came across Convoy *HX-106*. Its 41 ships from Halifax were homeward bound for Liverpool with an eleven strong escort. One of these was HMS *Ramillies*, a First World War battleship carrying a mass of armament including eight 15-inch guns. Marschall knew that *Ramillies* with her 21 knots top speed could not match *Gneisenau's* 31 knots. He could flee *Ramillies'* fearful guns if he wished. But he chose to attack with the aid of *Scharnhorst*.

He first ordered *Scharnhorst* to approach *Ramillies*. His intention was to draw off the warship, leaving *Gneisenau* to move in to attack the convoy.

According to the German historian Bekker, Lütjens had no knowledge of this plan. On seeing *Scharnhorst* approaching *Ramillies,* in direct contradiction to Raeder's orders, Lütjens angrily signalled: 'Break away! Am withdrawing south.' For him an order was an order to be followed blindly. A more flexible admiral would have recognised that a 31-knot ship could safely edge towards a 21-knot ship when they were 14 miles apart. Instead, the ships turned south while Convoy *HX-106* sailed on unmolested.

After this failed attack, the two raiders continued sailing in the Atlantic and succeeded in sinking 22 ships.

Had Raeder proved his point? He was jubilant once *Gneisenau* and *Scharnhorst* were safely back in port. But how did the 22 vessels sunk compare to 138 merchant ships sunk by the U-boats in the same three months? We can only make rough assumptions about cost. The two warships carried around 3700 men between them. Their fuel consumption was prodigious. The cost of keeping these two ships in the North Atlantic for three months must have far exceeded the few U-boats on patrol. (Dönitz had only 18 operational boats in January.) In terms of cost per ton of merchant shipping sunk, *Operation Berlin* was surely a failure.

It was also a failure when measured against Raeder's own rationale for the sortie. He had declared that his capital ships would lead to 'the annihilation of merchant shipping *bound for Britain*'. But this was unachievable as long as he restricted his commanders to attacking independent sailings or very weakly defended convoys. His massive ships were effectively limited to hit-and-run tactics. Essentially Raeder was conceding that the Allied escorts were too good at their job. It was not safe for his ships to take on the convoy defences.

The one success that the Reich could claim from Operation Berlin – and all its big-ship sorties – was the monumental strain that this placed on the Royal Navy's surface fleet. Once a battleship or cruiser was known to be on the high seas, every Royal Navy ship that could be prised from other work was sent to join the search. But, however we value the merits of the operation, its true weakness was soon to show. It relied on berthing the ships in the French Atlantic ports. And they were within range of British bombers.

While the surface raiders were failing to justify their very expensive outings in late 1940, the U-boat campaign was still showing no sign of forcing Britain to request an armistice. (Hitler and Raeder still saw winning the war as a matter of months rather than years.) Raeder held a series of meetings with Hitler in late 1940 at which he gained the Führer's commitment to the use of all available naval and air forces to disrupt British supply lines. Not only did Hitler agree to speeding up U-boat production but he also agreed to 'constant' Luftwaffe attacks on British destroyers. This never happened, in part because Göring usually frustrated any agreement that diverted his forces from his own operations.

Whatever Hitler might have agreed to in theory, in practice he favoured Luftwaffe bombing of Britain's cities and industrial facilities rather than merchant ships. But it was a policy that took him no nearer to crippling Britain than did the U-boat attacks on shipping. For all the horrific sights of burning buildings, rubble-filled streets and shattered houses, Hitler's bombing campaign had a negligible effect on production. In the crucial aero industry, with its 120,000 machine tools, only 700 had been destroyed and 5000 damaged. In Birmingham only 15 per cent of factories needed any repairs. In Southampton the Spitfire factories were badly damaged but within days were back running at full capacity.

## A perilous fall in imports

Churchill, though, knew that the U-boat war was a growing threat to Britain's production of war materials. Imports were falling steadily. In the week beginning 8 June imports had totalled 1.2 million tons whereas the average for the last three months of 1940 had fallen to 800,000 tons per week. Oil imports were a particular worry. By the autumn they were half their May-

June level, now covering only two-thirds of consumption. (Dönitz never appreciated how vulnerable Britain was to a sustained attack on oil tankers compared to more general attacks on merchant shipping.) Taking the year as a whole, it had been disastrous for Britain. Over one thousand ships had been sunk, totalling four million tons of shipping. This was a quarter of Britain's merchant fleet.

The shrinking merchant fleet was only one of the reasons for falling imports. An important but less obvious one was the increased turnaround times for ships in port. At Liverpool turnaround in February had been 12 ½ days; by July it was 15 days and in October it had slowed even further to 19 ½ days – an increase since February of over 50 per cent.

The fact was that, at the end of 1940, Britain was losing the U-boat war.

# 17 Dönitz at bay

## January to March 1941

### Tonnage 'decisive to the war'

The first half of 1941 was a struggle for Dönitz as he tried to stretch his meagre fleet of U-boats to match the magnitude of his task. His distribution of boats on 1 January suggests that he was having severe maintenance problems. Only six U-boats were at sea. Of the rest, ten were at Lorient; six were at Kiel; and five were 'ready for preparations'. Despite this scanty fleet, Hitler expected it to play a significant role in the war. On 6 February he issued one of his rare naval directives under the title *Operations Against the English War Economy*. He emphasised the importance of reducing 'enemy tonnage' which was 'so decisive to the war'.

Despite Hitler's support, Dönitz protested that he was beset 'with almost impossible tasks'. He had too few U-boats, and, he said, the building programme 'had as yet no effect on the fighting group'. It had become impracticable to carry out attacks near the coast since it was too easy for Allied forces to locate U-boats there. Yet, as he pointed out, hunting the oceans with so few U-boats was a hopeless task.

### 'We cannot go on like this'

While Dönitz was bemoaning the weakness of his position, a change in organisation was taking place in Britain that was to have significant consequences later in the war. Until early 1941 Western Approaches Command had been based in Plymouth. Back in August 1940, when Churchill was brooding over the rising shipping losses, he queried whether the losses in the Western Approaches were 'being grappled with the same intense energy' as had been the case with the magnetic mine. 'We cannot go on like this,' he told Pound, as he went on to suggest that the command should be nearer the main merchant traffic. 'Perhaps on the Clyde,' he concluded.

Six months later, the Western Approaches Command opened for business in Derby House at Liverpool on 7 February 1941. The command's new home, was no small affair. Over 1000 personnel worked in the huge building. Its heart was the massive operations room, deep underground beyond the reach of bombing. One wall of the high-ceilinged room was a towering map of the North Atlantic on which every allied and enemy warship and every convoy in the area was marked and tracked. A bevvy of Wrens ran up and down telescopic ladders, moving ship and U-boat markers to newly reported positions. At floor level Wrens and officers received minute by minute reports of sightings, actions and sinkings.

*Derby House, Liverpool, headquarters of the Western Approaches Command from February 1941 onwards.*

Noble's office had one wall of plate glass so that he could glance at the battle situation without even leaving his desk. Next door to him was his colleague Air Vice-Marshal James Robb of No. 15 Group Coastal Command, which provided air cover to Noble's convoy escorts.

## Convoys powerless against air attacks

In early 1941 the Focke-Wulfs of Group 40 continued to have some success in their attacks on the convoys, particularly when cooperating with the U-boats. Convoy *HG-53* had left Gibraltar on 5 February and came under U-boat attack at 4.00 am four days later. The 2000-ton cargo ship *Estrellano* and the smaller *Courland* were both sunk by *U-37*. The contact soon brought five Focke-Wulf 200s to the scene. The heavy fire from the escorts did nothing to deter the bombers as they homed in on the cargo ship *Britannic* with its 3000 tons of iron ore. She was soon hit and quickly sank. Not long after that the *Jura*, carrying 2800 tons of pyrites, suffered the same fate. Then Hauptmann Fritz Fliegel landed two bombs on the Norwegian *Tejo*, one of which destroyed the wheelhouse and the bridge. The commodore, in the merchant ship *Dagmar*, had to abandon ship and transfer to another vessel. This was an impressive achievement for KG-40. It proved that when Dönitz had access to air support the Bay of Biscay was a perilous place for convoys.

Just over two weeks later Convoy *OB-290* from Liverpool and bound for Halifax, Nova Scotia, also came under air attack. Its commodore was the retired Admiral R A Hornell. His glory years as a commander of a torpedo boat during the First World War were perhaps over, but the 64-year-old admiral, who had no foreknowledge of a possible attack, had been keeping his convoy in tight formation on that day. He was, though, concerned about a straggler that had fallen behind. These precautions against U-boat attack were standard procedure. There was nothing in the rule back to advise him on the hazards of attack from the air. He sighted the first plane from an enemy formation at 6.37 pm. His ships came under fire almost immediately. It was, he said in his report, 'a carefully planned and well executed low level bombing attack'. Ships on both the wings and the centre column came under fire as the Focke-Wulfs skimmed over the convoy at 150 to 200 feet. He watched helplessly as several ships were hit.

On the 5000-ton *Samuel Blake* men were at the 4-inch AA gun and the machine guns when the attack took place. The AA gun spouted two rounds at a Focke-Wulf as it passed over the vessel at a height of 50 feet. Its tracer showed hits on the plane, but the aircraft flew on as it dropped a bomb onto the *Samuel Blake*. The bomb hit and dented the after-deck before bouncing to the No. 4 hatch on the port side, where it made a second dent. Next it smashed into the galley bulkhead, significantly damaging its fittings, before it finally bounced into the sea, where it harmlessly exploded. Throughout this drama, a gunner in the Focke-Wulf was spraying machine gun fire up and down the *Samuel Blake*. The ship's carpenter, who was at the AA gun, hit the plane again, damaging its undercarriage, while yet more bombs fell into the sea.

When the brief attack subsided, Hornell ordered the convoy to disperse. *Samuel Blake* steamed on and reached Halifax, Nova Scotia, on 7 March. Accounts of the sunk and damaged ships vary but at least three ships were sunk and men died on at least six of the vessels. In his report Hornell noted that, 'Against such attacks as these, it is impossible for the Commodore to take any precautionary or safeguarding measures.'

*The Battle of the Atlantic becomes official*

With no good news from the Atlantic, Churchill raised the profile of the campaign by devising the term 'The Battle of the Atlantic'. His first formal use of the words was on 6 March 1941, in his role as Minister of Defence, when he issued a directive with the heading: 'The Battle of the Atlantic'. He began by confidently declaring that 'The next four months should enable us to defeat the attempt to strangle our food supplies and our connection with the United States.' He singled out 'the Focke-Wulf and other bombers' as the greatest peril and emphasised the importance of Coastal Command in combatting them: 'The U-boat at sea must be hunted, the U-boat in the building yard or in dock must be bombed. The Focke-Wulf and other bombers employed against our shipping must be attacked in the air and in their nests.'

It was good morale-boosting talk but lacked any detail on how the U-boats could be tamed with existing resources and technology.

*Admiral Sir Percy Noble with the complement of HMS Stork at Liverpool, 9 December 1941.*

### Dönitz: 'Our real weakness'

While Noble was busy establishing the Western Command in the north, Churchill was goading his commanders to more imperative action, and Raeder was worrying about U-boat production. The forecast increase for the second quarter of 1941 was 18 boats – just six a month. Output for the third quarter would be only 15 boats. If he were allocated more workers, Raeder told Hitler, output could rise to eight boats a month. He particularly wanted these extra boats since a trial of Italian submarines working alongside the U-boats in the Atlantic had shown them to be of no value to the Kriegsmarine. (The Italian commanders were too timid in their attacks.) Meanwhile, things were so bad that Dönitz gave up consecutive numbering of boats, so that new boats were receiving numbers like *U-570* (launched March 1941) and *U-754* (launched July 1941). He later admitted that, 'These numbers were used solely ... to conceal our real weakness.'

As Raeder sought to increase U-boat production, Dönitz pondered the poor performance of his boats in March. With five boats lost and only 240,000 tons sunk, a new initiative was needed. He decided to move his boats around, first to the south of Iceland, then to the south-west of Iceland. But his difficulty in locating convoys and the expertise of the Allied escorts held the U-boats in check. He would not see the large sinkings that he thought would win the war until his boats were free to attack United States' coastal convoys.

*Enigma yields its secrets*

In early 1941 the Bletchley Park code-breakers were at last able to decipher some of the Kriegsmarine Enigma. Very little of operational value resulted in the short-term, but Bletchley Park was steadily developing its understanding of Kriegsmarine Enigma and how it was used. Importantly they discovered that, while the Kriegsmarine Enigma machine still had the standard three rotor positions (it was later to have four wheels), any combination of seven wheels could be used in those positions. This made the Kriegsmarine Enigma vastly more difficult to decipher than the version used by the Wehrmacht and the Luftwaffe. Meanwhile the flow of intelligence from agents in occupied territories gave some insights into U-boat activity. In February 1941 Polish agents in Bordeaux began reporting U-boat departures. Later they did the same at other ports.

Bletchley Park's work was aided by two fortuitous and two planned retrievals of Enigma materials. The planned operations involved capturing two on-station German weather ships from the North Sea.

The earliest capture, though, was a lucky find. This occurred when a commando raid attacked the fish oil processing plant at Lofoten in Norway on 4 March 1941. One of the ships present was the German armed trawler *Krebs*.

After a bombardment that severely damaged the trawler, a boarding party took control of her. They were too late to seize the ship's Enigma machine – Lieutenant Hans Kapfinger had thrown it overboard before he was killed. But what they did find was even more important: a set of rotor wheels for an Enigma cypher machine *and* its code books. There was sufficient material for Bletchley Park to divert Allied convoys from wolf packs for a significant period.

In the case of the second seizure, it was the destroyer HMS *Griffin* which came across a German patrol boat off the coast of Norway. It was disguised as a Dutch trawler but a search of the vessel revealed hidden weapons as well as torpedo tubes. The crew had thrown a weighted bag of confidential material over the side but it had failed to sink. Inside were the precious Enigma keys for April. They had been seized too late to be of operational value but they enabled Bletchley Park to go back over old signals to understand how they could improve their methods.

The suggestion that German weather ships might be equipped with Enigma machines was made by Harry Hinsley (later Professor Sir Harry Hinsley and author of the mammoth *British Intelligence in the Second World War*). Hinsley was still studying for his degree at Cambridge University when he was recruited to Bletchley Park, where he became an expert on German radio traffic. It is said that he sank the *Bismarck*, so crucial was his intelligence. His first target was the weather ship *München*, from which valuable code books were recovered. Next followed the weather ship *Lauenburg*. These had been easy captures but the Admiralty dared not risk further raids of this kind. Any systematic raiding of weather stations would have looked suspicious. It would not have taken long for the Germans to deduce that Enigma was the object of the exercise. Accidental captures were to be the rule from now on. One of these was the taking of *U-110*.

We have already met Lemp and *U-110* when he sank *Athenia* at the start of the war. On 9 May 1941 Lemp had the misfortune to encounter the two British destroyers HMSs *Bulldog* and *Broadway*, accompanied by the corvette HMS *Aubretia*. Their incessant depth charges proved too much for *U-110*. When the boat rose to the surface Lemp and his crew tumbled out of the hatch, fearing that the boat was about to sink under the gunfire from the warships. At first they were unwilling to surrender, but the firing soon changed their minds. Thirty-two survivors – not including Lemp – were pulled out of the water and promptly put below in *Aubretia*.

*U-30 with Lemp and his crew returning from a patrol.*

With the submariners out of the way, Commander Joe Baker-Cresswell sent Sub Lieutenant David Balme to board *U-110,* with orders 'to get whatever you can out of her – documents, books, charts, and get the wireless settings, anything like that'. Balme was terrified as he descended the conning tower ladder, suspecting that the U-boat crew had set scuttling charges. In the dim light he could see an orderly boat with food on the table but not a seaman to be found. Balme and his boarding party spent six hours inside the boat, in the process, taking its Enigma machine and code books. Later *Bulldog* attempted to tow *U-110* back to port but an urgent call from the Admiralty ordered 'full speed ahead'. Eager minds at Bletchley Park were impatient to mine the secrets of Balme's booty.

## The hazard of the Atlantic ports

The spring brought more bad news for Raeder's capital ships. Only days after *Gneisenau* had returned to Brest following Operation Berlin, RAF bombers arrived on the night of 30-31 March. No damage was done but the presence of British bombers over a Kriegsmarine capital ship was a sign of dangers to come. A few days later *Gneisenau* survived a second attack as a bomb plunged harmlessly alongside her into the waters below. It was now obvious to the RAF that *Gneisenau* was a reachable target.

After the second attack, *Gneisenau* was moved from the dry dock to the harbour. She had barely tied-up, wreathed in camouflage netting, when the next raid came at first light on 6 April. It was a two-wave attack. In the first wave were three mine-carrying planes. As they swooped low over their target they dropped their mines over the torpedo nets and the flak tower. How successful they were is not clear. Certainly they were not successful enough for the comfort of the second wave. This consisted of three Bristol Beaufort torpedo bombers. Each was carrying an 18-inch aerial torpedo. For the aircrew, there could hardly be a more perilous weapon to drop. Precision was essential. The planes had to stay level as they ran-in towards the ship. Their speed had to be steady. And the critical drop height of around 70-feet was terrifyingly low.

The three torpedo bombers were due to rendezvous before their run-in together. But the weather was foul and they failed to meet. Flying Officer Kenneth Campbell and his crew of Sergeant J P Scott RCAF, Sergeant W C

Mulliss and Flight Sergeant R W Hillman found themselves alone in the dimly growing dawn light. Campbell remembered his orders: 'at all costs'. He could see that the first wave had not eliminated the harbour defences. If he couldn't run in with the other planes, he would run in alone. He turned his Beaufort and began his approach.

Campbell was no novice. He had been in the University Flying Corps at Cambridge. By the time he joined the RAF in September 1939 he was a graduate in chemistry. By the time of the Brest attack he had already torpedoed two German merchant ships and survived an aerial battle with two Messerschmitts.

Campbell had to select his line of attack with care since *Gneisenau* was protected by a low mole. She was also surrounded by banks of AA-guns. These he could not avoid as he brought his Beaufort low and steady in his attack run towards the ship. The flak filled the air and must have been tearing at the plane, but the Beaufort's high-strength alloy frame held as Campbell and his men neared the drop distance of 670 yards.

Away went the torpedo. It sped through the dark harbour waters and slammed into *Gneisenau* near her rear main battery turret. An explosion ripped into the vessel's plates and 3000 tons of water began to pour into her.

So far, so good. Campbell's next hazard was the terrain. His run was along a line that led directly into a range of hills. His Beaufort could not climb fast enough to escape in that direction. He banked. The underbelly of his turning plane offered a sizeable target to the flak gunners. Within seconds Campbell's plane was out of control. It plunged into the ground taking with it Campbell and his men. None of them survived. Campbell duly received a posthumous VC with a citation which referred to his 'pressing home the attack at close quarters in the face of withering fire, on a course fraught with extreme peril, this officer displayed valour of the highest order'.

The damage to *Gneisenau* was considerable. Her propulsion system was rendered inoperable. Her plating and propeller shafts were seriously damaged. And her electronic systems had been shattered by the force of the explosion. But the worst damage was to Raeder's strategy. His belief in battleships and battlecruisers was exposed as naïve. The only safe place for a battleship to operate in World War Two was a place beyond the reach of enemy aircraft. Any battleship within aircraft range was a liability rather than an asset. (A fact that the British learnt when they sent off *Prince of Wales* and *Repulse* without air support to fend off a Japanese invasion of Singapore in late 1941.)

Campbell's war ended that day as did *Gneisenau's*. She was repeatedly bombed by the RAF until finally she was ordered back to Germany for repairs. When these were more or less completed in February 1942, she was bombed yet once more. *Gneisenau* never sailed again.

# 18 Three aces down

## March 1941

The first three months of 1941 were full of setbacks for Dönitz. The worst of these was the spectacular disaster of losing three of his best commanders in quick succession.

In the early stages of the war, the departure of a U-boat was fêted with a military band, flowers and bunting. After nearly a year-and-a-half of war, departures were just one more part of the dreary, draining routine of war. There was no sense of the U-boat war being won. Many of the boats showed the ravages of the sea as the red streaks of undercoat showed beneath the peeling grey paint. Their guns and deck paraphernalia were rusting and the decks glistened with the slimy green of algae.

But Kretschmer's achievement of reaching 242,000 tons sunk with the torpedoing of the Dutch steam ship *Farmsum* on 7 December 1940 made his latest departure something special. As he stood to attention with his men on *U-99's* deck on 22 February 1941, his leaving was serenaded by the on-shore band, which then transferred to a steamer to accompany the U-boat to the open sea. The strains of *The Kretschmer March* were to be the last sounds of Germany for Kretschmer until his return to his homeland six years later.

Kretschmer was about to join in some of the most remarkable wolf pack actions of the war. Four boats took part in the first of these: *U-99*; *U-47* (Günther Prien); *U-70* (Joachim Matz); and *U-A* (Hans Eckermann). Prien was another U-boat ace. Many had expected him to reach the mythical 250,000 tons before any other commander. But his total of just over 160,000 tons was more than enough to make him one of Dönitz's star performers. It was a fearsome concentration of talent.

As usual Dönitz was directing the wolf pack by radio. It gathered ahead of the outward-bound Liverpool convoy *OB-293* of 37 ships, accompanied by two destroyers and two corvettes. Accounts of the battle are confused, but at least the outcome was clear. The tanker *Athelbeach* was sunk as was the cargo vessel *Dunaff Head*. The motor tanker *Mijdrecht* was badly damaged but limped on to Rothesay Bay and survived the war. But the puzzle of the battle was the giant (for those days) 20,000-ton tanker *Terje Viken*. Exactly what happened is not certain. One version has it that *U-47* torpedoed the ship but failed to sink it. Later it was found by *U-99* and sunk by Kretschmer.

It was, though, the fate of the U-boats that particularly marks this battle. *U-99* escaped. *U-A* was damaged but also escaped. *U-70* was forced to the surface and sunk by gunfire. And *U-47* disappeared with no further radio contact. Thus, in one action, Dönitz had lost two U-boats and one ace commander (Prien) for sinking just over 30,000 tons of shipping. Had Dönitz known how close he was to losing another ace he might have ordered *U-99* to return to base. *OB-293* had cost him dear. *HX-112* was to demand a yet higher price of Dönitz.

With Prien presumed lost, Kretschmer continued his patrol. A destroyer that he sighted on the horizon proved too fast for an attack. Various propeller noises were picked up by *U-99's* hydrophones over the next few days but it was not until 16 March that Kretschmer found himself in the middle of Convoy *HX-112*. Its 41 ships were escorted by the destroyers HMSs *Walker* and *Vanoc*, together with two corvettes.

Two of the five U-boats present were commanded by Dönitz's aces: Kretschmer in *U-99* and Joachim Schepke in *U-100*. Between them they had sunk over 400,000 tons of allied shipping. Could they further crown those achievements? Or would this be a convoy too far?

The battle could hardly have gone better for Kretschmer. With his usual calm precision he sank three tankers: *Fern* (6500 tons), *Bedouin* (8000 tons) and *Venetia* (6000 tons). He topped this performance by sending the cargo ships *Korshamn* (7000 tons) and *J B White* (7000 tons) to the bottom. *U-99's* last torpedo had been expended. Kretschmer's men were exhausted after 48 hours of action. He was relieved as the convoy passed ahead of him. At last his men could get some desperately needed rest.

*Kapitänleutnant Joachim Schepke who died when HMS Walker rammed and sank U-100.*

Joachim Schepke had had less luck. He had scored a hit on a tanker but, despite a resultant fire, it continued on its way and reached port safely. At 1.30 am on 17 March the escorts located *U-100*. Schepke ordered a crash-dive and stayed down while Commander Donald Macintyre in HMS *Walker* pounded the boat with depth charges. Later *U-100* surfaced in the expectation that all danger was past. Almost immediately it was spotted by *Vanoc*. The destroyer turned towards Schepke's boat and rammed at high speed. Schepke and the *U-100* were no more. Dönitz had lost a second ace in this patrol.

Meanwhile Kretschmer had fallen back. *U-99* was wallowing amongst the debris of battle. But he was not alone. The ear-splitting alarm rang through the boat. A tired look-out had failed to spot an approaching destroyer in the darkness. A crash-dive followed. In minutes *Walker's* asdic had found *U-99* and the depth charging began.

Macintyre had received his first anti-submarine command in 1935 and had commanded his first destroyer in 1937. HMS *Walker* was his first command as Senior Officer Escort. He was about to prove how well deserved his promotion was. Kretschmer had survived many depth charges in the past. But Macintyre's accurate drops were too much for *U-99*. Soon its instruments were smashed, the men were ankle-deep in sea water, and fuel oil was leaking into the boat. And, worst of all, *U-99* was listing. It was time to surface. Kretschmer ordered blowing the tanks, but the boat failed to respond. Down and down it went until it was at the staggering depth of 700 feet. Finally the boat responded. It rose erratically. Kretschmer fought to stabilise it at 200 feet but the boat had a mind of its own as it lurched uncontrollably to the surface. By the time Macintyre saw *U-99,* it was lying helplessly on its side.

During these last hours of the battle, the Lorient headquarters had been frantically signalling '*U-99* and *U-100* report position at once'. On the surface Kretschmer was finally able to reply: 'Two destroyers – depth charges – 53,000 tons – capture – Kretschmer'. It is said the Dönitz read this as meaning that Kretschmer had sunk two destroyers as well as some merchant shipping. What shouts of joy there must have been in these final hours before Dönitz learnt the truth.

As Kretschmer clambered onto the deck of *Walker*, a pistol was shoved into his face and his binoculars were wrenched from him. (Macintyre laid claim to these and was still using them at the end of the war.) As to Kretschmer, all he could look forward to was life as a prisoner of war in a camp in Canada.

*Captain Donald Macintyre who forced U-99 to the surface and captured Otto Kretschmer together with his binoculars.*

The greatest loser in this patrol was Dönitz. He had lost three of his top U-boat commanders as measured in terms of tonnage sunk. Between them they had accounted for over 600,000 tons of shipping. His men had much to learn if they were to outwit the allied convoy escorts.

Visitors who came to see Admiral Dönitz in March 1941 found him a changed man. The loss of three ace commanders, the lack of replacement boats and the diminished sinkings left him in low spirits. He had always feared that the U-boat war had begun with too few boats. Nineteen-forty was to have been the year that lead to Britain's rapid capitulation. Instead, by the Kriegsmarine running a half-hearted campaign, Britain had been given the time for its commanders to learn the arts of anti-submarine warfare. In 1941 there was still no victory in sight.

# 19 Operation Rheinübung

## May 1941

*'Gaining local and temporary command'*

Despite the *Gneisenau* disaster, Raeder had not lost faith in his surface raiders. By early April 1941 he was ready for their next operation. Two factors might explain his obdurate determination to hazard his capital ships once more. First, *Bismarck* and *Prinz Eugen* were ready to sail, and *Tirpitz* was not far behind. These were core elements of his dream fleet. They had to have some use. Then there was Hitler's increasing interest in the role of air power. Raeder needed something to make the Führer take more notice of the Kriegsmarine. His latest ships were the obvious thing. Nevertheless, the Grand Admiral appreciated that he needed a new strategy. Since he did not have large enough surface forces to dominate the Atlantic, he would use what he had to destroy older allied warships on convoy protection. He called this strategy 'gaining local and temporary command'. He was to demonstrate this new approach by risking *Bismarck* and *Prinz Eugen* in the Atlantic.

Raeder's decision to send out such a small force met with widespread criticism and alarm. Admiral Günther Lütjens, who was to lead the raid in *Bismarck,* declared the plan to be a 'piecemeal' venture. 'There is a powerful case,' he told Raeder, 'for waiting at least until *Scharnhorst* has been repaired – if not until the crew of the *Tirpitz* have finished their training.' (The Kriegsmarine had a six-month training period for new ships.)

The risk that Raeder was running was heightened by the differing endurances of *Bismarck* and *Prinz Eugen*. *Bismarck's* low endurance would limit her radius of action; *Prinz Eugen* could roam far afield. Effectively, the two ships would work as *loan* ships.

These restrictions compelled Raeder to once more impose contradictory and restrictive terms of engagement. As in previous capital ship sorties, the key objective was 'the destruction of the enemy's carrying capacity'. Lütjens was only to engage warships 'in furtherance of this objective, and provided such engagement *can take place without excessive risk*'. (This was strangely at variance with Raeder's new 'battle group strategy' which emphasised the need to sink allied battleships.) Meanwhile Admiral Marschall, an ex-fleet commander, advised Lütjens to depart from Raeder's orders if circumstances justified this. Lütjens sealed his fate in his unbending response: 'There have been two Fleet Commanders who have lost their jobs owing to friction with the Admiralty, and *I don't want to be the third*. I know what they want, and I shall carry out their orders.'

One person, though, did have doubts and could have stopped the disaster that was about to unfold: Hitler. He visited *Bismarck* and *Tirpitz* on 5 May but showed little interest in either vessel. Not even Lütjens' excited catalogue of the Bismarck's technical wonders was able to arouse the Führer's curiosity. Hitler did, though, mention the risk of 'torpedo planes from British aircraft carriers' in the Atlantic. It was clear that he thought the operation unwise but he never expressed his concern directly.

For Raeder's plan to work, it was essential that the two warships should reach the convoy lanes without being detected. Lütjens appreciated this, so it is hard to understand why he ignored Air Group North's warning not to approach the Atlantic via the Denmark Strait between Iceland and Greenland – this narrow waterway was under constant Allied observation. Instead, Group North advised Lütjens to use the Iceland-Faeroe passage. In ignoring this advice Lütjens was to lead *Bismarck* to disaster.

There were also other ways of impairing the operation. One was the Kriegsmarine's pre-operational air surveillance of Scapa Flow over several days. The British Admiralty had drawn its own conclusions from this unusual activity and ordered increased patrols in the Denmark Strait – before *Bismarck* had even set sail.

*Admiral Günther Lütjens, who had little faith in Raeder's Operation Rheinübung but enough loyalty to obey and sail on the near suicidal outing.*

*Bismarck* was to sail with three handicaps. First, she had a young crew – many were on their first ship; Lütjens could be certain that the crews of the Allied capital ships would be better trained and more experienced. Second, when the ship had been tested for manoeuvrability with locked rudders, he found that her course could be held 'only with great difficulty'. And finally, during her fuelling before departure, a fuel hose had ruptured. Fuelling was stopped and *Bismarck* sailed without full bunkers. (Lütjens later failed to take the opportunity to refuel at sea before leaving Northern waters.)

*Bismarck* put to sea at 2.00 am on 19 May 1941. The following day she was sighted at 1.00 pm by the Swedish cruiser *Gotland*, which reported her presence to the Swedish Navy. Late that evening the Admiralty in London received a report of the exit of 'two large warships, escorted by three destroyers, five escort vessels, ten or twelve aircraft'. This report came from Captain Henry Denham, British Naval Attaché in Sweden. Denham was no ordinary attaché. During the war he gained a reputation for fearless defiance of the Nazis as he scooped up intelligence from his Swedish contacts. His obituary described him as 'one of the key sources of British intelligence in the Second World War'.

*The battleship Bismarck. Her 42,000 tons were sunk by a flimsy 2-ton Fairy Swordfish plane – the culminating evidence of the uselessness of Raeder's surface fleet.*

The news of the sighting was flashed to Admiral John Tovey, Commander-in-Chief of the Home Fleet since November 1940. He had been present at both the Battle of Jutland and the Second Battle of Heligoland Bight during the First World War, so he had solid experience of major actions. Within hours, he had ordered the battlecruiser HMS *Hood* and the battleship HMS *Prince of Wales*, along with six destroyers, to the Denmark Strait. He held his other warships at Scapa Flow on stand-by, ready to join the chase once the intentions of *Bismarck* and *Prinz Eugen* became clear.

Three days later the heavy cruiser HMS *Suffolk*, searching in thick weather with intermittent fog, found *Bismarck*. Her radioed contact report to the Admiralty was picked up by the German Naval Intelligence Service, B-Dienst, deciphered and radioed back to Lütjens only a short while later. Lütjens now had the confirmation that his choice of the Denmark Strait had been unwise.

### The Battle of the Denmark Strait

*Suffolk* began to shadow *Bismarck* until greater forces could be assembled. Nevertheless she briefly exchanged fire with her protagonist. Neither ship scored any hits, but the force of *Bismarck's* guns put her own forward radar out of action – this was, strangely, to prove advantageous to *Bismarck* in the short term. *Prinz Eugen* now moved forward to the head of the line, so providing forward radar cover.

It was 5.35 am on the following day when *Hood* and the *Prince of Wales* sighted *Bismarck*. Vice Admiral Lancelot Holland, in command of the Battle Cruiser Squadron, ordered the two ships into action. They were in a difficult position, being fine on *Bismarck's* starboard bow, so they were only able to use their forward guns. After about 15 minutes of action, Holland ordered both ships to concentrate fire on the leading ship, which he took to be *Bismarck*. His mistaken identification meant that *Prinz Eugen* took the brunt of the salvoes, while *Bismarck* was left free to fire on *Hood*. The first shell struck the battlecruiser at 5.56 am, causing a fire amidships. Four minutes later she was straddled by a salvo. *Bismarck* had found her range. *Hood* could not hope to survive.

Kapitänleutnant Burkard von Müllenheim-Rechberg was in his gun director station on *Bismarck*, which gave him a limited view of the battle. From his headphones he heard the Second Gunnery Officer, Helmut Albrecht, shout,

'The *Hood*!' Müllenheim-Rechberg looked through his gunsight: 'The sight I then saw is something I shall never forget. At first the *Hood* was nowhere to be seen; in her place was a colossal pillar of black smoke reaching into the sky. Gradually, at the foot of the pillar, I made out the bow ... projecting upwards, a sure sign that she had broken in two.'

The German ships now turned their guns on the *Prince of Wales*. The first shell to strike her holed her below the waterline. This was followed by the destruction of her compass platform, killing many key personnel. Other damage quickly followed, seriously affecting the ship's guns. The uninjured Captain John Leach decided to withdraw, being convinced that his ship was no longer capable of inflicting any further serious damage on the *Bismarck*.

According to some of *Bismarck's* survivors, Ernst Lindemann, *Bismarck's* commander, tried to persuade Lütjens to pursue and sink the *Prince of Wales*. Lütjens rejected this suggestion without giving any reason. In the hours following the battle he engaged in lengthy radio communications with the German Admiralty but offered no comment on his action. When the end was near three days later, he called for a U-boat to pick up his records – a deed that strongly suggests that these contained some self-justifying material. But no U-boat came. We are left to surmise his intentions. However his action was entirely within the spirit of Raeder's orders. He was to attack the British supply lines and avoid action on 'equal terms'. His over-literal adherence to his orders allowed the *Prince of Wales* to survive. She was compelled to retire from the battle but three months later she would carry Churchill to his Atlantic Charter meeting with President Roosevelt.

The news of *Hood's* sinking and Bismarck's survival was given to Churchill when he woke on the morning of 24 May. An anxious-looking private secretary came into his bedroom. 'Have we got her?' said Churchill. The simple 'No,' was a harsh blow for the Prime Minister.

*Bismarck* had received three hits in the Battle of the Denmark Strait. One of these had holed her below the waterline, letting in over 1000 tons of water and cutting off access to 1000 tons of fuel. Her flooding left her with a 9-degree list to port and 3-degrees down in the bow. To avoid damage to her bulkheads Lütjens reduced her top speed to 28 knots. Meanwhile her wake was a highly visible streak of oil.

At 8.01 am Lütjens decided to abandon his raiding operation. He was to make for Brest – it was only 600 miles away to the south. His one worry was the dogged attachment of *Norfolk* and *Suffolk*. They kept station through any amount of snow, rain or fog, guided by their superior radar. At 3.40 pm Lütjens released *Prinz Eugen*. *Bismarck* was now alone.

### The forces gather

Meanwhile, the British Admiralty had detached precious warships from convoys to assist in the search and destruction of the *Bismarck*. The majority of them never reached the scene since the end came so quickly. The most important detachment was the withdrawal of Force H from Gibraltar. That force had been awaiting the arrival of a convoy for escort, but sinking the *Bismarck* came first. Critically, Force H included the aircraft carrier *Ark Royal*.

The clash on 24 May began before the arrival of Force H, when Swordfish planes from the carrier HMS *Victorious* were despatched to attack *Bismarck*. *Victorious* had only been in commission for two weeks so her crew and her pilots were ill-experienced. The nine torpedo planes met a furious response from *Bismarck's* AA-guns but the guns failed to bring down a single plane. Equally, the Swordfish failed to damage *Bismarck* significantly: one torpedo detonated on the armoured belt but did not penetrate the hull. A carrier attack, so feared by Lütjens, had proved harmless. Shortly afterwards *Bismarck* and the *Prince of Wales* briefly exchanged fire to no effect. And then the *Bismarck* disappeared. It looked as if Lütjens would make Brest despite the British presence.

Throughout 25 May – Lütjens' birthday – the British ships had no sighting of the great ship. What they did have was direction-findings from the three radio signals that Lütjens made on that day. These had confirmed the Admiralty in its suspicions that Lütjens was making for Brest.

*Force H showing HMS Renown and HMS Ark Royal as seen from HMS Sheffield.*

It was not until 10.30 am on 26 May that a Catalina, piloted by the American Ensign Leonard 'Tuck' Smith from Coastal Command, found *Bismarck*. Having located her, Smith descended to 2000 feet to get a clearer view. As his plane came out of the clouds, 'we were met by a terrific anti-aircraft barrage from our starboard quarter', he recalled. Almost immediately the Catalina was damaged by *Bismarck's* AA fire. Smith dropped his depth-charges and took to evasive movements.

Although Smith reported the sighting to Tovey, contact with *Bismarck* was soon lost again. The situation now looked desperate for Tovey. His prey was within one day's sailing of the cover of Luftwaffe planes. She had to be sunk before those planes could reach the Allied warships.

Tovey was saved by the arrival of *Ark Royal* from Force H. Her Swordfish rapidly tracked down *Bismarck*. A flight of planes was soon swooping down on her. Away went the torpedoes but not one hit was scored. Except that the ship that the Swordfish had attacked was HMS *Sheffield*. No one had told Force H that *Sheffield* lay between them and *Bismarck*. At 7.10 pm a second flight of fifteen Swordfish took off from *Ark Royal*, this time heading for the correct target. One torpedo caught *Bismarck* amidships but the armoured belt limited the damage. Then two planes approached *Bismarck* on the port beam near the stern. They turned to port. They were flying so low that George Herzog's gun could not depress low enough to hit them. He watched helplessly as two torpedoes splashed into the water. Müllenheim-Rechberg was following the action as best he could in his enclosed director station. His eye was on the rudder repeater: it read 'left 12 degrees'. And it stayed at 'left 12 degrees'; the Swordfish torpedoes had jammed *Bismarck's* rudder. Müllenheim-Rechberg knew what this mean; he would not be disembarking at Brest. In fact, he would not be disembarking anywhere friendly at all.

On 25 May Lütjens had received birthday greetings from Hitler. With *Bismarck* now mortally crippled, short of fuel and unable to steer, the award of the Knight's Cross reached him at 3.51 am on 27 May. The citation read 'for sinking battle cruiser Hood. Hearty congratulations'.

At 6.35 am that morning Korvettenkapitän Ottokar Paulssen in *U-557* was passed a radio message:

EMERGENCY ALL U-BOATS WITH TORPEDOES TO
PROCEED AT ONCE AND AT FULL SPEED TOWARD
BISMARCK GRID SQUARE BE 29

His boat turned south and raced through a wind-swept sea.

On board *Bismarck,* damage control parties were feverishly attempting to bring parts of the ship back into use and to stem the flooding – there were even suggestions on how to rig up a temporary rudder. But Lütjens was a crushed man. He took no steps to conceal his defeat as he told his men that they could take anything they wanted from the ship during the night. That could mean only one thing.

### 'Two battleships port bow'

Meanwhile, Tovey had figured out that *Bismarck's* movements had to be caused by rudder damage. In a handwritten note to Captain Wilfrid Patterson in HMS *King George V* he said, 'The sinking of the *Bismarck* may have an effect on the war as a whole out of all proportion to the loss to the enemy of one battleship. May God be with you and grant you victory.' The rest of the night was otherwise uneventful apart from some desultory exchanges of fire.

Müllenheim-Rechberg had been awake all night when, at 8.45 am on 27 May the alarm bells rang throughout *Bismarck*. He was on the bridge at the time. As he left for his action station he heard one end of a telephone conversation: 'two battleships port bow'. He correctly assumed these to be *King George V* and *Rodney*.

*King George V* opened fire around 8.45 am, with *Rodney* following a few minutes later. *Norfolk* and *Dorsetshire* soon joined in. But it was a one-sided battle: *Bismarck* was unmanoeuvrable so could not take up an appropriate firing position. The nearest she got to a hit was to land a shell close to *Rodney*, which did little damage. By 10.00 am *Bismarck* was a wreck.

Those who could reach *Bismarck's* deck from below could barely recognise their ship. There was no sign of the anti-aircraft guns and searchlights. The guns, gun-shields and all the controls had vanished.

*Bismarck* was now listing badly. The First Officer, Fregattenkapitän Hans Oels, ordered 'Abandon ship'. Men began to take to the water. Müllenheim-Rechberg waited for as long as possible so as to limit the time he might spend in the cold water. Once in the water, and 150 metres away from the ship, he turned and saw Lindemann standing on the forecastle, making no attempt to leave. *Bismarck* was now lying on her side. At 10.39 am she went beneath the waves. An hour later Paulssen received another message from Lorient:

BISMARCK VICTIM OF CONCENTRATED ENEMY FIRE
ALL U-BOATS IN VICINTIY TO SEARCH FOR
SURVIVORS

By the time *U-557* reached the site of the sinking on the next day, all Paulssen found was oil and debris. *Bismarck* had carried over 2000 men. Only 114 survived.

### Failure of the surface raiders

For Hitler, the calamity of *Operation Rheinübung* lay in Lütjens' failure to sink the *Prince of Wales* after having sunk *Hood*. But the responsibility for the loss of the *Bismarck* must lie with Raeder. He took the risky decision to allow her to sail (effectively) alone and then hobbled Lütjens with orders that led him to withdraw from an engagement with the *Prince of Wales* that he would surely have won.

Raeder, though, still defended his big-ship policy, reminding Hitler that destroying Atlantic commerce was the overriding objective in the North Atlantic. Hence the surface ships had to avoid any situation that would impede destroying merchant ships. Battleships were only to engage enemy warships of the same strength. Only when battle was 'unavoidable' were they to engage. Then, and only then, such engagement was to be 'all out'.

One person had a particular interest in the failure of the surface raiders: Dönitz. He knew how many construction workers were occupied in building and repairing these ships. Ever since the start of the war his cries for more U-boats had been ignored. He still had fewer than 40 boats at sea at any one time. With *Scharnhorst* crippled and *Bismarck* sunk he had the evidence that he needed. He declared that he wished 'to contradict the view that our battleships and cruisers are indispensable to the Atlantic campaign ... these ships no longer play a vital role in the present war, and consequently should no longer have a call on repair facilities urgently needed by the U-Boat Arm'. He reinforced his comments by referring to the need to increase the effectiveness of the U-boat service.

In retrospect we can see that mid-1941 was a critical moment in the Atlantic battle. Sinkings for the last three months of that year were to prove to be only just over 60 per cent of the 1940 tonnage figure. As the Allies improved their anti-submarine techniques, so it took more U-boat sea-hours to sink one ton of merchant shipping. This raised the strategic question: was it still possible for the U-boats to win? If tonnage sunk per boat per day was falling, was it possible to build enough boats to compensate? It was at this critical moment that Raeder made a war-losing decision. He accepted Dönitz's faith in the U-boats. Between the two of them they would repeatedly petition for increased boat construction. They would get their boats in huge numbers. But Dönitz had been wrong. It would prove impossible to build boats fast enough to compensate for the falling per boat performance. 'More of the same' when that same was proving ineffective was strategic error number five. The Allies, meanwhile, were persevering in their search for new technologies.

As to the future of the large ships, it was Hitler who had the last word. He had never been keen on his big ships being sent out to chase lumbering merchant vessels. For him, as for Kaiser Wilhelm II, a big fleet was a symbol of world-power status. It was for flaunting at naval reviews in peace time and for all-out battles in war. With Raeder's ships having failed to give Hitler the glory for which he yearned, the Führer turned against his admiral. From now on he would be the one to authorise big-ship operations. In his autobiography Raeder recalled that, 'his instructions to me considerably circumscribed my use of such heavy units. *The first thing he forbade was the sending of any further surface ships into the Atlantic.*' (Emphasis added.)

169

Operation Rheinübung had one final lesson for the surface raiders: their vulnerability to air attack. *Bismarck* had been sunk by tiny Swordfish planes when at sea. And other, larger, planes could reach these ships even when they were in harbour. Had *Bismarck* survived the second hunt and reached Brest, there was a good chance that Allied bombers would have hit her before she was once more sea-worthy. It was, after all, precisely in one of the French Atlantic ports that *Gneisenau* had come to grief. *Prinz Eugen* was to suffer the same fate in July 1941. An armour-piercing shell tore through her bridge, deep down into the ship, putting her out of action until the end of the year. It was, therefore, a near certainty that any large capital ship moored within reach of British bombers would meet the same end.

And there were other ways in which the Royal Navy could disable capital ships. While *Prinz Eugen* was in Brest the Royal Navy scoured the seas for her supply ships. Six tankers were sunk, so making long ocean forays impossible for the Kriegsmarine.

Despite the uncomfortable truth as to the dubious value of the Atlantic ports to capital ships, Raeder continued to argue that even solo sorties by the largest ships could both tie down allied warships and disrupt the flow of convoys. In a flight of fancy he even told Hitler that the warships could force Britain to seek peace that summer.

# 20 Calm before the storm

## April to December 1941

### Victory in sight?

When Churchill reviewed the progress of the war in the House of Commons on 9 April 1941, he was in an optimistic mood. Buoyed up by being able to announce victories over the Italians in North Africa, he allowed himself to foresee victory in the Battle of the Atlantic, saying:

> Once we have gained the Battle of the Atlantic and are certain of the constant flow of American supplies which is being prepared for us, then, however far Hitler may go, or whatever new millions and scores of millions he may lap in misery, he may be sure that, armed with the sword of retributive justice, we shall be on his track.

Was Churchill so unaware of what was to come? Merchant sinkings so far that year had averaged 40 per month. Nineteen-forty-two sinkings would be at two-and-a-half times that level. His optimism was wildly premature. At least, though, a week later he warned that the press should not overrate North African victories: the Atlantic was the decisive arena.

### Air support for the U-boats

After the disaster of losing three aces for little gain in March, Dönitz moved his U-boats further west and out of the reach of Allied air support. He was quickly rewarded with an attack on Convoy *SC-26* from 2-5 April. This convoy of 23 ships was *en route* from Halifax to Liverpool when it encountered a wolf pack of nine U-boats. Ten merchant ships, totalling 52,000 tons, were sunk and the escorting armed merchant cruiser was seriously damaged. Although Dönitz lost one U-boat he drew comfort from the overall success of the attack. His fear that he had lost his three aces to some mysterious new technology evaporated. He was confidently back in business.

There followed a brief period when the Luftwaffe showed a short-lived interest in the battle, with considerable success as in the case of Convoy *OG-69*. B-Dienst, the German Naval Intelligence Service, had intercepted a report of the passage of this convoy on 24 July. Focke-Wulf 200 Condor aircraft successfully located it on the same day and Dönitz despatched a pack of eight boats to the scene. Seven ships totalling 11,000 tons were sunk. This tonnage was not large but Dönitz was delighted by the cooperation of intelligence, air support and his U-boats. This was how he believed the U-boat war should be conducted. But with no planes under his direct control, such cooperation was at the whim of Göring. As for the U-Boat Arm, Dönitz was pleased that his mainly inexperienced boats had triumphed despite the strong defence put up by the escorts. This, he said, 'can be taken as a proof that methods of training in use are right'. On the Allied side the attack had been a disaster. This Liverpool to Gibraltar convoy had been heavily escorted by varying ships at different times. There were about nine escort corvettes and anti-submarine warfare trawlers with the convoy at the time of the attack yet not one U-boat suffered any damage. However, Göring's cooperation was to prove fickle. Later in the year – on the very day of the Japanese attack on Pearl Harbor – he showed his inherent hostility to cooperating with the U-Boat Arm, saying, 'U-Boats needed the co-operation of air reconnaissance only as long as U-Boat numbers are small.' He also declared that Raeder 'would never have the Naval Air Force he so much desired'.

Boat numbers, though, remained an issue for Dönitz and Raeder. The agreed target size for the U-boat fleet was 300 boats but progress towards that number was near to invisible. In July Raeder warned Hitler that, at the current building and loss rates, the target would not be reached until July 1943. He asked for another 25,000 workers to be allocated to U-boat construction. (It took 2400 worker-months to produce one U-boat.) Hitler demurred, saying there could be no increase in manpower until 'after the end of the war in the east'. At the time this seemed an acceptable reply – Russia was due to be subdued by December. In practice the war with Russia was becoming an inexorable drain on Germany's manpower. By January 1942 the demands of the Wehrmacht for more men on the Russian front resulted in skilled workers being taken from the shipyards. Completion dates for new boats were becoming 'indefinite'.

*Hermann Göring, Reich Minister of Aviation, at the Nuremberg Trials. He had no faith in the U-Boat Arm and repeatedly refused to supply planes to protect U-boats from Allied air attacks.*

### A new ally

Until April 1941 the Allied escorts in the Atlantic were largely British and Canadian. The United States patiently forbore the activities of German vessels on their side of the Atlantic. This patience broke on 10 April 1941. The United States destroyer *Niblack* was taking on board survivors from a sunk merchantman when a U-boat surfaced. Commander Denis Ryan took no chances and immediately depth-charged the U-boat, which disappeared.

Germany now knew that, although there was no declared state of war between the two countries, the US was ready to act with the Allied powers in her own defence.

Three weeks later the United States entered into a formal agreement with the Allies to report all their sightings of German vessels in the Western half of the Atlantic. Towards the end of May, American forces occupied the British bases in Iceland, so allowing the British flying boats based there to be moved to the Western Approaches. And in early July, America took a step which made her position barely distinguishable from being formally at war.: she announced that she would guarantee 'the safe arrival at destination of all the material being furnished by the United States to nations whose security is essential to the defense of the United States'. The statement added, 'Axis naval and air forces … deemed potential threats … will be attacked wherever found.'

This was all part of President Roosevelt's 'everything short of war' policy in support of the Allied cause. It was the best that he could do when both Congress and the American people were determined to keep out of the war. Roosevelt patiently waited for the right incident to rally his country behind him. When in September 1941 a U-boat fired on a United States destroyer, he exploited the incident to the full.

As usual in war, there are conflicting accounts of what happened. The German version comes from the reports of Korvettenkapitän Georg-Werner Fraatz. He was on patrol south of Iceland in *U-652* when he detected enemy aircraft. It was 8.40 am when he crash-dived after reporting his position. This signal was intercepted by the British. At 10.32 am a plane reached the U-boat's location and dropped depth-charges.

Meanwhile an American destroyer had arrived on the scene. Fraatz assumed that it was responsible for the charges and he retaliated with two torpedoes. The destroyer successfully pulled away without damage. In this version, Fraatz was acting in self-defence, as permitted by Hitler's orders.

The Americans did not see it like that. For them it was a direct unprovoked attack. President Roosevelt exploited the details in his fireside chat on 11 September, saying: 'In spite of what Hitler's propaganda bureau has invented, and in spite of what any American obstructionist organization may prefer to believe, I tell you the blunt fact that the German submarine fired first upon this American destroyer without warning, and with deliberate design to sink her.' There was only one way to read this. America had covertly entered the war. Her planes and destroyers were to stand side-by-side with the Allied patrols to protect ships of *all* nations. Nazi Germany was no longer a mere nuisance on the oceans: it was an enemy of the United States of America.

## Breakthroughs in anti-submarine methods

The year 1941 saw a burgeoning of Allied anti-submarine technologies, with significant advances in code-breaking, radar, and escort vessels.

By the middle of the year the code-breakers at Bletchley Park were finally reading German naval Enigma fast enough to be operationally useful. These signals included communications between the U-boats in British Home Waters and their headquarters at Lorient. F H Hinsley later wrote that, 'the situation was profoundly altered' by this breakthrough. The decrypts sped from Bletchley Park to the Admiralty's Operational Intelligence Centre in London where they were interpreted into useable intelligence. By June every signal to and from the U-boats was being deciphered. On the basis of this, convoys were rerouted away from the wolf packs, and, in some cases, escorts detached from one undetected convoy to one at risk of a wolf pack attack. For example, on 23 June, Bletchley Park found that a wolf pack had been sent to attack Convoy *HX-133*. By the time the pack met the 64 merchant ships, they were being protected by an escort of 20 vessels. This huge force limited losses to five merchant ships and resulted in the sinking of two U-boats. It is estimated that in 1941 alone 300 ships were saved through intelligence of this type. In the first three weeks of June, the U-boats made no convoy sightings as the convoys were diverted away from the wolf packs.

The ease with which Bletchley Park was reading German naval Enigma at this time created a problem of its own. Between 3 and 21 June eight U-boat supply ships were sunk as a result of Ultra intelligence. In the following week seven more supply ships were sunk along with some weather ships. It would not be long before Raeder and Dönitz realised that such a spate of precision sinkings could only mean one thing. The Admiralty backed off. From then on, Ultra intelligence was acted on more cautiously. Preserving the secret of Ultra had to take precedence over success in particular operations.

Code-breaking, though, was a two-way activity. In October 1941 the B-Dienst broke the British Naval Combined Cypher No. 3. This could have been catastrophic for the Allies since the cypher was used for, amongst other things, the Atlantic convoys. But the U-Boat Arm could only use ten per cent of the B-Dienst deciphers – the rest arrived too late to be of operational value.

Bletchley Park and the Operational Intelligence Centre had problems, too. In the autumn the U-Boat Arm introduced new grid square references – the code used to disguise U-boat locations in the Atlantic. This led to an alarming rise in merchant sinkings in late August and September 1941: Convoy *OG-71* lost 10 ships; *SC-42* lost 16; and *HG-73* lost 10. It took several weeks for Bletchley Park to resolve this problem, after which sinkings fell again. In November, sinkings had fallen to a quarter of the September level. This episode was a startling demonstration of how dependent the escorts were on both Bletchley Park's decrypts *and* on the correct interpretation of the decoded messages.

Alongside code-breaking triumphs, radar was developing fast in 1941. In March, Type 271 10cm radar began to be fitted to ships, with the Flower-class corvette HMS *Orchis* being the first recipient. This radar could detect a surfaced U-boat at 5000 yards and a periscope at 1300 yards. It proved to be highly successful and was fitted to hundreds of ships.

This is a suitable point to include the story of the invention that made 10cm radar possible – the cavity magnetron.

Many of the technical difficulties of radar had been mastered by 1939. ASV Mk I went into production, followed by Mk II which used the same wavelength but was much more reliable. But the 1.5 m wavelength could not detect a partially submerged U-boat, where only the top of the conning tower or the periscope was above water. That needed 10cm radar. Edward Bowen's attempts to produce this were frustrated by the limitations of vacuum tubes: they just would not produce a strong enough 10cm signal. Then came the breakthrough: the magnetron. The magnetron was first demonstrated on 21 February 1940 by John Randall and John Boot in their laboratory at Birmingham University, delivering a 9.8 cm wave at 400 watts power. Randall had arrived at the initial design after a long period of trying to improve vacuum tube performance. One day he decided to go back to first principles and looked at the work of Heinrich Hertz (1857-1894). It was in 1887 that Hertz had demonstrated his oscillator – a device that created a radio wave by means of a wire ring with a gap in it. Randall thought about the ring and then imagined a three-dimensional version of it to create a metal tube with a break down its length. In a moment of inspiration that he could never explain, he realised that a series of his broken tubes, linked together in a circle would make a powerful oscillator. By putting his metal tubes in a ring with the breaks facing inwards he could prevent the signal escaping and force it to spin round and round inside the device. As it spun, so it would increase in power. He had imagined the cavity magnetron.

The next step was to gain American support in manufacturing magnetrons. The precious device was in Bowen's charge when he was one of the seven top men in the Tizard Mission to the United States in September 1940. They carried with them details of all Britain's key scientific and technical breakthroughs. Bowen's magnetron was so important that it had its own Army escort. Tizard and Bowen had rightly realised that the magnetron was to prove critical to winning the U-boat war.

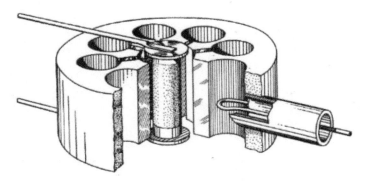

*A schematic diagram of a cavity magnetron showing the resonating cavities and the output device. (BSTJ 25: 2. April 1946).*

Even without the benefits of 10cm radar, significant improvements were being made to the Allies' anti-submarine strategies in the second half of 1941. By the middle of the year there were fewer sinkings of independent ships after the Admiralty raised the minimum speed for independents from 13 to 15 knots. Also, most of the slower ships were now forced into convoys. Sinkings of independents fell from 120 in April to June, to 25 in July to September. Sinkings of ships in convoys rose, but this increase was due to the increased number of ships being convoyed.

Amongst the new anti-submarine methods were the catapult ships. One of these was the 6000-ton cargo banana boat *Erin* which had been requisitioned in 1940 and renamed HMS *Maplin*. She was to become the first catapult ship to bring down a German plane.

On 1 August 1941 *Maplin* sighted a Condor approaching a convoy. Lieutenant Robert Everett's Hawker Hurricane was speedily catapulted into the air in pursuit of the enemy. Everett, was a 40 year-old Australian who had farmed in South Africa and had experience both as a charter pilot and as a professional jockey. Nine minutes into the air, he had caught up with the Condor, flying alongside it at a distance of 600 yards. The rear gun of the Condor opened up but the shots were falling below and behind Everett's plane. Everett manoeuvred round to the starboard beam of the attack, where he found himself the target of three machine-guns. He turned away, firing short bursts until he was behind the Condor. As he followed the plane he continued firing his guns until his last round had gone. Now unarmed, he watched as bits flew off the Condor. A wing broke free and the enemy plane spiralled into the sea. As Everett ditched his Hurricane near to *Maplin*, it turned over. But he survived and was awarded a DSO. The catapult ship had become the latest weapon with which to protect the convoys.

Within a month of Everett's success, the first escort carrier went into service. HMS *Audacity* was originally a German merchant ship with the name *Hannover*. Captured in March 1940 she was now an escort carrier with eight Martlets from 802 Squadron of the Fleet Air Arm.

Under Commander D W Mackendrick *Audacity* had a short life, escorting just three convoys. She came to an end just before midnight on 21 December 1941 when working with Convoy *HG-76*. Escort carriers were designed to give daylight protection to convoys. During the day Mackendrick had kept two Martlets patrolling over the convoy. (Even though they rarely sighted a U-boat, their presence still forced the boats to stay submerged.) When darkness fell, he withdrew *Audacity* from the convoy. In this state she was vulnerable to U-boat attack. It was Korvettenkapitän Gerhard Bigalk in *U-751* who found her. He fired four torpedoes, one of which hit *Audacity*. He reloaded his bow tubes and fired two more torpedoes, both of which hit their target. Fifteen minutes later *Audacity* sank by the stern with a loss of 73 crew members. Amongst her survivors was the pilot Eric Brown, who received a DSO for his bravery in defending *Audacity*. Brown still holds the world record for the number of deck take-offs (2407) and landings (2271). Later in the war he became a test pilot, eventually flying 487 different types of plane. Commander Bigalk also distinguished himself in the action, being awarded the Knights Cross.

Despite the short operational life of *Audacity*, the escort carriers were a critical factor in protecting convoys in seas beyond the reach of land-based air cover. U-boats in the vicinity of these carriers had two choices in day time: submerge or be spotted and bombed.

In August the growing strength of Allied air power was demonstrated on 27 August 1941 when a Coastal Command Hudson captured a U-boat. *U-570*, under the command of the inexperienced Kapitänleutnant Hans-Joachim Rahmlow, was into the fourth week of its first patrol, with no sinkings to its credit. The rough sea was obscuring the periscope so Rahmlow ordered the boat to surface to give him a better view of the area. It was in this position that the Hudson sighted *U-570*. The pilot saw the boat submerge but dropped smoke floats before reporting the sighting to Iceland. With insufficient fuel to stay on patrol, the plane returned, to be replaced by a Hudson piloted by Squadron Leader J H Thompson. By the time that Thompson arrived, *U-570* was just surfacing. The boat crash-dived but Thompson's depth charges brought the boat to the surface almost immediately. Rahmlow's resistance collapsed in the face of the damaged boat and his panicking crew. Making no attempt to submerge again or escape, he radioed to Lorient: 'Am not able to dive, and am being attacked by aircraft.' He ordered his men to put on their lifejackets and line up on the boat's deck. There he took off his shirt and used it as a flag to signal his surrender. Thompson circled the U-boat as he waited for a Catalina to relieve him. From there on a relay of planes kept watch on *U-570* until a trawler arrived at 11.00 pm to take off the crew. Later that day a destroyer took the boat in tow. On its arrival in Iceland the damage was found to be slight. After repairs, *U-570* was commissioned into the Royal Navy as

HMS *Graph*. The crew ended up in a prisoner of war camp, where they were tried by a Court of Honour and found guilty of cowardice.

## Captain Frederic John Walker

Another development in this period was of immense importance. It was not a machine or a weapon, but a person. Commander Frederic John Walker was the most successful anti-submarine operator of the war. Many knew him as 'Johnnie'; for others 'Walker' was sufficient to identify him throughout the fleet. He had joined the navy in 1909 and served in surface ships during the First World War. In 1924 he was one of the first officers to attend the Antisubmarine Warfare Training School, HMS *Osprey*, when it began work. No one doubted that Walker was a brilliant commander but he was also independent-minded. He had so transgressed the norms of subservient behaviour towards senior officers that when war broke out he had to wait until October 1941 to receive a command. He was given the 36th Escort Group of two sloops and six corvettes, based at Liverpool. Commanding in the sloop *Stork*, he and *Stork* were about to become the most talked about pairing in the Royal Navy.

The Admiralty's instructions to escort commanders emphasised that their prime duty was 'to ensure the safe and timely arrival of the convoy'. Walker thought this to be a pusillanimous approach to escort work. Seeing off the U-boats was only half the story for him. The full story involved destroying them. 'U-boats are the chief menace to our convoys,' he told his escort captains. 'I cannot emphasise too strongly that a U-boat sighted or otherwise detected is immediately to be attacked continually without further orders, with guns, depth charges and/or ram until she has been destroyed or further orders received.' This was revolutionary. The Royal Navy did not encourage initiative. Rather it expected officers to await orders. And now Walker was telling his subordinates, 'Don't wait. Act!' It was this philosophy that would make Walker the most successful escort commander of the Battle of the Atlantic.

It was in the attack on Convoy *HG-76* that Walker first tested his innovative methods. Despite the loss of *Audacity* in this battle, it is regarded as the first significant Allied victory in the Battle of the Atlantic. Thirty-two ships, accompanied by 24 escorts came under attack from ten U-boats. Four out of five of the U-boats that were sunk were accounted for by Walker's escort group. Cooperation was central to Walker's methods, as he demonstrated in his attack on *U-131*. When the first sighing was made, Walker, in *Stork*, ordered three destroyers and a corvette to join him in the chase. From 9.00 am to 1.30 pm they relentlessly depth-charged *U-131*. In a severely damaged state Arend Baumann took his boat down to 600 feet and set a course away from the convoy. But when fumes and leaks forced *U-131* to the surface two hours later, there was Walker. HMSs *Stork*, *Blankney* and *Exmoor* opened fire. The combined depth charge damage and eight cannon holes forced *U-131's* crew to surrender. The scuttled boat slipped beneath the waves. Walker's long time away from the convoy during the chase, and his emphasis on U-boat destruction rather than convoy protection had paid off. The boldness of his attack won him the DSO with a citation mentioning his 'daring, skill and determination … in the face of relentless attacks from the Enemy'.

Walker's methods were a paradox. He emphasised the need for initiative but taught his commanders to work as a team. These two potentially antithetical qualities were tied together by his standard procedures. These were proven methods of getting the better of the U-boats. Two examples will suffice to show his ingenuity in attack. First, his Operation Buttercup. The purpose of Buttercup was to turn an attack *by* a U-boat into an attack *on* the U-boat. Walker argued that once a U-boat had hit a ship it either hung around in the dark on the surface or raced off *on the surface* at full-speed. Either way it was near enough to be taken. On the command 'Buttercup' his escorts turned night into day with all the rockets and star shell at their disposal. This compelled the

U-boat to sink. 'Once submerged,' said Walker, 'the destruction of the U-boat is simplified.'

Buttercup proved a success when Convoy *HG-76* came under attack, At first Walker struggled to work out the locations of the attacking U-boats. Then HMS *Stanley* – six miles from *Stork* – reported 'Torpedoes passing astern'. Walker raised his glasses to his eyes just as *Stanley* disappeared 'in a sheet of flame' at 4.00 am. He shouted the order 'Buttercup'. All the escorts turned outwards and the sky blazed with the light of rockets and star shell. Walker raced towards where *Stanley* had sunk (but no nearer than half a mile for fear of injuring survivors in the water) As *Stork* neared the area where *Stanley* had been, Walker's asdic operator reported a 'certain' U-boat. Ten depth charges set to detonate at depths from 50 to 150 feet shot from *Stork*, without any sign of contact with a U-boat. In came *Stork* for a second run. But before Walker could off-load a second round of charges, *U-574* broke through the waves at 200 yards from the ship. Walker ordered the helm over to the meet the submarine. The command 'full-ahead' rang down to the engine room. But *U-574* still had some life in it. For 11 minutes its commander Dietrich Gengelbach turned and turned as he attempted to escape *Stork's* towering bow. The scene was brightly lit by snowflake as *Stork's* 4-inch guns thundered away. She was now closing on *U-574* and too close for the guns to continue firing. At this point First Lieutenant Gordon Gray grabbed a Lewis gun and sent a hail of fire into the U-boat's conning tower. But still *U-574* was afloat with her crew below. Finally Walker was able to home in on the boat. He described the final moment, '*U-574* hung for a second on *Stork's* stem before rolling off and scraping underneath her until reaching the stern where she was greeted by a pattern of depth charges set at shallowest settings. These blew her to pieces and even rocked *Stork* dangerously.' *Stork* picked up 16 survivors from a crew of 44. Gengelbach is believed to have shot himself and gone down with the U-boat's wreckage. So ended his and *U-574's* first and only patrol.

*Stanley* was their only sinking. Buttercup was soon adopted as official advice – the first of many contributions that Walker would make to escort tactics.

Walker's 'creeping attack' was equally audacious in its rejection of Admiralty procedures. It was a means of getting around a weakness in a standard attack: U-boats were fitted with hydrophones for picking up the sound of the propellers of another vessel. It was almost impossible for a single escort vessel to get near enough to a U-boat to attack without being detected in this way. But the hydrophones could not detect the propeller noise from a very slow escort vessel. Walker took advantage of this by using, typically, three escort vessels for an attack. Two – the attackers – had their asdic turned off and approached the U-boat at five knots. At this speed they made too little noise to be detected. Their path was guided by a third destroyer, acting as a decoy, running her asdic and going at speed. Walker pulled off this ruse on 24 June 1943. On this occasion he directed the attack from the bridge of *Wild Goose*. Walker studied the asdic echoes being received by *Wild Goose* and radioed directions to HMSs *Wren*, *Woodpecker* and *Kite*, which were creeping at 5 knots towards the echo source. *Wren* was the first vessel to reach the U-boat's location. Her depth-charging brought no visible result so Walker sent in *Kite* and *Woodpecker* for a barrage attack. It took over 50 depth charges before the U-boat's wreckage began to surface. Throughout this attack the U-boat commander would only have been aware of *Wild Goose*, the one ship that was *not* attacking.

### Pressures on the Kriegsmarine

With the U-boat bases on the Atlantic coast fully operational, the U-Boat Arm was well-established for the coming acceleration of the war. But it would be a long time before the concrete bunkers would appear. For now, both the U-boat pens and the Atlantic docks were ready targets for air attacks. The first serious attack came in July.

The target was the 19,000-ton heavy cruiser *Prinz Eugen*, which lay in Brest harbour. An armour-piercing bomb penetrated into the control centre of the ship, so rendering all her guns inoperable. Sixty men, including the First Watch Officer Otto Stooss lost their lives. It took to the end of the year to repair the guns.

In response to this raid on Brest – the first of many – a massive air raid defences operation was immediately mounted. The two dry docks were covered in 15,000 square metres of netting and 800 smoke-making machines were brought in. These required 550 men to operate them, supported by 200 boat crew. On top of this, the yard had to refill 800 bottles of smoke every day. Alongside these defences, key areas of the dockyard were camouflaged with 1000 tonnes of paint and 200,000 rush mats. Even after all this work, the Kriegsmarine dared not keep *Scharnhorst* and *Gneisenau* together. *Scharnhorst* was sent away. Despite all the camouflage at Brest, the RAF were not fooled by the tanker that had replaced *Scharnhorst*. Three days later they located her at La Pallice and landed five bombs on her at a cost of losing twelve planes.

Dönitz had other problems in the closing months of 1941. After the brief period of Luftwaffe support and his untrammelled freedom to dispose his forces as he wished, he suddenly found life much harder. The planes had gone off to support the Russian campaign, as had many of his boats. He railed against what he saw as 'a complete lack of understanding, particularly by our political leadership of the essential characteristic of U-boat warfare'. He cited the eight boats that had been sent to the Baltic but '[had] found practically no targets'. Then he mentioned boats that had been sent to the Arctic at a time when there were no convoys there. And finally he complained that 'Again and again German auxiliary cruisers, blockade runners, supply ships and prizes were given U-boats as escorts.'

Calm before the storm

There were, though, some occasions when Dönitz was prepared to let boats go in the interests of the wider war. One of these occurred in September 1941 when Field Marshal Rommel was losing up to 70 per cent of his supplies as the British Mediterranean Fleet sank ever more Italian supply vessels. Dönitz agreed to the detachment of some of his boats, saying, 'the measure was unavoidable, for the threat to the Africa Corps had ... to be defeated'. Hitler's detachment proved its worth as the U-boats took a devastating toll of British capital ships. On 13 November the carrier Ark *Royal* was torpedoed by *U-81* and sank the next day. Just over a week later the battleship HMS *Barham* was sunk by *U-331*. Then the light cruiser HMS *Galatea* was caught by *U-557*. Over one thousand men were lost in these three ships.

*HMS Ark Royal under attack in November 1941. Her sinking helped justify Hitler's order to move U-boats from the Atlantic to the Mediterranean to support Rommel's Afrika Korps.*

The withdrawal of U-boats to the Mediterranean came at a cost. In September the U-boats had sunk 203,000 tons in the Atlantic. The figures for October and November were 157,000 and 62,000 tons. Despite this impairment of the Atlantic battle, another 15 boats were taken from the Atlantic in November to be permanently stationed across the Strait of Gibraltar.

The concentration of so many U-boats in the Mediterranean and around Gibraltar was not without its consequences. The Strait was narrow and heavily defended; the sea was shallow and subject to air patrols over the clear waters. It was a perilous place for submarines. Between the sinking of A*rk Royal* and the end of the year, one-third of the U-boats attempting to enter the Mediterranean failed to get through the Strait; four were lost in the Strait and four had to turn back as a result of bomb damage.

Towards the end of 1941 the labour shortage in the U-boat repair yards was an increasing worry for Dönitz. The time taken to bring a new boat to operational readiness had lengthened from three to four months. He warned, 'Some remedy must be found, as when the number of operational boats increases greatly in the near future the demands for repairs will increase sharply.'

In the same month the U-Boat Arm became concerned about the quality of the men being sent to the boats. The young men now being recruited needed 'longer intensive training' said Eberhard Godt, Dönitz's Chief of Operations. Oddly, having acknowledged this deficiency, Godt went on to complain about U-boats being removed from Norway and the Baltic to be used for additional training of recruits. These were the early signs of overstretch in the Reich. The Russian campaign would place impossible demands on Germany's labour supply. Dönitz and Godt had to accept that many of their finest men had already died in the U-boat war. Replacing them would become increasingly difficult.

But even with these difficulties, Dönitz's boats were still capable of massive destruction. Convoy *SC-42* was on its way from Sydney, Nova Scotia, to Liverpool when *U-85* found it on 9 September off Greenland. Fourteen U-boats from the *Markgraf* pack gathered to attack. The attack lasted four days, with most of the action taking place at night. The four escorts struggled to keep the U-boats away from the 65 merchantmen but with little success. Sixteen ships were sunk, totalling 69,000 tons with only two U-boats sunk. This was the worst attack on a convoy since Convoy *SC-7* in October 1940, with which this book opened. There were mitigating circumstances for the Allies. Although the U-boat attack was anticipated with the aid of Ultra intelligence, Convoy *SC-42* was hemmed in by ice to the north and unable to detour to avoid the wolf pack. Other nearby convoys which were able to divert successfully escaped the wolf packs.

## On the cusp

At the end of 1941 neither side in the Atlantic battle had reason for satisfaction.

The Allies were keeping merchant sinkings below crisis level, but with no sense that they were about to defeat the U-boats. Meanwhile, the Allied armies were confined to operations in North Africa. On the eastern front Soviet troops had succeeded in counter-attacking the German Army. Moscow had proved an objective too far. The war was, at best, a stalemate.

Things looked equally bleak for Dönitz. He was still desperately short of U-boats. Production was rising slowly but of his fleet of 220 boats, only 22 were out in the Atlantic. Training, working-up, trials and travel to and from the convoy routes accounted for a good number. Others had been diverted to the Mediterranean. Sinkings measured by tons per day per boat were falling rapidly, while the Eastern Front demanded an ever greater share of the Reich's resources. But despite this dismal outlook, the battle was about to turn in Dönitz's favour.

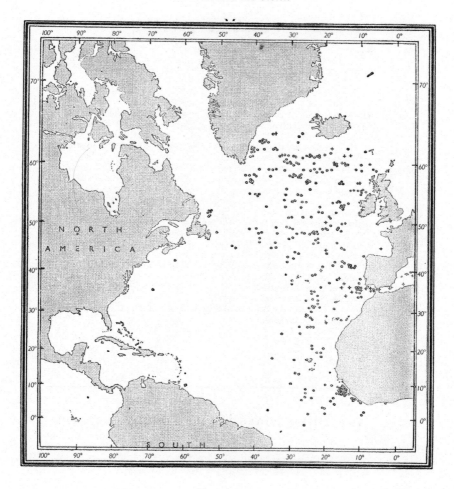

Map 2. Sinkings Mid-March 1941 to 31 December 1941. 0 = Merchant ship;
+ = U-boat.

# 21 The Second Happy Time

## January to April 1942

### *Pearl Harbor*

Since October 1941 hundreds of Japanese aircrew had been training in low-flying raids at Kagoshima Bay in Japan. Their task was to fly at 160 knots while at a height of only 165 feet. Their target would be Pearl Harbor in Hawaii, home of the United States Pacific Fleet.

Meanwhile the United Kingdom struggled under the burdens of war. In 1938 Britain had imported 68 million tons of raw materials and goods. By 1941 imports had fallen to 26 million tons. No two figures were a better testimony to the continuing mortal threat of the U-boats. Pearl Harbor could not come too soon for the United Kingdom.

The Japanese carrier aircraft raid on Pearl Harbor on 7 December 1941 was intended to be a pre-emptive attack to destroy the aircraft carriers based there and so leave Japan free to conquer the Dutch East Indies and Malaya. Their disappointment on finding the carriers USSs *Enterprise*, *Lexington*, and *Saratoga* absent that morning did not prevent them from inflicting a humiliating defeat on America that day.

As Pilot Commander Mitsuo Fuchida's first-wave attack planes crossed the coastline of Oahu Island he saw the harbour in the distance. His cry of 'Tora, tora, tora': Tiger, tiger, tiger went back over the radio to the Japanese carriers. It was the code that confirmed that Oahu had been taken by surprise. In the slaughter that followed, four of the eight battleships were sunk or capsized (USSs *Arizona*, *California*, *Oklahoma* and *West Virginia*). The remaining four suffered considerable bomb and torpedo damage which, in the case of USS *Nevada* was very severe. (Yet only USSs *Arizona* and *Oklahoma* would not be salvaged.) There had been serious damage to two cruisers: USSs *Helena* and

*Raleigh*. A third cruiser, the USS *Honolulu*, got off more lightly. Two destroyers, USSs *Cassin* and *Downes*, were damaged beyond repair, while USS *Shaw* had suffered non-mortal damage. There was also damage to some auxiliary vessels. In all 19 vessels had been hit, or damaged by fire and debris from adjacent ships. Additionally America lost 188 aircraft and a further 159 were damaged.

*US battleships sinking at Pearl Harbor, 7 December 1941. America's entry into the war brought little relief to the embattled British escort vessels and their crews. The worst was yet to come.*

The Japanese losses were slight: 29 planes and six submarines (of which five were midget submarines). Fifty-five airmen had lost their lives, as had nine men on the midget submarines. Over 100 planes were damaged. But it was a small price to pay for the massive destruction inflicted on the United States Pacific Fleet and the island's defences. The Japanese were content enough with the result to order their advance into Malaya, Thailand, Hong Kong and the Philippines on the following day. In January 1942 the Dutch East Indies, New Guinea and the Solomon Islands were added to the list. But Admiral Isoroku Yamamoto's comment on the attack was a more prescient summary of that morning's devastation: 'I fear all we have done is to awaken a sleeping giant and fill him with a terrible resolve.'

When Raeder heard how easily the Japanese had wrought massive destruction on the world's largest fleet, he shuddered at this reminder of just how weak *his* fleet was. The war, he wrote that day, 'came five years too soon'. Japan had humbled the mighty United States, so opening up huge possibilities for conquest in the Far East. Yet Raeder had no force to send.

Raeder comforted himself with the fact that the Allies were now fighting on two fronts, so there would be fewer Allied warships in the Atlantic. This, surely, was the moment to force the Atlantic Battle to a conclusion. But he was always more ambitious than events merited. Rather than intensify his Atlantic campaign, he proposed to mount amphibious operations in the Mediterranean. Presumably Dönitz knew nothing of this hare-brained scheme: he was too busy planning his attack on United States' east coast shipping. Operation Drumbeat was to give his commanders a chance to put their lack-lustre performance of November and December 1941 behind them. Their triumphant accomplishments in the first two months of the New Year were to be the harbinger of a year of unrelieved naval disaster for the Allies.

## Operation Drumbeat

Four days after the Pearl Harbor attack, Joachim von Ribbentrop, Germany's Foreign Minister, asked the United States Ambassador to call on him at his office in the Wilhelmstrasse. Von Ribbentrop read out Germany's formal declaration of war on America, although, in typical Nazi fashion, the note accused the Americans of having 'created a state of war'. This, though, was just a formality for the press. Two days earlier Hitler had lifted the restrictions on U-boat attacks on merchant ships in the Pan-American Safety Zone on the United States' east coast. The Atlantic battle that had been confined to the eastern half of the ocean was now to spread to the full vastness of that mighty sea.

In taking on America, the Reich had assumed a risk on the same scale as that of its invasion of the Soviet Union. The magnitude of the American response to war was made clear by President Roosevelt on 1 January 1942 when he announced the building of 8 million tons of shipping in that year and 10 million in the following year. Added to this was the modest British output of 1.3 million tons of new merchant shipping in 1942. Here was a monumental challenge to Raeder and Dönitz: his war-winning target of sinking 700,000 tons a month had leapt to over 900,000 tons a month.

Nevertheless, Dönitz gleefully predicted that his boats would catch the Americans unawares. Just how unawares was to prove astounding, especially given the extraordinary weakness of his U-boat fleet. He had only 55 operational boats in the Atlantic, of which 60 per cent were in dockyard hands. That left just 22 boats for his new war, although Hitler only allowed him to deploy six.

The Reich's war with the United States began at 1.49 am on 12 January 1942. The 9000-ton *Cyclops* was an ageing merchant ship, built in Glasgow in 1906. She had twice been attacked by U-boats during the First World War but had evaded them on each occasion. She had departed from Auckland in New Zealand on 1 December 1941, passed through the Panama Canal, bound for Halifax, Nova Scotia, where she was to join an escorted convoy across the Atlantic. It was in her unescorted state that Commander Reinhard Hardegen in *U-123* caught her in his periscope. Hardegen was an experienced commander, now on his sixth patrol. He had already sunk seven ships and was eager for his eighth. Until that day, Hardegen had had to search hard for his ships, so he was astonished to find the eastern seaboard of the United States and Canada lit up as if there were no war, with no sign of any anti-submarine precautions. The ships even had their navigation lights switched on, while the lightships helpfully continued to guide coastal traffic.

Hardegen took his time in the undefended waters as he manoeuvred *U-123* into position. He was close enough to rely on one torpedo. It scored a firm hit between the number six and number seven holds of *Cyclops*. She began to settle but she showed no signs of sinking. However, Captain Leslie Kersley thought that *Cyclops* was no longer seaworthy so he ordered 'Abandon ship' while his radio operator sent out a distress call. The boats swung out and his crew of 96 officers and men, together with seven naval gunners and 86 Chinese seamen as passengers stepped into them.

With the boats in the water Kersley had second thoughts about his ship. She was stable. Perhaps she could be saved. Back he went with a large part of the crew to see what could be done to rescue her. Kersley's decision had horrific consequences. Hardegen, seeing that his prey refused to sink, fired a second torpedo. The *Cyclops* broke in two as the torpedo exploded in the depths of the vessel. Five minutes later she had gone. With her had died around 40 crew members and nearly 50 passengers. For those who survived, help was not far away. HMCS *Red Deer*, a brand new 700-ton minesweeper, was soon on the scene and speedily picked up the 95 survivors.

The ease which Hardegen sank *Cyclops* heralded a new phase in the war, which the U-boat men would dub 'The Second Happy Time'.

In the first wave of Operation Drumbeat, which lasted until early February, 23 ships were sunk, totalling over 150,000 tons. After his sinking of the *Cyclops*, Hardegen noted in his war diary: 'It is a pity that there were not 10 to 20 U-boats here last night, instead of one. I am sure all would have found ample targets. Altogether I saw about 20 steamships, some undarkened; also a few tramp steamers, all hugging the coast.' Dönitz described these attacks as 'a complete success'. He marvelled at the display of coastal lights and the total lack of any defences. The few lone patrolling destroyers made no attempt to attack the U-boats, while the merchant masters chattered away on their radios as if the war were still on the other side of the Atlantic.

Dönitz sent out a second wave of five boats at the end of January to take over from the returning first wave. At the same time he shifted the area of operations to the Venezuelan coast, which was thick with tankers bringing precious South American fuel oil to Britain. From Britain's point of view, there could be no worse place for the U-boats to congregate. Hardegen had sunk three tankers and damaged a fourth during his patrol in this area, and the losses continued as other U-boats homed-in on the tankers. By mid-March Churchill was telling Harry Hopkins, President Roosevelt's chief diplomatic adviser, that he was 'deeply concerned at the immense sinkings of tankers west of the $40^{th}$ meridian and in the Caribbean Sea'. January sinkings were 221,000 tons; February, 365,000 tons; followed by 88,500 tons in the first 11 days of March. Churchill declared that 'drastic action of some kind is necessary'. He even went so far as to suggest a temporary halting of tanker sailings.

*An American vessel is the victim of the Second Happy Time.*

The early reports from U-boat commanders off the American coast revealed a complete absence of war-readiness. All the merchant ships appeared to be sailing independently. Their ship handling was 'clumsy', reported Karl-Heinz Moehle, commander of *U-123*. The escort commanders were so inexperienced as to leave the vessels in a peacetime state of readiness.

Whereas the war had started slowly for the British in the last few months of 1939, the United States was plunged overnight into war on a massive scale on 7 December 1941. After Pearl Harbor, the Japanese rampaged westwards. By early January the American naval base at Cavite in Manila Bay was in Japanese hands. Next the Japanese forced American surrenders at Wake and Guam. Later they drove the Americans out of the Philippines. Until the Battle of Midway in early June 1942, America was in danger of a monumental defeat in the Pacific. Only the United States Navy could prevent this catastrophe. Inevitably, the east coast of the United States was left poorly defended as warships were despatched to the Pacific Ocean. Meanwhile, on the east coast, the United States urgently needed to establish convoys, even if its destroyers were to be thinly spread. Except that is not what happened. There were to be no convoys.

The man responsible for this bizarre decision was Admiral Ernest King, Commander-in-Chief of the United States Fleet. King has been described as 'perhaps the most disliked Allied leader of World War II'. He is undoubtedly one of the most controversial of the Allied leaders in that war. Some rate him as one of the greatest naval commanders of all time; others find little to praise in him. He announced his refusal to introduce convoys in his characteristic dogmatic style:

> It should be borne in mind that effective convoying depends
> upon the escorts being in sufficient strength to permit their
> taking the offensive against attacking submarines without ...
> exposing the convoy to other submarines ... Any protection
> less than this simply results in the convoy's becoming a
> convenient target for submarines.

And that was that. All the experience of 1917-1918, and the British and Canadian experience of the new war was tossed aside. Was King truly unaware

196

that hardly a single convoy of the war had had anything approaching 'sufficient strength'? Was he really unaware of the horrific rate of sinking of the independent sailings compared to that of even the weakly escorted ships?

Fortunately Churchill was a man who based his judgements on facts and experience. He surrounded himself with scientists, statisticians and operational research people so he immediately recognised the horrific consequences of a 'no escorts' policy. This put him in the unusual position of offering ships to the Americans rather than begging for them for himself. He offered Roosevelt 'twenty-four of our best-equipped anti-submarine trawlers and ten corvettes … the utmost we could spare'.

While targets were easy to find for the U-boats on the eastern side of the Atlantic, the boats were operating at vast distances from their bases. To enable them to stay on patrol for significant periods, Dönitz introduced supply and replenishment U-boats, which were known as 'milch cows'. The first – *U-459* – had a surface displacement of 1700 tons. These boats were unarmed, except for their AA guns, since every available corner was used for a typical cargo of around 450 tons of fuel, along with torpedoes, ammunition and spare parts for U-boats. They also brought fresh food and even had on-board bakeries so that U-boat crews could enjoy freshly baked loaves. (Standard U-boat bread came in tins.) And, if needed, a U-boat crew could make use of the doctor that each milch cow carried. Initially the milch cows proved a success, with 14 boats being refuelled off Bermuda in April. But the ten that were produced had a precarious existence since they were always a priority target for the Allies. Two were sunk on their maiden voyages before they had even supplied one U-boat. Only *U-549* supplied more than 6 boats, making a total of 72 supplies.

It was on 1 April 1942 that the United States finally began limited convoying. Even so, the Americans were still tardy in their anti-submarine activities. In mid-April U-boat commanders reported that United States' destroyers started hunts but soon gave up. The tenacious persistence of men like Walker had yet to feature in the United States Navy.

When Dönitz reviewed the patrols off the American coast at the end of the first three months of the year, one figure stood out: not one U-boat had been lost. (In fact *U-85* had been lost the day before he wrote the report but he was not then aware of its sinking.) There was no other territory where U-boats could operate so insouciantly. On the basis of the merchant sinkings reported to him by his commanders (much higher than the true figures) Dönitz concluded that 'it was better to use the U-boats off the American coast than in the Central Atlantic, despite the long journey which this entailed'.

But the peak had passed. Despite the presence of the first milch cow, and despite Dönitz now having around 17 boats on patrol, sinkings were diminishing. United States antisubmarine activities were improving by mid-April and belated convoying kept target ships within narrow lines. The Second Happy Time was coming to an end.

Of this period, the American historian Samuel Eliot Morison said, 'the massacre which the U-boats were able to "enjoy" along the Atlantic coast in 1942 was as great a national disaster as if saboteurs had blown up half a dozen of our biggest munitions factories'. But by May 1942 Operation Drumbeat was only a nasty blip as the United States regained control of its eastern seaboard. The price had been high: 1.2 million tons of shipping had been sunk off the east coast and total Allied losses in this period had been 2.6 million tons. This was more than for the full twelve months of 1941. The war at sea was approaching a crisis.

### 'And sink the U-boats!'

It was during Operation Drumbeat that the retired Vice admiral Cecil Usborne made a suggestion that was to have far-reaching consequences for the Battle of the Atlantic. Throughout his career Usborne had shown a talent for innovation. He had served as Assistant Director of Naval Ordnance in the early

1920s and as Director of Naval Intelligence in the early 1930s but was ignominiously deprived of his post after the Invergordon Mutiny in 1932, when about 1000 sailors had staged a strike over their pay. To his surprise, he was called back to the Admiralty in November 1941 to be Naval Adviser on U-Boats to the First Sea Lord.

Pound despatched Usborne to the Western Approaches Command in Liverpool with orders to find out why its performance was so poor. A few days later Usborne was back in London in the office of the Second Sea Lord, Admiral Sir Charles Little. Usborne described the state of affairs at Derby House in Liverpool. Although Admiral Noble would not admit it, the escorts were doing a poor job because their commanders had never been trained to work together. (Tobermory only provided basic, single-ship working.) Usborne recommended the creation of a 'tactical table' at which escort ship commanders could fight and analyse attacks on convoys. Pound ordered the immediate setting up of a Western Approaches Tactical Unit (WATU) to develop anti-U-boat tactics and to train escort commanders. The Tactical Unit was to prove one the most powerful weapons in the Allied anti-submarine armoury.

It is not clear why the 43-year-old Captain Gilbert Roberts was chosen to command the unit. He had had a routine sea-going career, culminating with promotion to the rank of captain and the command of the destroyer HMS *Fearless* in 1937. Within weeks of taking up that command he had been invalidated out of the navy with tuberculosis and was told that the navy was unlikely to need his services again. So he was surprised to receive a telegram from Admiral Little commanding him to pack an overnight bag and attend the Admiralty the next day. When Roberts was shown into Little's office he found that Usborne was also in attendance. Two admirals meeting one out-of-work captain signalled a meeting of considerable importance. Little and Usborne were in sombre mood as they revealed to Roberts the Government's closely guarded secret: the Allies were losing the Atlantic battle. Sinkings were exceeding replacement ships. Food and war supplies were being swallowed up by the ocean at an unsustainable rate. Roberts was given his brief for setting up the tactical unit. To underline the importance and the urgency of his task, Usborne took Roberts across Horse Guards Parade to be ushered into the Prime Minister's presence. Churchill was blunt in his orders to Roberts: 'Find out what is happening in the Atlantic, find ways of getting the convoys through *and* sink the U-boats.' The Western Approaches Tactical Unit was in business.

Noble stood aside in the creation of the Tactical Unit – indeed it seems it was created against his wishes as Roberts found when he arrived at Derby House to begin work. Noble made some contemptuous remarks about Roberts' background and dismissed him, saying. 'Well, you can carry on with it but don't bother me. I am busy.' Fortunately for Roberts, Noble's chief-of-staff, Commodore J M Mansfield, Cdr , did all he could to help, including ensuring that Roberts had the staff he desired. Most importantly, Chief Yeoman Bernard Rayner was brought from Portsmouth to be Chief Signalman.

The unit began with Rayner, two lieutenant commanders, four Wren officers (Elizabeth Drake, Jane Howes, Jean Laidlaw and Nan Wailes) and four Wren ratings. This small team set to work and soon gained the confidence of escort officers and, importantly, Noble.

To understand why this unit had such a high proportion of Wrens, we need to take a closer look at the unit's core activity: 'the game', as it came to be known. The game was played on the floor of a large room with no windows. (Roberts had made only one significant change in Usborne's plan for a tactical unit: the table had become the floor.) Around the sides of the room were cubicles made by hanging pieces of canvas from wooden frames. Each of these represented an escort vessel. The trainee officers were placed inside each cubicle with only a small slit through which they could see a tiny portion of the battlefield laid out on the floor – this was to replicate the limited view that a commander had of a convoy battle. The Wrens moved escort ships and U-boats around on the floor according to the commands of the officers, who could only communicate with the Wrens by pencil and paper on message chits. As battle followed battle, the officers learned how to interpret a battle scene, even when they could see only a fraction of the action. Slowly they learnt where best to position their ships, where a U-boat might be, and how it might act. Soon the Wrens – who were present at every battle – knew more about escort tactics than did their trainees. This led them to work by themselves to solve tactical problems, so adding to the range of tactics that could be passed on to escort officers. And, just as Walker had his Buttercup and other tactics, so the Tactical Unit developed a range of similar methods, including Raspberry, Pineapple and Step-aside. Raspberry, for instance, was a counter-attack method to sink a U-boat as it hid at the rear of the departing convoy after having attacked in the middle of the convoy.

The unit was never more than a dozen or so strong, but it trained over 5000 officers from the navies of the Allied powers. Some came before their first posting; others were experienced escort commanders. The Tactical Unit proved successful. In 1941, 35 U-boats had been sunk; the figure for 1942 was 86. While there were many factors that contributed to this success, there is no doubt that the tactical training of escort commanders played an important part. Amongst its trainees were Lieutenant Prince Philip of Greece and Denmark (later the Duke of Edinburgh); Peter Scott the famous ornithologist; and Nicholas Monsarrat, who later wrote *The Cruel Sea*.

*Ups and downs in anti-submarine warfare*

The establishment of the Western Approaches Tactical Unit bode well for the escorts in January 1942. Yet just one month later Western Approaches suffered a grievous setback. The Kriegsmarine introduced a new fourth wheel and reflector for the naval Enigma machines. (The reflector was a device to enable an Enigma machine to be used both for encryption and decryption.) For the next ten months, Bletchley Park was unable to read radio traffic between the U-boats and their headquarters. During that period the escorts would have to rely on the growing range of anti-submarine technology and methods. However, 1942 was a year of highly significant developments in anti-submarine warfare, including end-to-end convoys, better radar and a breakthrough in direction-finding

End-to-end convoying was the first development in 1942, beginning in January. A convoy leaving Britain would have a British-based escort to the mid-Atlantic, where it would be met by a Canada-based one. The first beneficiary of this approach was Convoy *SC-67*, which consisted of 28 merchant ships with 13 escorts. On 10 February *U-591* reported its sighting to Lorient. Dönitz despatched *U-136* and *U-213* to attack. These were inexperienced boats, under orders not to attack if they encountered a strong escort. Only *U-136* risked attacking, succeeding in sinking a merchant vessel of 4000 tons and the Canadian corvette HMCS *Spikenard*. In view of the horrors that 1942 was to bring for the Allies, this small result was grossly misleading. At this stage of the war, even a strongly-escorted convoy could expect many sinkings. The tactics needed to face down a more experienced wolf pack were yet to be developed.

Otto Kretschmer was one of the first U-boat commanders to discover another innovation in Allied escort procedures: ASV II radar. In early April 1942 his *U-333* was to be one of the first of its victims. He was proceeding to American waters. It was its third day at sea. Six lookouts were on the bridge. Visibility was good but there was low cloud overhead. Without any warning – not even the feint noise of an engine – an aeroplane came hurtling towards the boat. Although it had come out of the clouds, it was perfectly lined up on *U-333* as if it had seen its target from afar. The men fell down the ladder as Kretschmer yelled 'Dive!' The hatch slammed shut as air rushed from the ballast tanks. The boat had descended about 30 metres when it was rocked by two bombs. Bulbs shattered, fuses blew, valves sprang leaks, and every loose item flew through the air. *U-333* had been bombed by a plane that no lookout had – or could have – seen. Kretschmer knew that only radar could have found his boat through thick cloud. And so accurate was the find that it had to be a new type of radar. His boat survived the attack but Kretschmer knew that he had a lucky escape from a new mode of detection.

*Otto Kretschmer with the crew of U-99 celebrating his Knight's Cross in August 1940. He was the most successful U-boat commander of the war with 46 ships sunk (273,000 tons) and 5 damaged (38,000 tons). He was captured in March 1941 and remained a prisoner of war until 1947.*

Despite its potential, this radar was not a great success in sinking U-boats in its early days. It did an excellent job, though, at keeping them submerged.

Yet another powerful search technology was coming into use at this time: HF/DF direction finding. On 27 March 1942 *U-587* was returning to its base after sinking five ships off the Canadian coast. It was Korvettenkapitän Ulrich Borcherdt's second patrol. He had 23,000 tons sunk to his credit. Ahead of him he sighted a convoy. He knew the routine. He reported his sighting to Lorient and prepared to shadow the convoy while Dönitz despatched a wolf pack to join him. The signal was barely despatched when he saw a warship – HMS *Leamington* – pass his position. Thinking that he was undetectable, Borcherdt made another report to Lorient. The warship turned. She was heading his way. Borcherdt ordered a crash-dive but the depth charges were soon pulverising U-587. She sank without a single survivor.

Did Borcherdt have time before he died to wonder how his boat was found so quickly? The answer was High Frequency Direction Finding (HF/DF), commonly known as 'Huff-Duff'. Land-based direction finding had been in use for years. It worked by having two listening stations a known distance apart. Their two independent bearings from a radio signal were then used to calculate by triangulation the exact position of the radio source. In theory such land-based systems could be used to inform escort vessels of the location of a U-boat that had used its radio. In practice it was too slow to give U-boat locations in real-time. The Allies' breakthrough came with the invention of a single ship-based receiver that used two aerials placed close together. Although both aerials physically pointed to the same bearing, the signals they received had minute phase differences. These enabled the precise bearing of an object to be calculated. (The human ears work in a similar way, so allowing us to locate a sound source.) In the case of *U-587*, it was HMS *Keppel's* HF/DF that located the U-boat and passed its bearing to HMS *Leamington*.

*Retreat from the Atlantic ports*

While Dönitz's U-boats were enjoying almost risk-free attacks off the American east coast, problems were looming at the Atlantic ports. The dockyards were coming under increasing Allied bombing attacks. Hitler, worried about his two precious battlecruisers, *Gneisenau* and *Scharnhorst*, ordered their return to Germany. At 9.14 pm on 11 February 1942 the two vessels left Brest to embark on their famous 'Channel dash'. To their grave embarrassment, the RAF and the Royal Navy failed to sink these two prizes as they passed through the Channel, although both were damaged by mines. They reached their home ports on the night of 12/13 February. The seamanship was brilliant, but the 'dash' was effectively a retreat for the Reichsmarine. By early 1942 it was clear that Brest was of little value to the Kriegsmarine's capital ships. At best it was useful as a last resort for emergency repairs. The port's fitting out had consumed vast resources, including the relocation of valuable machine tools from Germany. Now those facilities were near to unusable by the large ships.

Six weeks later the vulnerability of the Atlantic bases was once more exposed – this time by the raid on St Nazaire. The raid's origin lay in a ship that had not yet put to sea: the *Tirpitz*. If she were ever to be in need of major repairs when in the Atlantic (as *Bismarck* had been) the only place she could go to was St Nazaire, where there was a large enough dry dock to take the vessel. The raid's objective was to destroy the dry dock and the harbour facilities before *Tirpitz* had even put to sea. At the heart of the raid was HMS *Cambletown*, loaded with 1500 tons of explosive, which was to ram the 35-feet thick gates of the dock. *Cambletown* succeeded in ramming the gates and her explosives detonated a short while afterwards. The cost in men was high. The large raiding flotilla had carried over 600 seamen and commandoes. Of these 169 were killed and more than 200 captured. Much had gone wrong on the Allied side, but the raid was a brutal shock to Hitler. The Allies had proved that the French coast was vulnerable.

The St Nazaire raid provoked panic in the U-boat high command. The U-Boat Arm's imposing *Villa Kerillon* and Dönitz's own house, *Chateau des Sardines*, were within easy access from the waterfront. The next raid might well have been an attempt to kidnap Dönitz himself. The command fled to Paris in undignified haste. In the 20 months of their occupation of the ports Dönitz and his staff had built a tight community of seamen, repair workers, ancillary services and accommodation. Attacks on seamen by the French were rare and relations with the local community were generally satisfactory. And Dönitz's presence enabled him to more than command his men: he supported and nurtured them. Overnight, the St Nazaire raid had turned Dönitz's smooth and compact operation into a community on edge, now managed at distance. All the sailors' rest homes along the Atlantic coast were closed down. And harbour protection boats were taken for coastal protection duties. The British naval planners could never have imagined the panic that they had caused at the highest levels in the Reich.

### Allied gloom

In March 1942 Pound carried out a major review of the Atlantic battle since the outbreak of the war. The results were sobering.

Top of the list of problems was the shortage of escort vessels. When the British and Americans met to review their requirements in early March 1942, they concluded that Britain needed 725 escorts, of which she had 383, leaving a shortage of 342. The Americans needed 590 vessels, possessed 122 and so lacked 468. These staggering shortfalls reveal that the United States was even less well prepared for war than Britain had been.

But new escort vessels would not in themselves win the battle. That needed a new approach to escorting. The Royal Navy had a long tradition of ships boldly putting to sea to fearlessly hunt down Britain's enemies. Daring, courage and determination delivered victory. But not in this war. The loan ship heroically hunting down its adversary was a thing of the past. Now, finding the enemy depended on more than valiant seamen. Coordinated working, air search, radar and training in antisubmarine warfare were just as important. It is surprising that the Admiralty took so long to recognise this truth. Their short-lived search groups had proved a disaster in the early months of the war. And their most successful commanders – men like Walker – used methods that involved training escort officers in new forms of synchronised attack. At least, though, in his Western Approaches Tactical Unit, Pound now had a key component of the move from vague hunting to precision search and attack. But the battle would take Britain to the very verge of collapse before these new methods yielded the results that they promised.

.

# 22 Dönitz triumphant

## May to December 1942

*Return to the Atlantic*

At 1 May 1942 Dönitz had a total of 292 U-boats, of which 124 were frontline – the others were on trials or being used for training. Eighty-five of his operational boats were Atlantic-based. These figures were a huge increase on his 57 boats in September 1939, but even so, the daily average of boats at sea was only 48.8; and only 9.87 were in operational areas. The reality of operating U-boats was that for most of the time they were in harbour, or in transit to and from their operational areas.

As the Second Happy Time drew to an end in spring 1942, Dönitz reassessed his boat distribution. He knew from signal intercepts that the Allies were now routing Atlantic convoys along a great circle in the north. (This being the shortest route, it exposed them to the minimum possible period of attack.) Noting that his 16-20 boats in the Norway area had sunk only 40,000 tons in March and April, Dönitz concluded that his Atlantic boats could quadruple that tonnage. The move to the North Atlantic quickly followed. It was to yield spectacular successes and bring despair to the Allied escorts.

One of Dönitz's earliest forays proved amply rewarding, while also exposing the feeble response of the Allied escorts. Convoy *ON-92* was outbound from Liverpool for North America. It had departed on 6 May and on the next day had met its Mid-Ocean Escort Force led by Commander J B Heffernan in USS *Gleaves*. The escort was handicapped from the moment that it met the convoy since none of its ships was fitted with either HF/DF or 10cm radar. Only the rescue ship, HMS *Bury*, carried HF/DF and only the Canadian corvette HMCS *Bittersweet* was fitted with Type 271 radar.

On 11 May, HMS *Bury's* HF/DF found three U-boats circling the convoy. Her commander reported the sightings to Derby House, which passed them on to Heffernan in *Gleaves*. British practice at this point was to execute a sharp course change followed by zigzagging. Instead, Heffernan chose to follow United States Navy practice by taking *Gleaves* and the cutter USCGC *Spencer* on a sweep ahead of the convoy. They found one U-boat and dropped depth charges without any success.

While *Gleaves* and *Spencer* were away from the convoy, *U-124* had manoeuvred into a striking position. Its commander, Commander Johann Mohr, had already sunk 18 ships. He took two more in minutes as his torpedoes first hit the 7000-ton *Empire Dell* and then the 5000-ton *Llanover* at around 2.00 am. All but two men from the two ships were picked up by *Bury* and the corvette HMCS *Shediac*.

*Gleaves* and *Spencer* were still away from the convoy when *U-94* arrived and sank the Panamanian 5500-ton *Cocle*. Kapitänleutnant Otto Ites, who had been in U-boats since 1938, had now sunk his tenth ship. His attack was followed by the return of *U-124*, which sank the Greek steamer *Mount Parnes*, laden with Welsh coal. Shortly afterwards, the 5500 ton *Cristales* succumbed to one of Ites' torpedoes. Both ships went down without loss of life.

On the following day convoy life returned to the dull routine of scanning the horizon, maintaining equipment, and station keeping. Night fell. The U-Boat Arm had demonstrated how invulnerable it was in its close actions against the convoy, while the escort had shown itself to be too weak to keep the enemy at bay. Convoy *ON-92* was now in a state of high tension. Its only hope of escape was the deteriorating weather as the winds rose and the seas mounted.

In the darkness after midnight, the attacks began again. The coal carrying 4500-ton *Batna* had six naval gunners for her protection. They had no chance of sighting *U-94* in the dark through the pall of the cold Atlantic spray. One torpedo. One man dead. One more ship went to the bottom.

But *U-94* had not finished. Its next prey was the 4500-ton Swedish *Tolken*. Another torpedo from the wolf pack took the seventh ship of the night. Still Otto Ites wanted more. As the crew of *Tolken* lowered the ship's boats, *U-94* closed in, as if to board the steamer. The crew turned to their guns and fought off the threatening U-boat.

At last the convoy's ordeal was over. It had faced a wolf pack of eight or nine boats and had lost seven merchant ships out of the 46 that sailed. These were grievous figures. And the message behind them gave cause for sombre thought back home.

The success of the wolf pack had owed everything to the weaknesses in the escort system: the escorts lacked HF/DF and 10cm radar; Heffernan was following tactics that British experience had shown to be worthless; nor did he know how to benefit from the one credible sighting report from HMS *Bury*; and the escort was far too small to take on a sizeable wolf pack.

And what could the Allies do? There were no short-term answers. HF/DF and radar were being fitted to ships in large numbers, but they were of little value until the men became proficient in their use – a process that took months. Escort ships were coming down the slipways, but not fast enough. And escort-carriers were on the way, but slowly. Until all these deficiencies could be mastered, the U-boats were to be near to invincible. The second half of 1942 was to be an ordeal that would threaten Britain's capacity to remain in the war.

### The success of air cover

The Allied breakthrough in anti-submarine tactics began slowly in mid-1942 with the development of air cover in the Bay of Biscay. The Atlantic coast bases were all within reach of Allied planes. No U-boat could put to sea or return to base without passing through the Bay. The unavoidable concentration of the boats as they passed in and out of harbour made them easier to locate. As Dönitz gloomily said, '[the Bay] has become the playground of English aircraft ... there is no defence against Sunderlands and heavy bombers'. He saw no solution to this problem, being convinced that British radar developments would lead to the loss of all his boats. He added, 'It is sad and very depressing for the U-boat crews that there are no forces whatever available to protect a U-boat, which is unable to dive owing to a/c bombs'. While Dönitz's forecast was true for the long term, it reads oddly for something written in June 1942. The merchant sinkings for June to November of that year were to be the highest of the war.

What Dönitz wanted more than anything else in mid-1942 was air cover for his boats during their passage through Biscay. In early July he pressed his case on Göring at one of their rare meetings. Dönitz justified his demands for additional air cover and more boats by claiming that his boats were sinking 700,000 tons a month – the level that he thought was necessary to defeat Britain. This total was based on reports from his U-boat commanders, which were inevitably subject to error. In fact the true figure for the first seven months of the year was 508,000 tons a month sunk by U-boats – nowhere near his target. Göring, who had a low opinion of the value of the U-Boat Arm, for once accepted Dönitz's plea. He allocated an additional 24 Junkers 88s to the Luftwaffe Atlantic Command.

Despite the additional air cover of the Junkers 88s, Allied planes continued to harass the U-boats in Biscay. In August, Dönitz complained: 'Outward and inward-bound boats in the North Sea and Biscay are exposed to grave danger by daily, even hourly, hunts by aircraft.' In July and August he reported that four boats were sunk by planes and others had been damaged. He was even more alarmed to discover that, in addition to the coastal attacks, there were now long-range planes reaching out into the Atlantic. He lamented, 'this has made the operation of boats very difficult and in some cases no longer worthwhile'. This was remarkably perceptive of Dönitz. The current rate of sinking by his boats superficially indicated an all-conquering U-boat service. But Dönitz was able to see the looming threat of the Allies' superior technology.

His fears were confirmed little more than a week later when a wolf pack was shadowing a convoy. At 9.00 am an air escort appeared and forced all the

U-boats to submerge. By twilight they had lost contact with the convoy. It was not until 3.00 pm that the boats found the convoy again, at which point it was too late to manoeuvre into an attacking position. The attack was broken off with three U-boats damaged by air action. In 1941 a contact between a wolf pack and a convoy would have proved deadly for the convoy; from now on, Allied air cover would never be far from the U-boats' hunting grounds. Dönitz understood this. He called it the 'unfavourable air situation' and foresaw that it would be the U-boats' nemesis unless Göring would provide more air cover. But that was the one thing that both Hitler and Göring repeatedly failed to supply – this was strategic error number seven in the U-boat war.

Objectively speaking the second half of 1942 was the peak of Dönitz's war, but his mood varied greatly during this period. In May he was in an optimistic frame of mind, writing: 'U-boat losses are extraordinarily small.' Success was just 'a matter of bringing out the (new) boats form the Baltic as fast as possible'. By August, pessimism had set in as he battled 'ever increasing difficulties' and 'intolerable losses'. He concluded 'our chances of victory in the U-boat war' were now diminished. Part of his problem was the diminishing efficiency of the U-Boat Arm. In October 1940 his boats had been sinking 900 tons per boat per day; by August 1942 they were down to 149 tons per boat per day.

### Dönitz: 'Be hard.'

By September 1942 Dönitz was fearful of defeat, despite all he had achieved in building up the unappreciated U-Boat Arm. For three years he had single-mindedly sought to maximise tonnage sunk. With the might of American industry now in the war, his dreams of sinking vessels faster than they could be built were fading. He needed a new tactic. He found it sometime in September 1942. America and Britain could replace ships with ease. Crews were another matter.

The first indication we have of Dönitz encouraging his men to commit murder comes from the evidence of Midshipman Peter Heisig at the Nuremburg Trials after the war. He recalled a speech that Dönitz had given to his group of trainees in late 1942. Dönitz had referred to the one million tons of new shipping that the Allies were turning out every month. 'The bottleneck of the Allies lay only in the problem of personnel for these newly built ships,' he told his recruits. Heisig's deposition continues: 'He therefore demanded that we should from now on carry on total warfare against ship and crew. That meant, so far as possible, no seaman from a sunk ship was to get home any more ... After the sinking of a ship, every possibility of rescue must be denied to the crew, through the destruction of every means of saving life.'

If we accept Midshipman Heisig's account, it is clear that Dönitz left little room for ambiguity in his verbal orders. In print he was more cautious. He yearned to prevent survivors of sunk merchantmen and escort vessels from returning to sea. But the nearest that he dared go to in writing was his order of 17 September 1942 which reminded his commanders that 'attempts to rescue the crews of ships sunk are in direct contradiction to the most primitive rules of warfare after sinking enemy ships and their crews'. He added: 'Orders dealing with bringing captains and chief engineers back remain unchanged.' He concluded: 'Be hard. Think of the fact that the enemy in his bombing attacks on German towns has no regard for women and children.'

Dönitz was not a man to issue vague or confusing orders so we must presume that the ambiguity in these orders was deliberate. Aware of the propaganda value to the Allies of the Kriegsmarine directly ordering the killing of survivors, Dönitz resorted to ambiguous suggestion. Those U-boat commanders who wished to could interpret the words 'rescue contradicts the most fundamental demands of war for the annihilation of enemy ships and crews' as an excuse to kill men in rafts and boats. Testimonies later collected by the Allies confirmed that additional verbal instructions left the matter to each commander's own conscience. But, if they did murder survivors, they were not to record the action in their log books.

*Midshipman Peter Heisig giving evidence at the Nuremberg trials.*

These hard-hearted orders were reinforced by Hitler's remarks at a Reich's Chancellery meeting on 28 September. He was troubled by the American claim to be able to launch one million tons of shipping per month. His response was to declare: 'Even if it were possible for the enemy to launch hulls relatively quickly, they would still lack engines, auxiliary engines, further items of equipment, and above all, personnel to man these ships.' Dönitz, who was present at this meeting, shared Hitler's view that killing seamen was the only way to beat an enemy with the industrial might of the United States. There is, though, no evidence to suggest that many commanders took advantage of Dönitz's hints.

*Battle in the balance*

During the second half of 1942 Dönitz's boats sunk an average of 500,000 tons a month in the Atlantic. From the Allies' viewpoint that figure was horrendous. But for Dönitz, who had declared that he needed to sink 700,000 tons a month in order to throttle British trade, it was not enough. So by late 1942 he was intensifying his analysis of the poor (as he saw it) performance of his boats.

His greatest concern was the devastation wrought by Allied air cover. It was so effective that his boats had to search out convoys at the point where they left air-cover – the Mid-Atlantic Gap. This often required two days of high-speed chasing in order to get ahead of a convoy for a night attack position. And the growing use of Allied radar forced his boats to stand well clear of the escorts. 'Operations against convoys had thus become much more dangerous,' Dönitz remarked. Patrols were also taking an increasing toll on his men: 'after two or three operations ... the strain on the crew made it imperative that the boat should return to base'.

Towards the end of the year, the weather brought havoc to the U-boats, making operations almost impossible for days on end. High seas smashed over the U-boat bridges. Lookouts were once more chained to the bridge to avoid being swept into the sea. Sighting ships in blizzards and icy rain was all but impossible. As a result the 730,000 tons sunk in November were followed by 330,000 in December and 203,000 in January 1943.

These storms were equally horrific for the men on the escorts and the merchant ships. Howard Goldsmith, who served on the corvette HMS *Snowflake,* described how 'inch-thick iron stanchions ... were bent at right angles ... as if a giant hammer had hammered them'. Ships' boats disappeared and the meat lockers, welded to the decks, were swept away leaving just the vestigial welding marks where they had been.

A final problem that Dönitz faced at this time was that of manning. He had started the war with well-trained men – many had had earlier naval experience. By mid-1942 he had to accept lower recruiting standards and shorter periods of training. (Of his 311 boats in early June, 124 were on trials and 59 in use for training.) Nor was training straightforward. There was no way that his training boats could enter the North Sea, and even the Baltic Sea was not safe. The Allies were so successful in mine-laying there that, as Dönitz told Hitler in September 1942, the mining 'might be fatal to U-Boat training'.

By this stage of the war Dönitz was so short of commanders that he recruited Luftwaffe pilots in a period when bombing was in a lull. They were given a brief and inadequate training and proved to be of little value. This is not surprising. Dönitz knew from experience that good commanders were an elusive commodity. We have seen how, in several battles, a few commanders were responsible for the majority of the sinkings: 80 per cent of sinkings came from 20 per cent of commanders. The special abilities that enabled a commander to hunt down and sink ships were hard to find. To add to these difficulties, the lower-deck was also problematic by mid-1942; there were not enough experienced men to fill the petty officer posts. Dönitz had no choice but to promote men prematurely.

Herbert Werner, who received his commander training in late 1943, noted the poor quality of his fellow recruits. He had been in the Kriegsmarine since 1939 and at sea in U-boats since 1941. Yet only two of his fellow trainees came from the U-Boat Arm, and not one of them had taken part in a war patrol. He remarked: 'They all lacked the essentials that only combat could provide.' There was no way that even the 'exhausting schedule of hair-raising manoeuvres' was going to produce another generation of ace commanders.

The net effect of these factors was a steep decline in the quality of his U-boat crews. These lightly-trained recruits could hope to complete no more than two or three 3 patrols before they went down with their U-boats. Dönitz's war was getting tougher by the day.

Throughout 1942 the balance of forces swayed from one side to another as U-boat numbers rapidly increased, while Allied anti-submarine technology speedily developed. Both sides were giving prominence to air support. And each side had to fight harder and harder to avoid succumbing to its adversary.

Britain's short-term position remained precarious throughout 1942, under the constant threat to its food supply and imports of war materials. That America's presence in the war more or less guaranteed eventual victory was little comfort as merchant sinkings soared in the autumn of 1942.

For Germany, it was the long-term prospects that looked threatening. The threat from the east was on an unimaginable scale. But in the west, too, Hitler feared the consequences of invasion. In particular, he feared the loss of his Atlantic bases. To thwart this threat he ordered the construction of 15,000 bunkers to protect the Atlantic shores. But in the short-term it was allied technology that Hitler should have feared as years of research and development were about to deliver stunning results.

# 23 Developments in anti-submarine warfare

## Mid-1942

### Glints of hope

The raw statistics of merchant ships lost and U-boats sunk made grim reading for the Allies during 1942. Yet it was exactly at this time that all the ingredients of their victory were being put in place. High on the list was acquiring and equipping aircraft for U-boat hunting.

### Air support for convoys

It was Pound who first pressed hard over the need for air support for the escorts in May 1942. He watched in exasperation as Air Marshal Harris of Bomber Command indulged in massive bombing raids on Germany that brought no obvious return. Meanwhile 272 merchant ships had been lost in the previous three months. His frustration burst out in a paper to the War Cabinet on 10 May 1942. Pound insisted that he could only 'safeguard our vital sea communications' if he had '[an] increased number of aircraft of the right type'.

Pound's paper received no response. In early June he was forced to use his last weapon: the threat of the Board's resignation, a move last used in 1893 to compel the Chancellor of the Exchequer to accept the naval estimates. With this threat in the background Pound now demanded that the chiefs of staff provide 'an immediate increase in the strength of the land-based air forces working with the Navy'. Rear Admiral Patrick Brind (Assistant Chief of the Naval Staff) and Air Vice Marshal John Slessor were asked to study the matter. They soon recommended the provision of an additional 72 long range reconnaissance planes and 36 Lancaster bombers for Coastal Command.

But there were enemies within. As soon as Harris heard of this allocation he moved to quash it. He called Coastal Command 'merely an obstacle to victory' and insisted that the only way to win the war was 'to concentrate our air power against the enemy's weakest spots'. He gave, as an example, the

1000-bomber raid on Cologne on 30 May. Harris had claimed that this raid would wipe out the city, yet it only destroyed 5.2 per cent of the buildings. A 1000-bomber raid on Essen on 1-2 June destroyed 11 houses and killed 15 people.

Churchill initially sided with Harris. In yet another paper of 5 October Pound emphasised that 'we have lost a large measure of control over our sea communications'. Still Churchill would not budge, declaring that 'the Bomber offensive should have first place in our effort'.

*Marshal of the Royal Air Force Sir Arthur Harris, who used his great persuasive powers to prevent Western Approaches Command from having bombers for sinking U-boats.*

The air support discussion had now run on for six months, during which time 768 merchant ships had been sunk. Tankers were being sunk at a faster rate than they were being built, while merchant ship construction was just about matching sinkings. Pound refused to give up as he now addressed his pleas to the recently formed Anti-U-boat Committee. At a minimum, said Pound, Coastal Command needed 40 long-range aircraft.

Air Chief Marshal Portal finally gave way. Except that the planes remained elusively unavailable. It would take the appointment of Max Horton (Chapter 24) to prise them out of the reluctant hands of Harris.

The Admiralty's case for bombing U-boats rather than German cities was supported by operational research. This showed that one long-range Liberator bomber would save six merchant ships in its lifetime. That same bomber sent over Germany would drop 100 tons of bombs and kill 12 civilians. Operational research had first been developed before the war at the Bawdsey Research Station in Suffolk as a means of improving the performance of Britain's radar chain. It used mathematical analysis to improve decision-making. But, in 1942, operational research was only just proving its power to guide strategy. Few people trusted it. Harris certainly did not. Regrettably, he was a law unto himself and much admired by Churchill. As a result the Royal Navy had to scream for every plane it got, while Bomber Command squandered war resources on mostly fruitless missions.

At least, though, the Admiralty made good use of the minimal air support that it managed to acquire. By August Dönitz was bemoaning the assault on his U-boats: 'The number of British aircraft in the eastern Atlantic has increased and a great variety of them is seen … U-boat traffic off the north of Scotland and in the Bay of Biscay is gravely endangered.' He particularly noted that the planes 'are equipped with an excellent location device'.

Flying Officer M A Ensor gave a bold demonstration of the power of air attack in November 1942 when flying his Hudson out of the Gibraltar air base. He was at 7000 feet when he spotted a U-boat. Ensor dived, taking the plane down to 70 feet. The boat's conning tower stood out above the waves, guiding Ensor to his target. He dropped four depth charges, of which one at least detonated. Still low over the U-boat, the plane was rocked by the force of the blast. Sergeant Roe watched the U-boat as its bow rose out of the waves. Half-a-minute later it had sunk. But the Hudson had taken severe damage. The blast from the depth charge had blown it upwards to 300 feet, torn off the rudders and elevators, jammed the aileron, and bent the tips of the wings. Ensor refused to accept defeat as he took the plane up to 1500 feet and set off for Gibraltar. He was finally defeated by a failed engine, which forced him and Roe to bail out. Ensor's DSO citation read: 'Squadron Leader Ensor, gallantly supported by Sergeant Roe, displayed courage and devotion to duty of a high order.' Ensor already had two Distinguished Flying Cross awards.

(The problem of depth charges damaging the planes that dropped them was later addressed with the development of an air-dropped 300 lb Torpex depth charge, set to fire at a depth of 25 feet.)

## Radar and Leigh lights

By mid-1942 the search planes were benefitting from the combination of 1.5 m radar and Leigh lights – the latter being a search light invented by Wing Commander Humphrey de Verd Leigh. This combination made night attacks on surfaced U-boats possible. The radar enabled a plane to home in to within a mile of a U-boat, at which point the pilot switched on his Leigh light. A lone U-boat, quietly charging its batteries while on the surface at night, would suddenly find night turned into day as a 50 million candle-power light picked out the boat. Before a crash-dive could even be attempted, bombs would be dropping around it.

It was on the night of 3-4 June 1942 that Wing Commander Jeaffreson Greswell became the first pilot to use Leigh's new device. He was flying a Vickers Wellington bomber of No. 172 Squadron over the Bay of Biscay when his light found the Italian submarine *Luigi Torelli*. Greswell brought his plane down to 50-feet, while his co-pilot, Flying Officer Lloyd Trigg, kept the light on the submarine. It was a perfect run as Greswell dropped a depth charge either side of the boat. The huge splashes were caught in the beam of light but the charges sank too far before detonating, and so failed to sink the *Luigi Torelli*. Even so, the submarine was badly damaged and had to limp back to the safety of a Spanish port. Greswell's Leigh light then picked out the *Morosini*. He brought his plane over this second boat and again dropped depth charges. These also detonated at too great a depth, so Greswell turned back to attack the submarine with machine gun fire. The boat survived, but disappeared sometime in early August while returning to its base in France. Greswell's first use of the Leigh light had not brought dramatic results, but it did prove how effective the light was in forcing U-boats to dive. Once under water they could neither attack planes with their AA-guns nor continue to charge their batteries.

The contribution of radar to sinking U-boats was confirmed by operational research. A study of United States data of searches over the eastern seaboard found that it took 660 hours of flying with visual recognition to detect a U-boat. In day time, using radar, a U-boat was found for every 466 hours in the air. But radar triumphed at night when 161 hours were enough to locate one U-boat. In the Trinidad area, the average flying time with radar to find one U-boat at night was just 50 hours. It was figures such as these that both justified shifting planes from bombing German cities and spelt the end of the U-boat threat.

U-boat sinkings quadrupled after the introduction of the Leigh light from three in June to twelve in July. Nevertheless, the Allies were still losing the battle since Germany was building U-boats faster than the Allies were sinking them. In July Dönitz's net gain was nine boats.

By the middle of 1942 Allied methods of detecting U-boats were a significant factor in Dönitz's operations. With surface attacks now favoured by his commanders, the boats were more exposed to Allied detection. It became ever more necessary for his fleet to take counter-measures as both aeroplanes and escort vessels were increasingly successful in locating the boats. The simplest response to a sighting was to submerge. It was highly effective but severely disrupted operations. Submerged boats were generally too slow to chase convoys and less likely to maintain visual contact with one. As a counter-measure, submerging had to be regarded as a last resort. This left the U-boat commanders desperate for a means of detecting Allied radar so that they only needed to submerge when under its threat.

*A Leigh light, so feared by U-boat crews when surfaced at night to charge their batteries.*

Within three months of the Allies using radar to locate and follow U-boats, the U-Boat Arm was installing its Metox receiver in the boats. These receivers could detect the presence of 1.5 m radar at a distance of up to 12 miles – sufficient time to crash-dive. It proved to be startlingly effective Almost immediately after its introduction Allied pilots began to report the mysterious disappearance of their targets. In June 1942 Allied planes were sighting about half of all U-boats in the Bay of Biscay. In July, Metox came into use; by October, Allied sightings had dropped to 20 per cent. In the short-term there was no technological fix for this. It would need 10cm radar to defeat Metox.

One drawback of Metox was its distinctive diamond-shaped aerial – known as a Biscay cross – which stuck out high above the conning tower. It had to be taken into the boat before diving – not an easy operation in a crash-dive.

## HF/DF

HF/DF was also proving effective in locating U-boats from their radio transmissions. Even the experienced Cremer became one of its victims. He was on patrol in the Atlantic when he saw smoke on the horizon. He radioed his report of a possible convoy to Lorient before moving closer to begin shadowing. Convoy *SL-118* was on passage from Freetown to Liverpool. Its 34 vessels were escorted by five warships. With *U-333* on the surface, too far from the convoy to be spotted, Cremer calmly scanned the merchant ships, concentrating on where to position his boat until a wolf pack could gather. Then his eye caught a strange aerial on the mast of one of the warships. His musing on what the purpose of this aerial might be was interrupted by a low-flying bi-plane approaching his stern. Cremer ordered a crash-dive. For the moment *U-333* was safe. Soon, though, he heard propellers overhead, followed by the body-breaking blasts of depth charges. The boat was being shaken, banged and torn to pieces by four warships. It was some hours before Cremer could shake off his pursuers. His boat was leaking badly, while his men were running up and down collecting water in buckets and pouring it into the main bilge to be pumped out. It was gone midnight when *U-333* surfaced to find an empty sea. As Cremer concluded 'my three day effort to maintain contact with the convoy was in vain'. His boat limped home, its propeller shaft glowing hot as his men dripped oil on it round the clock.

## Depth charges and hedgehog

Not all U-boats could be caught by aircraft so the Admiralty continued to develop its ship-based weaponry. New depth charges that could work down to 500 feet were introduced, along with Hedgehog. Hedgehog was a mortar-throwing device, mounted in the prow of an escort vessel. It could throw 24 mortars with contact detonators at a U-boat ahead of the vessel. These detonated on hitting the boat's hull – one or two hits were usually enough to sink the boat. This weapon proved more efficient than the traditional depth-charge, which would often detonate without damaging its target. On average for every 60 depth charges dropped, one U-boat was sunk. Only 47 Hedgehog attacks were needed to secure the same result.

*U-333 seriously damaged after being located by HF/DF. It's brief radio transmission sufficed to reveal its location. Cremer's skill as a submariner enabled him to bring the wrecked boat back to base.*

## Code-breaking

The one area where the Allies not only made no progress at this time but actually went backwards was naval code-breaking. In February 1942 the U-boat service had introduced a fourth wheel to its Enigma machines. Overnight the flow of intelligence on U-boat operations ceased. This had little impact during the Second Happy Time since so many U-boats were hunting independently. But when Dönitz sent his wolf packs back to the North Atlantic, the loss of intelligence became serious. It is impossible to estimate just what impact this dark period had, for three inter-locking reasons: first, Dönitz had an increasing number of U-boats; second there was the direct loss of intelligence on boat movements; and third was a more subtle loss. At this time, B-Dienst was reading the British Naval Cypher No. 3. Had Bletchley Park been able to decipher Enigma at that time, they would have discovered that Dönitz had access to a mass of information on Allied shipping movements. But, just as Germany was unwilling to believe that anyone could crack Enigma, so the British were unwilling to believe that the Germans could crack Naval Cypher No. 3.

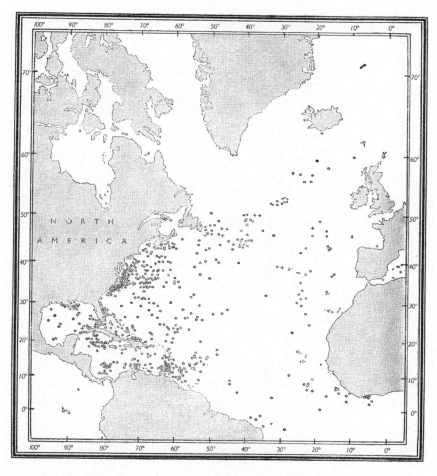

*Map 3. Sinkings January-July 1942: o = Merchant ship; + = U-boat.*

# Part 3: Triumph of the hunted

## 24 Dönitz's nemesis

### Late 1942

*The turning point*

The last two months of 1942 saw one event that highlighted the capacity of the Allies to overcome the worst that Dönitz's boats could do, and another that was to ensure the defeat of the U-boats themselves. We shall look at these in turn.

*The Torch landings*

At dawn on 8 November 1942 a Western Task Force landed at three beaches in Morocco. It was the first assault of Operation Torch – the Allied invasion of North Africa. Over a period of eight days 107,000 men were landed from 500 transports under the protection of 350 warships. It was the greatest amphibious action ever at the time. The safe passage of these troop convoys across the Atlantic and from Glasgow was a powerful testimony to the skills of the escort vessels that protected them across a hostile sea.

The Torch landings caught Dönitz unawares. It was 6.30 am when news of the landings reached the U-Boat Arm. On 1 November he had 368 U-boats in commission, of which 160 were in the Atlantic Ocean. Yet his boats had failed to dent the capacity of the Allies to land their troops at places and times of their choosing. The first of Dönitz's nearby boats were not able to reach the landing beaches before the next day, with others arriving in the following two days. He realistically declared that, 'Prospects of success should not be regarded too highly' since the water was shallow and there would be a heavy aircraft presence alongside destroyer and corvette patrols.

*Torch landings, November 1942. Only one major vessel of the 850 ships involved was sunk by a U-boat.*

Dönitz's prediction proved correct. The only significant sinking from his U-boats was the escort carrier HMS *Avenger*, with the loss of over 500 of her crew. Dönitz, meanwhile, lost eight U-boats in the early days of the landings. In his memoirs he justified his failure to seriously disrupt the landings, saying, 'any precautionary concentration of U-boats might well have been at the wrong place – or at the right place at the wrong time'. This would have resulted in 'a very material diminution of effort in our war on shipping'. He also blamed the intelligence service which, he said, '[had] failed throughout the war, to give the U-boat command one single piece of information about the enemy that was of the slightest use to us.' (This was clearly an exaggeration, but B-Dienst was much less successful than Bletchley Park in providing intelligence of high operational value.)

The second event that was to prove fatal to Dönitz's U-Boat Arm was a change of personnel at Western Approaches Command.

### Admiral Max Horton

Admiral Max Horton's credentials for his appointment to the Western Approaches Command were impeccable. His forceful personality was also exactly what was needed at this desperate moment in the Atlantic battle.

*Admiral Sir Max Horton (left) with Sir John Tovey, Commander-in-Chief, Home Fleet.*

At the start of the First World War the then 31 year-old Lieutenant Commander Max Horton was in the submarine HMS *E-9*. Within six weeks of the opening of hostilities *E-9* had torpedoed the German light cruiser *Hela*. Not long after that, Horton sent the German destroyer *S-116* to the bottom. Following his time in the North Sea, Horton was moved to the Baltic, where he continued to distinguish himself as an aggressive submarine commander.

Given this background it is not surprising that, in December 1940, Pound had chosen Horton to be Vice Admiral Submarines. He had been offered the prestigious command of the Home Fleet but turned it down because he would not have had control of his own aircraft. His refusal was typical of a man who put his own convictions ahead of his career. His stubbornness was not always an attractive quality but was to prove providential at the Western Command.

Pound had a very high regard for Horton's abilities. In one letter he wrote, 'Thank God we have not to guard our convoys against the attacks of your submarine Commanders.' Quite possibly Horton might have stayed in that post throughout the war. After all, he loved his work and had no desire for a change. But then came one of those butterfly wing-flapping moments when small events can have great consequences. Admiral Andrew Cunningham had been taken from his command of the Mediterranean Fleet to be Supreme Commander, Allied Expeditionary Force for Torch, based in Washington. With the Torch landings safely accomplished, Pound wanted Cunningham back in the Mediterranean so he needed a new man for Washington. His choice fell on Admiral Sir Percy Noble from the Western Approaches Command. Pound was in no doubt that Horton was the man to replace Noble. Even so, Horton obeyed Pound's command with great reluctance. Submarines were his life. He was not to know that as he stepped over the threshold of Derby House in Liverpool he was about to prove that he was one of the greatest admirals of all time.

It is hard to understand why neither Churchill nor Pound saw Noble's weaknesses for the post that he had held since early 1941. Noble was conscientious and orderly – qualities useful in a good administrator – but not enough to be on the front line of the Battle of the Atlantic. Horton, on the other hand, was an arrogant and aggressive commander, who could never tolerate anything other than perfection. In addition to these qualities, so indispensable for the coming battle, he brought with him his intimate acquaintance with the world of submarines. In the opinion of Captain Stephen Roskill, official historian of the naval war, 'There was no living officer who better understood the U-boat commander's mind, nor could more surely anticipate what his reactions to our countermeasures would be.'

It is hard to describe Horton's abilities without moving into the realms of hyperbole, yet we have to accept what those who worked with him had to say. Commander R A B Phillimore of the Fleet Air Arm said that Horton was 'a technician who completely mastered the scientific discoveries and devices brought in to aid the ships and aircraft' and 'a man of immense drive who refused to accept frustrations, delays and objections to any scheme on which he had made up his mind'. Horton's qualities were even recognised by his enemy. Dönitz called him 'an outstanding submarine captain of the First World War and Flag Officer, submarines in the second'.

Of all the qualities that Horton brought to his new job, his determination to never accept defeat was perhaps the most important. Nor would he accept defeat from his officers, as the experience of Commander Martin Evans of the escort training yacht *Philante* showed. It was after D-Day. The U-boats, concentrated in home waters, had become ultra-cautious. With the aid of their newly installed snorkels they spent long periods in shallow water, where the rocks hindered their use of asdic. Commander Evans grew frustrated at the lack of progress at detecting snorkel-using boats and told Horton that he 'could see no chance of the situation improving'. Horton fiercely responded, saying, 'You are never to say such a thing outside this office.'

It was fortunate that Horton brought a sound sea-going reputation to Liverpool in November 1942 since he had little else to recommend him. He was ruthless in his methods, driving his staff without any consideration for their feelings or self-respect. One shipping industry leader declared him to be 'uncongenial'. He was not alone in this assessment. Horton was selfish, too. On arrival at Liverpool he declared that he would play golf in the afternoon and bridge in the evening before arriving at work at 11.30 pm. His officers were commanded to adapt to this routine. He justified this diktat on the grounds that the battles that the command oversaw mostly took place at night. Nevertheless he gave the impression that he enjoyed inconveniencing his staff in this way.

One person who brushed off Horton's imperious style was his Wren flag lieutenant, Miss Kay Hallaran. Hallaran was British by birth but had been brought up in America. She was a natural with people and deftly managed the impatient and demanding officers who bombarded her boss with queries and requests. Her calm demeanour and cheerful manner doubtless sheltered Horton from a good deal of bother. Equally, she protected officers from some of Horton's harsh treatment.

Uncongenial as he could be, Horton had a good eye for talent and an inquisitive interest in new ideas. By the time that he arrived at Derby House, Captain Gilbert Roberts had been running courses at his Western Approaches Tactical Unit for nearly a year. Horton had no idea what this strange outfit was. His approach to Roberts was typically blunt, 'And what do you think you do on my staff?' Roberts diplomatically responded, 'Why don't you come up and see properly?' ('Up' because Horton's command centre was below ground at Derby House; the Tactical Unit was above ground level.) Horton took up Robert's offer, saw the importance of his work, and signed-up to take the full one-week course.

Although Horton was witheringly censorious of slackness and incompetence, he also understood that patrols could push commanders beyond the limits of human endurance. A young commander who had damaged his ship when severely sleep-deprived, shivered in his boots as he approached Horton for a reprimand. But one look was enough for Horton to order the young man to his own bedroom. 'I will look after your ship,' said Horton. And the exhausted commander slept for eighteen hours.

Horton had an instinctive understanding of the cruel demands of an escort command. Once with a convoy, officers and men were on high alert 24 hours a day. A missed or late sighting, a misinterpreted asdic response, or the failure to correctly anticipate a U-boat's movements, could spell disaster not only for the escort vessel, but for the convoy too. Horton knew the strain that this put men under. He never assumed that the technical developments would lessen the pressure, nor ease the punishing tiredness. Hence he believed that the sea war would be won by whichever side had the highest morale. Such a level of morale would enable escort commanders to 'rise above all tragedies and set-backs'. For this, each commander had to have 'complete confidence in his shore organisation'. This Horton achieved not only through his demanding administrative methods, but by regularly going to sea in the small escort vessels.

### Support groups and escort training

Horton now occupied Noble's office with its plate glass wall looking out onto the battle situation wall deep below ground in Derby House. Next door to him was Air Marshal Sir L H Slatter, Air Officer commanding No. 15 Group Coastal Command, which provided air cover to Horton's convoy escorts. Whether Horton needed Slatter to tell him the truth about the markers on the battle map or not we don't know. But he was soon telling London. His job was impossible, he told the Admiralty, without a huge reinforcement of long-endurance destroyers and long-range aircraft to support his escorts. Without these 'a very serious situation will develop on the Atlantic lifeline'.

We have seen that Air Chief Marshal Sir Charles Portal had agreed to supply these planes. But Churchill, under the influence of Lord Cherwell (his scientific adviser) and pressure from Air Marshal Harris, had refused to move any bombers from Bomber Command to Coastal Command. In October, when some planes seemed to be on offer, Churchill ruled that all the new radar sets were to go to Bomber Command. For six months Churchill, Portal, Noble,

Pound and Harris had exchanged papers and minutes without the Admiralty's need for bombers ever being conceded. Captain Stephen Roskill, who interviewed many of the senior naval officers after the war, concluded that it was the failure of Pound and Alexander to stand up to Churchill that accounted for these wasted six months. Yet, within days of Horton arriving, the planes were granted. We are left to imagine for how much longer the planes would have been denied to the Command without Horton in post.

By 25 November Horton had allocated his first seven planes to search areas from Biscay in the south to Iceland in the north. Relieved as he was at the fulsome, if belated, response of the chiefs of staff, Horton knew that planes alone were not sufficient to turn the battle. There was, he noted, a lack of coordination between sea and air forces in the hunt for U-boats. 'The only way to defeat the U-boat was to attack in strength with aircraft and warships trained together,' he told the Admiralty on 19 November 1942. This particular letter was written on Horton's first day at the Western Approaches Command. He was not the sort of man to wait long for a reply; the Admiralty soon learnt that Horton was both demanding and impatient. (He had perhaps studied the techniques of Britain's greatest reforming admiral, John Fisher, who was First Sea Lord 1904-1910 and 1914-1915. Fisher bludgeoned his political masters with letters and memoranda as if he were distributing confetti, yet each carried a full broadside of his imperative demands.)

After just a few weeks in his new post, Horton elaborated on the problem of training escort officers. He summarised his conclusions in a long minute to the Admiralty. Apart from one polite reference to Noble, his minute was a condemnation of the methods then in use. While he accepted that there were 'many examples of well trained and equipped groups, resolutely led,' he drew attention to 'convoys suffering disastrous loses'. These, he said, were 'escorted by a collection of ships strange to one another, untrained as a team and led by an officer inexperienced in convoy protection'. He was unhesitating in his belief that every escort group had to be 'led and managed by competent officers' and 'equipped with the latest devices'. Only then would the loses fall.

Horton also mentioned one particular problem that needed sensitive handling. The best escort commanders were often rewarded with promotion, and then left their ships to fulfil some other role. He was adamant that such officers 'should not be removed on promotion, since their loss must entail a falling off of efficiency,' he told the Admiralty.

The promotion problem interacted with another manning issue. Escort duties lacked glamour. Few naval officers aspired to the role. Captain Gilbert Roberts put the point forcefully in a lecture that he gave after the war at Trinity College, Cambridge: 'the glamour of the Fleet and the attraction of Destroyer Flotillas, the cruisers, the carriers, and the traditional paraphernalia of fleet life meant that few of "the quality" were left over for command in the escort forces'. Horton understood this problem and, despite his abrasive exterior, he did all he could to make his commanders feel supported and wanted.

The Escort Support Group was central to Horton's plans for defeating the U-boats. Using long-endurance destroyers, accompanied by escort carriers, these groups were to act independently of the convoy escorts. With their emphasis being on offensive action, Horton could direct them to those convoys under threat from a major attack. By March 1943 Horton had the first of his first five support groups in operation under the command Commander G N Brewer. The other four groups were commanded by Captain F J Walker, Captain J A McCoy, Captain A K Scott-Moncrieff, and Captain E M C Abel Smith.

The Escort Support Groups soon proved their worth. In one case a Support Group spent 27 days at sea during which it went to the aid of five separate convoys and refuelled six times. Six U-boats were sunk as a result.

*Convoy ONS-154*

By Christmas 1942 Horton had only been in post for six weeks. That was not long enough to put an end to the recurring nightmare of unequal convoy battles. Convoy *ONS-154* reminded him of why he was at Derby House and how far the Allies still were from mastering the U-boat threat.

Those men and women who served at sea and abroad never forgot where they were for each Christmas when away from their home country. Over 2000 men were on board the freighters and the escorts of Convoy *ONS-154* when it departed Liverpool on 18 December 1942. The escort was one Canadian destroyer and five Canadian corvettes, accompanied by an oiler and a rescue ship.

The early part of the convoy's passage was uneventful, with Christmas Day being happily free from attack. It was on Boxing Day that *U-662* found the convoy. Its commander, Wolfgang Hermann, radioed the contact and prepared to shadow the convoy. *U-356,* commanded by the 23-year-old Günther Ruppelt, was the first of 20 boats to arrive. In the early hours of the 27 December Ruppelt sank both the 6000-ton *Empire Union* and the 2500-ton *Melrose Abbey.* Six men, including the master, were lost from the *Empire Union* and seven from *Melrose Abbey.* The latter went down with 70 bags of mail along with her cargo of 3500 tons of coal.

Three hours later *U-356* was ready to attack again. Ruppelt's first target was the Dutch freighter *Soekaboemi,* which he damaged in a torpedo attack. A short while later *U-356* made its last kill as it sent the British freighter *King Edward* to the bottom, going down in three minutes. By now the escort had found *U-356.* Four warships pounded it with depth charges. *U-356* was no more. Its first patrol and that of Günther Ruppelt was to be their last.

On the night of 26-27 December the 7000 ton oiler *Scottish Heather* had dropped behind in the chaos of the previous day's battle and the inaccuracies of zigzagging. She was ordered to cease zigzagging and close up to her station.

It was while *Scottish Heather* was making a straight run to her station that Wolfgang Leimkühler in *U-225* saw his chance. A single torpedo halted the oiler – she failed to sink but she had to leave the convoy, so depriving ships of vital refuelling.

By the night of 27-28 December about 18 U-boats were prowling in and around the convoy. Ship after ship was sunk. In the midst of the battle HMS *Fidelity* suffered engine failure. Her presence was an oddity, not being part of the escort. She was a Special Service Ship, fitted out for use by the Special Operations Executive. On board was a company of 40 Commando. She fell behind but restarted her engines the next day. Now sailing alone she was spotted by *U-435* on 30 December, torpedoed and sunk. Her crew, the commandoes, and the men rescued from *Empire Shackleton* all died. Only a handful of men, out in a torpedo boat, survived.

This was the last great convoy battle of 1942. In all, 20 U-boats had attacked a convoy of 50 merchant ships. Thirteen ships were lost and only one U-boat had been sunk. It was a poor escort performance and bade ill for 1943.

*A disastrous year*

The year 1942 had been a naval disaster for the Allies. Over 1000 merchant vessels had been sunk by U-boats in all waters. Sinkings by all methods were over 1300 ships. U-boats had destroyed over 6 million tons of shipping; total shipping lost in all waters was nearly 8-million tons. Allied replacements were seven million, so there was a net loss of one million tons of shipping over the year. There was a small triumph at the end of 1942. For 40 despairing months since September 1939, month after month the U-boats sank merchant tonnage at a faster rate than it could be constructed. Then, in December, new construction finally overtook the losses from U-boat kills. It was a flicker of hope in one of the darkest moments of the war.

Behind these figures lay a frightening truth that threatened Britain's capacity to keep on fighting; her bunker fuel stocks were down to 300,000 tons

– less than three months' consumption. There was an emergency naval reserve of one million tons, but to use that was the equivalent of firing the last bullet on the battlefield. The navy was within weeks of having to tell Churchill that its ships would have to remain in harbour for lack of fuel.

On the German side, at the start of the year Dönitz had had 91 operational boats in all sectors; he ended the year with 212 operational boats.

There was not a single operational figure that pointed to any means by which the Allies might stem the inexorable advance of the U-boats.

The Battle of the Atlantic was surely lost.

And yet, the cumulative strategic mistakes of the Kriegsmarine had left it helplessly vulnerable to what Horton was about to unleash on them. They had no answer to new tactics; no answer to 10cm radar; no answer to HF/DF; and no answer to air power. The Type VII U-boat, based largely on First World War technology, was about to discover how antiquated it was.

# 25 Raeder's despair

January 1943

*A demoralising New Year*

Although the terrifying storms of late 1942 had deprived several wolf packs of convoy sightings, early January 1943 saw one of Dönitz's most successful attacks of the war. For once he had put tonnage aside and had taken an interest in the contents of a convoy. All nine vessels in Convoy *TM-1* from Trinidad to Gibraltar were tankers, filled to capacity with vital fuel oil.

*U-124* discovered the convoy by chance on 29 December 1942. As soon as Commander Johann Mohr's report reached Lorient, Dönitz despatched a wolf pack of ten boats. It was a rare opportunity to deprive the Allies in North Africa of supplies essential to their attacks on Rommel's forces.

Bletchley Park had a partial view of what was happening and warned Commander Richard Boyle in HMS *Havelock*, that a U-boat was nearby. On 3 January *Havelock* found an asdic echo. Boyle ordered a change of course. While the change was in progress, *Havelock* picked up another echo at 5000 yards. The echo quickly disappeared but the presence of a U-boat was confirmed by a hit on the 8000-ton tanker *British Vigilance*. Carrying aviation fuel, she burst into flames, leaving not one survivor. The towering blaze revealed a U-boat on the surface. The tanker *Empire Lytton*, loaded with 12,500 tons of aviation spirit, turned towards the U-boat in an attempt to ram it, but missed the boat by a few yards. Boyle ordered a Raspberry attack to sink the U-boat as it hid at the rear of the departing convoy. On this occasion, Raspberry failed and the unknown boat escaped.

There were no further attacks during the next four days. During this period the U-Boat Arm made a change in their Enigma code settings, leaving Boyle with no warning from Bletchley Park of the full-scale wolf pack attack that fell on the convoy on 8 January. Dönitz in his memoirs admitted that 'luck was entirely with us'. The convoy made one of its night turns; dawn found it

240

steaming right into the centre of the line of waiting U-boats. In the ensuing slaughter the tankers *Albert L Ellsworth* and *Oltenia II* were both sunk. The crew of *Ellsworth* were lucky though, getting safely into the boats while their ship burned around them. Not one man was lost – there were 17 dead from *Oltenia II*.

*One of the seven tankers in Convoy TM-1 that fell prey to wolf pack Tümmler (Dolphin).*

The worst day of the battle was on 9 January, with *Empire Lytton*, *Minister Wedel* and *Norvik* being sunk. Two days later the *British Dominion* went down to a torpedo from *U-522*. Only *Cliona* and *Vanja* entered Gibraltar harbour on 14 January. On the German side, two U-boats had suffered some damage, but none was lost to the U-Boat Arm.

This was a demoralising start to the year for the Allies. Losing seven out of nine vessels was a shattering rate of attrition. That the vessels were tankers made the loss even more devastating since it came just as the Allies were mounting huge land-based actions. Secure and plentiful fuel supplies were now the lifeblood of the Allied war.

Nine days later the combined chiefs of staff were in Casablanca to decide the next priorities for the war. In the light of the attack on Convoy *TM-1* their remarks on the U-boat war are not surprising: 'The defeat of the U-boat must remain a first charge on the resources of the United Nations.' We can presume that Chief of the Air Staff Portal did not reveal how recently he had prioritised bombing Germany over bombing U-boats.

### Upheavals in the Kriegsmarine

But all was not well on the Kriegsmarine front either. Raeder, in particular, was feeling low as Hitler poured more and more resources into the failing Russian front, to the neglect of the navy.

It was an action beyond the confines of the Battle of the Atlantic that triggered Raeder's resignation. The Battle of the Barents Sea in December 1942 involved a U-boat attack on one of the Arctic convoys to North Russia. The 15 merchant ships of Convoy *JW-51B* were bound for Murmansk with an escort of six destroyers. The day after being sighted by *U-354,* the convoy encountered the heavy cruisers *Admiral Hipper* and *Lützow*, accompanied by six destroyers. After a short battle, the German ships withdrew, having sunk the destroyer HMS *Achates* and a minesweeper. Meanwhile the merchant ships steamed on to arrive without further trouble at Murmansk on 3 January. This may read as a mundane incident – just one more minor convoy battle. But Hitler could not help comparing this attack to the one on Convoy *PQ-17* in July 1942. On that occasion an Arctic convoy was set upon by a massive German force which included nine U-boats, 17 surface vessels and a large number of planes. Twenty-four of the 35 merchant ships were lost. Now, in December, Raeder's latest attack had failed to sink a single merchant ship.

It was Raeder's misfortune that the first account of the Battle of the Barents Sea to reach Hitler came from a Reuters' report. The British press emphasised how mere destroyers had seen off a far more powerful force. Throughout New Year's Day Hitler snapped at anyone who came near him as he waited for an official account of the battle. By 5.00 pm his patience was at an end. He summoned Admiral Theodor Krancke, Raeder's representative at Hitler's headquarters, and let fly. His tirade alternated between berating Krancke for not producing a battle report, and condemning the humiliating performance of the capital ships. The ships were 'a needless drain on men and materials,' he declared, 'They will accordingly be paid off and reduced to scrap. Their guns will be mounted on land for coastal defence.'

When Krancke reported back to Raeder, the latter took fright and refused to go to Hitler's headquarters to give an account of the battle. Five days later, Raeder had reached his decision and went to see Hitler.

Raeder described the moment of his resignation in his memoirs:

> Very quietly, then, I requested Hitler to relieve me from my position as Commander-in-Chief of the Navy, since in his remarks he had indicated that he was dissatisfied, no longer had confidence in me ... I stated that I was now almost 67 years of age, and my health not of the best. It was time for a younger man to take over.

Hitler tried to persuade Raeder to stay in post, saying that he was not criticising the navy in general, but only the performance of the capital ships. When Raeder refused to retract his resignation, Hitler asked for his recommendations for a successor. Raeder suggested both Admiral Rolf Carls and Karl Dönitz. Carls was Chief of Naval Group Command North. He had briefly commanded *U-124* at the end of the First World War but was otherwise a big-ship man. His appointment would have represented a continuation of the

Raeder régime. Nevertheless, Raeder said that Carls was 'especially suitable' although he admitted that appointing Dönitz would emphasise 'the significance of the U-boat campaign as of war-decisive importance'. But, he remarked, appointing Dönitz would distract him from the U-boat war. Beyond that, Raeder declined to choose between the two. Despite Raeder's ambiguous remarks on Dönitz, Hitler selected him as his new commander-in-chief.

Dönitz was the obvious man to choose. One could almost say that, in January 1942, he was the *only* senior German commander who was winning his part of the war. His record of over 1300 ships sunk or damaged in 1942 stood out as the Reich's sole success of that year.

Raeder's contribution to the war had been far from brilliant. He was the big-ship man for whom the U-boats always took second place. He was also the man who had failed to make completing the aircraft carrier *Graf Zeppelin* a priority. Without carriers, his battleships and heavy cruisers were too vulnerable to air attack to sail beyond land-based air cover. If ever Raeder needed evidence of the imbalance of his shipbuilding programme, he had only to recall the fate of the *Bismarck*, sunk by a Fairy Swordfish plane weighing two tons and popularly known as a 'string-bag'.

Raeder was also the man who gave up his plan to have a separate naval air arm when the Z-Plan was conceived. In ceding air cover to Göring, Raeder had gained more resources for ship building, but he came to regret that decision. He aggravated this deficiency by failing to establish a good working relationship with Göring, who despised the Kriegsmarine's capacity to win the war and only gave it minimal air support.

Another of Raeder's weaknesses was his vacillating strategy. His priorities were variously focused on: retaining a fleet-in-being as a bargaining counter after a short war; proving that the navy was essential to the army (as in the invasion of Norway); making risky surface raids to prove the value of his big ships; and being involved in any action going, merely to raise the profile of his navy.

*The never-to-be completed Graf Zeppelin aircraft carrier.*

The U-Boat Arm received only sporadic attention from Raeder. It was not until July 1942 (when his surface-raiding strategy had stalled) that he finally recognised the criticality of the U-boat to the war. And, in the U-boat war, he and Dönitz failed to share a strategic goal. Dönitz thought that tonnage sunk was the way to defeat the allies; Raeder preferred attacking specific targets that would have a 'decisive impact'.

Raeder had had a combative relationship with the man who was to replace him – although any man would have found Dönitz difficult to manage. The latter was conceited and obsessively focused on *his* U-boats. .Not only was Dönitz convinced that only his boats could bring victory in the west, but he was also sure that he was the only man to bring this about. He fought hard for more U-boats, for the retention of trained men, for air cover and for combined working with the air services. It was not the job of his boats, he thought, to sort out the messes that the army got into in Norway, Crete or North Africa. Anything that took away resources from sinking tonnage in the Atlantic had to be resisted. Strategically Dönitz was right. The allied war in the west depended on the uninterrupted flow of food, fuel, arms and raw materials across the Atlantic. (And even goods from the east came via the Atlantic.) Every failure to sink a merchant ship was a failure to strangle the supplies that kept the Allies in the war in the west.

Difficult as he was, Dönitz was focused. Raeder could never match his clarity of thought nor his determination not to be deflected from what he saw as the only war-winning strategy. But what was a virtue when commanding the U-Boat Arm now threatened to be a weakness in running a navy. His new job called for a wider vision. His decision to retain direct command of the U-Boat Arm alongside his role as commander-in-chief suggested that he was unlikely to bring any new vision to the wider role.

Raeder, though, was a big enough man to see beyond the irritating side of his subordinate. When writing a formal report in 1942 he acknowledged that the U-boat war had the potential to be decisive. If this came about it would be 'primarily to the credit of Admiral Dönitz'.

### Grand Admiral Dönitz

As Dönitz took up his new post with the rank of Grand Admiral on 30 January 1943 he was in a 'master-of-all-he-surveyed' mood. At last he was in a position to prioritise U-boat production and to eradicate the bottlenecks and inefficiencies in the supply chain and the shipyards. He was confident that he would get what he wanted since the U-Boat Arm was the only bright spot on the Reich's far-flung battlegrounds. As he wrote a few days later, 'All has to be subordinated to this [the U-boat war] main goal.'

For now, Dönitz was in a triumphant mood. His decision to use his new powers as commander-in-chief to sustain to the utmost the U-Boat Arm is completely understandable. But did he really believe that Germany could win the overall war? The German armies were on the defensive in the east; the Allies were pushing back Rommel in North Africa; the Luftwaffe no longer had the strength to bomb Britain into submission. Yet nowhere in his writings at that time did Dönitz show the merest hint of the possibility of his country's defeat in the wider war. This hardly seems credible if he were to have spent any time thinking on the subject. The conclusion must be that he did not think on it. His capacity to focus on the task in hand was legendary. It was easy for him to see the war through the keyhole of the U-Boat Arm and to ignore the panorama of what was now a worldwide conflict. Also, as we shall we see when we come to 1945, Dönitz was a man who refused to recognise defeat even when all was lost. He was just the man the Kriegsmarine needed as it was about to face an Allied onslaught that he could never have imagined possible.

With the benefit of hindsight we can see that Dönitz's capacity to win the Atlantic battle was now severely compromised by the strategic errors of the past: the war had begun with too few U-boats; the expensive surface fleet was too weak to take on the Royal Navy; Raeder had squandered 57 surface ships on the distraction of the Norway invasion; Dönitz had failed to prioritise sinking Allied escort vessels; and Dönitz had fought a U-boat war of 'more of the same' rather than pursue new technologies. It was too late to avoid the consequences of these failings. Only the last strategic error – the failure to use planes to sink escort vessels – was still potentially reversible, but Göring was an unlikely saviour of a Kriegsmarine that had so mishandled its war.

Dönitz's first act as head of the navy was to issue orders for paying off the capital ships. All construction work was to cease on battleships, heavy and light cruisers, and aircraft carriers. *Hipper*, *Köln* and *Leipzig* were to be paid off as 'unserviceable'. Amongst the ships under construction that were abandoned was the *Graf Zeppelin*. Cancelling work on the Kriegsmarine's only aircraft carrier – the heart of an ocean-going navy by 1943 – was heavily symbolic of Germany's failure to build a fleet.

However, Dönitz was concerned at the propaganda value to the Allies of this massive mothballing of the Kriegsmarine, so the dismantling of guns and other equipment was to be done as each ship came up for its scheduled refit. (Later Hitler relented and allowed some of the big ships to be retained, in particular, *Tirpitz* and *Scharnhorst*, which were allocated to 'defend Norway against enemy landings'.)

Dönitz retained command of the U-boat Arm while Eberhard Godt became the chief operational officer, subordinate in every way to Dönitz. In the process Godt was promoted from kapitän zur see to rear admiral (lower half). This relatively lowly rank emphasised that Godt was Dönitz's tool. From now on Godt signed most of the War Log entries but, in many places, it is hard to tell whether the comments are those of Godt or of Dönitz.

The decommissioning plan and the retention of his role in the U-boat war, reflected Dönitz's continuing belief in the supremacy of the U-Boat Arm as the sole path to victory. His last entry in the War Log before handing over to Godt was defiantly determined. 'The tonnage war,' he wrote, 'must be accepted with open eyes and determined efforts made to concentrate everything possible on the main task, while accepting the gaps and disadvantages this will cause elsewhere'

# 26 The nearing crisis

## Early 1943

*Lorient in flames*

In early 1943 on both sides of the war there was a sense that the Battle of the Atlantic had reached a more serious and critical phase. Although there was now no shortage of U-boats, sinkings were not commensurate with the enlarged fleet. On the Allied side, the escorts were growing in number and skills, but victory was as elusive as ever. But the first shock of the year was delivered by the Allies.

Allied air power was growing rapidly in early 1943, with an increasing number of planes that could comfortably reach the Atlantic U-boat bases.

At 11.55 pm on the night of 14/15 January the sirens screamed out over the sleeping town of Lorient. A few minutes later the bleary-eyed residents heard the rumble of the engines of heavy aircraft. They paid little attention to this disturbance of their sleep. This was surely just another Allied air-drop of mines in the harbour entrance. There was no need to go to the shelters.

Twenty minutes later incendiary and explosive bombs began to rain down on the town, concentrated on the sectors of Nouvelle-Ville and de Merville. Within minutes, 80 houses were in flames. The civil defence workers rushed to the scene. One glance was enough for them to realise that the scale of the attack was beyond their means. They called in the dockyard fire brigade, and the brigades from the nearby towns of Vannes, Hennebont, Pontivy, Quimper, Quimperlé and Concarneau. Three-hundred-and-fifty officers and men battled the raging fires with over 20 engines.

By 11.30 am on 15 January the fires were under control. One-hundred-and-twelve houses and two churches had been reduced to smouldering rubble.

Later that day the planes returned for a second and much larger attack. 'It literally rained incendiaries,' said an eye witness. By 10.00 pm the firefighters were facing defeat. The principal water main was ruptured and the electricity supply was cut off.

A south-east wind was now fanning the flames. The air was unbreathable. Amidst the flaming buildings, men and women, many half-dressed, ran, clutching bags and suitcases. The struggle to extinguish the fires continued all through the day on 16 January and on through the night into the early hours of 17 January.

Finally, it was time to assess the damage. Eight-hundred more houses destroyed. The death toll was remarkably low at around 30 people.

*Lorient, uninhabitable after the early 1943 Allied bombing. The U-boat pens remained unscathed.*

The bombers returned on the nights of 23 and 29 January, then on 4, 7, 13, 16 and 17 February. Three-and-a-half-thousand houses (60 per cent of the town) had been destroyed. A now homeless resident recalled, 'from then on one could say that Lorient no longer existed'. The town was largely evacuated.

And yet, the part that mattered – the U-boat base – was barely affected. It had suffered no more than some minor interruption to U-boat repairs. The U-Boat Arm had previously marvelled at the failure of the Allies to bomb the boat pens during their construction. By 1943 the boats were safely under three-and-a-half metres of reinforced concrete. The Kriegsmarine did, though, abandon surface ship repairs at Lorient.

The bombing, which was meant to be strategic, proved to be no more than a minor nuisance to Dönitz. But it was a sign of the growing power of his adversary. And he knew as well as anyone, that air-power was becoming the decisive factor in the war.

### Winter war

Dönitz had no shortage of boats as he took over from Raeder. On 1 January 1943 there were around 400 boats, of which 24 had been commissioned in December. This resulted in 164 operational boats in the Atlantic – nearly ten times the number operating there at the start of the war. Although the Allies never had any precise figures for U-boat numbers, they were aware of the seriousness of the threat that they faced. Sinkings for the last three months had averaged over 110 ships and nearly 600,000 tons per month. The British Submarine Tracking Room warned (for 1943) of the 'potentially annihilating superiority' of the U-Boat Arm. 'The critical phase of the U-boat war in the Atlantic cannot be long postponed', the report concluded. They could not have been more right in their assessment of the threat nor more wrong in how quickly that threat would be overcome. The Allies were on the verge of one of the most spectacular turn-rounds in the history of warfare.

It was, though, winter. The storms that year were of an unusual ferocity. The ocean had become an immeasurable, hostile waste. Convoys were involuntarily scattered. Wolf packs were unable to form. U-boats searched in vain for their milch cows. And for those men condemned to stand on bridges, all they could see were mountainous waves, horrific troughs and terrifying peaks. Icy cold water combined with sleet and snow penetrated every item of their clothing. Waves crashed down on conning towers, beating the very breath out of the men. Merchant sinkings fell to less than half the monthly average of 1942.

The weather, though, was incidental to Dönitz's worries. The growing number of long-range Allied planes working in the Bay of Biscay was now the greatest threat to his boats. He was without intelligence on convoy routes and timetables, so these could only be found by chance. There were only two ways to sink these convoys, as he explained to Hitler in early February: more U-boats or more air cover. In the short-term he could increase the number of U-boats by speeding up trials of new boats, and repairs of operational boats. For this he needed his U-boat staff to be exempt from the army call-up. Hitler supported this request, saying he would discuss it with Field Marshal Keitel. Whether such a discussion ever took place is not clear. What is known is that the Reich was running out of manpower. Skilled workers were at a premium in all sectors of the war.

While Dönitz put his faith in 'more of the same' Admiral Horton, newly arrived in Derby House, was convinced that victory lay in something different. He was determined to put the latest technology into his escort vessels, to put his officers and men through improved training programmes, and to provide the escorts with new types of support. But this could not happen overnight. He knew there would be setbacks. The first serious one came in January 1943.

Convoy *SC-118* had left New York on 24 January. The 64 merchant ships soon linked up with their escort group of destroyers, corvettes and cutters. It was a well-protected convoy with up to 12 escorts for some parts of its passage. But, like so many convoys, its sailing was known to the German naval intelligence service. This was not enough to guarantee that the wolf packs would find the convoy. But they hardly needed to search for it. A seaman on the Norwegian freighter *Vannik* accidently released a pyrotechnic snowflake projector on 4 February. Its blaze of light in the early dawn sky was sighted by *U-187* from the wolf pack *Pfeil* (Arrow). Kapitänleutnant Ralph Münnich reported the sighting to Dönitz, who ordered several U-boats to the scene. Meanwhile *U-187* had sealed its fate by sending its radio message. HF/DF enabled the cutter USCGC *Bibb* and the 1500-ton rescue ship *Toward* to triangulate the U-boat's position. The United States destroyer *Beverly* lost no time in sinking Münnich's boat. Forty-five of her crew were rescued. Later that same day *Zagloba*, a Polish freighter, and the United States freighter *West Portal* both succumbed to torpedoes.

The following day a United States cutter and two United States destroyers joined the convoy. The few U-boats that approached the merchant ships that day were easily repulsed, resulting in damage to two of them. But this was the deceitful quiet before the storm.

Amongst the mass of lurking U-boats was *U-402* under the command of Korvettenkapitän Siegfried Freiherr von Forstner. The son of an aristocratic Prussian family with a long record of army and naval service, von Forster had signed up for the Kriegsmarine in 1930. His U-boat service had begun in that year, with his first command being in May 1941. He now had seven sinkings and two ships damaged to his credit. Von Forstner fell upon the convoy shortly before dawn on 7 February. Soon another five ships were at the bottom including, disastrously, the rescue ship *Toward*. SC-118 had been her forty-fifth convoy. In her career since starting rescue work in October 1941 she had saved the lives of 337 men.

Three U-boats had been lost in the battle but questions still needed to be asked about the failure of twelve escorts to prevent eight merchant sinkings. There was nothing new in the answers, though: twelve escorts were one thing; twelve escorts trained to work together were something else. The American warships that came from Iceland had not had the benefit of the British two-tiered training system (Tobermory and the Tactical Unit). Without the benefit of training in the sort of methods that Walker had pioneered, escorts were ineffective. And a final lesson of this battle was the need for merchant ships to carry supplies of depth charges to replenish the huge quantities used in combatting a wolf pack of 20 boats.

However, another convoy in early 1943 gave reasons for Horton to have faith in his deep commitment to training, particularly training in working together.

Convoy *ONS-165* left Liverpool on 2 February, bound for New York with about 32 vessels in the care of Commodore D A Casey. The escort group included the destroyers HMSs *Fame* and *Viscount*. This was a promising escort. *Fame* had sunk *U-353* when escorting Convoy *SC-104* in late 1942, and *Viscount* had sunk *U-661* around the same time. In short, *ONS-165* had a battled-hardened escort. Of the ships that kept up with the convoy, the Greek *Zeus* was the sole sinking. (Some accounts even state that the *Zeus* was a straggler.) Only the superior training and greater experience of this escort can explain how much better Convoy *ONS-165* fared than did *SC-118*.

But, however good the escort training was in February 1943, Horton thought it could still be better. To this end he set up an additional base for the Western Approaches Tactical Unit at Larne in Northern Ireland under Captain Joe Baker-Cresswell. As the commander of HMS *Bulldog* when *U-110* was captured in May 1941, Baker-Cresswell brought the appropriate aggressive style to the new unit. Based in HMS *Philante*, he organised group training of the most realistic kind possible. (This was the same *Philante* that Stephenson had commandeered for Tobermory and relinquished on the Fall of France in 1940.) When Commander Peter Gretton took his escort group to Larne in April 1943 prior to going on patrol, his commanders received the full fury of Baker-Cresswell's methods. *Philante* and some old submarines acted as targets while escort vessels chased them in mock-attacks. Gretton described how his ship fired live ammunition at a splash-target towed by another escort ship, both going at full-speed and making sharp turns. He recalled: 'For the towing ship, this exercise was alarming enough by day; by night it was suicidal.' The crews, he said, became 'intoxicated with excitement' and ended up firing at the towing ship. Nevertheless, Gretton raised the stakes by exercising with live depth charges. That proved a hazard too far and the exercise returned to using dummy charges.

# 27 Can it get worse?

## March 1943

### The largest convoy battle of the war

December 1942 had seen merchant ship losses fall to 400,000 tons. Such a drop was of little comfort to the Allies since the ferocious Atlantic weather always brought a lull in end-of-year sinkings. That lull continued into January with losses of 350,000 tons. Then came the horrific news: losses in February 1943 were 450,000 tons. This was slightly lower than the 500,000 tons for February of the previous year, but still unthinkably high. The Submarine Tracking Room's warning of the 'potentially annihilating superiority' of the U-Boat Arm seemed to be coming true.

And then came the largest convoy battle of the war.

The extraordinary size of this battle arose from two convoys being caught in the jaws of three wolf packs in the same area of the Atlantic Ocean.

The 60 merchant vessels of the slow convoy *SC-122* had left Liverpool on 5 March with New York as their destination. On 13 March the convoy rendezvoused with the mid-ocean B5 Escort Group, led by Commander R C Boyle in the destroyer HMS *Havelock*. The rest of the escort consisted of the United States destroyer *Upshur*, the frigate HMS *Swale* and five Flower-class corvettes.

Three days after *SC-122* had put to sea, Convoy *HX-229* left New York to follow much the same route, but at a faster speed. The convoy met its escort group, B4, on 14 March. Commander G J Luther was in the destroyer HMS *Volunteer*. This was to be his second passage across the Atlantic. With him were three destroyers – HMSs *Beverley, Mansfield, Cdr* and *Witherington* – plus one corvette.

German intercepts of Allied signals had alerted Dönitz to a large convoy but he was unsure of its route and timings. Then came a B-Dienst breakthrough on 13 March with a reasonably accurate location for Convoy *SC-122*. Knowing the size of this convoy, Dönitz called off an attack on a smaller convoy by the wolf pack *Raubgraf* (Robber Baron). Boats *U-468, U-435, U-603, U-615, U-600, U-458, U-664, U-84* and *U-91* were given positions for a patrol line across *SC-122's* route. At the same time, Dönitz ordered the wolf packs *Stürmer* (Forward) and *Dränger* (Pusher), which were further away, to move into the same area. In all, around 40 U-boats would descend on *SC-122* and *HX-229* in the next few days.

Dönitz had been fortunate in his timely receipt of intelligence. The Allies, though, were the victims of a great misfortune. Bletchley Park was reliant on signals from weather ships to yield the vital keys for decrypting Kriegsmarine Enigma messages. On 10 March the Germans changed the code used by these ships. Consequently the flow of messages to and from the U-boats became unreadable. (It was a cruel irony that Bletchley Park recovered from this setback on the very day that the *SC-122* and *HX-229* battle ended.) Without any up-to-date information on where the wolf packs were, the Admiralty was unable to divert the convoys away from danger. A crumb of comfort came from a direction-finding that located a U-boat near to *SC-122*. A diversion followed, but it was too late to avoid the gathering wolf pack.

At first, luck was on the side of the convoys. On 15 March Commander Boyle unknowingly took *SC-122* through the *Raubgraf* patrol line – neither side making any sightings. Then, during the night of 15-16 March Commander Luther similarly took *HX-229* across the same line with no sightings occurring. Dönitz ordered *Raubgraf* to move 15 miles to the south during the night.

Now luck switched to the U-boats. *U-653* from *Raubgraf* was in difficulties. During a storm her conning tower watch crew had been swept off into the sea. The boat was also short of fuel and down to its last torpedo. It was time to withdraw. As Commander Gerhard Feiler took his damaged boat home, he came across Convoy *HX-229* at 3.30 am on 16 March. The *Raubgraf* pack was ordered to pursue his sighting. That night the pack's boats sank three freighters. They took another five the next morning. Throughout these operations the *Raubgraf* boats saw no signs of any significant escort presence.

When day dawned Commander Luther found that there were now only 28 vessels in his convoy. Which had been sunk and which had parted from the convoy was impossible to tell. With most of the losses being on the starboard side, Luther reduced the convoy from eleven to nine columns and brought in the starboard remnants to fill columns seven to nine.

One-hundred-and-twenty miles away *U-338* was stalking Convoy *SC-122*. Kapitänleutnant Manfred Kinzel had taken command of his boat in June and was now on his first patrol as commander. In a brief period he sank four merchant ships. One of these was the 5000-ton *Kingsbury* with its cargo of building timber, soya and 2000 tons of bauxite.

Deane Wynne had come off his watch on *Kingsbury* at 8.00 pm. Before going below he stood on deck to admire the convoy. The night was clear as the ship ploughed her peaceful way. Once below, Wynne was soon asleep. It was five minutes past midnight when he was awoken by a massive explosion. The ship shuddered; the engine stopped. The ship's list told him there was no time to lose. He grabbed his life jacket and raced for the deck. His fear for his life was confirmed by the massive hole in the deck on the port side.

There were only two lifeboats. The port one was lowered. As it dropped into the water the painter severed and the boat drifted off into the darkness with just one man on board. The ship was now sinking fast. Wynne thought of the deadly vortex that would see the end of the ship. He jumped into the 30ft wall of the icy water. The ship quickly sank beneath the fearsome waves, along with her Master, William Laidler, and three seamen.

Alone in the sea, Wynne had no expectations of rescue. Half-an-hour later he banged into something. It was the dinghy that had drifted from the ship. Two men were clinging on to it: one was the 70-year-old chief engineer, the other a passenger. Wynne joined them. They were still clinging to the dinghy at 6.00 am when dawn broke. There on the horizon was the silhouette of a ship. And not just any ship. It was the rescue ship *Zamalek*. Wynne and his two companions would be amongst the 665 men and women that the *Zamalek* rescued as it sailed with 68 convoys between February 1941 and the end of the war.

*The Kingsbury, sunk by U-338. Derek Wynne and 42 other passengers and crew were saved by the British rescue ship Zamalek.*

Two more ships went down during the daylight of 17 March. The escorts were overwhelmed.

It was at 4.55 pm that the first aircraft arrived from RAF 86 Squadron at Aldergrove, Northern Ireland and 120 Squadron at Reykjavik, Iceland. They scoured the seas around the convoy, found six U-boats and dropped their bombs. There were no hits. But the planes had done their job: the U-boats stayed submerged and left the merchantmen alone. Later – presumably when the planes had gone – the last four sinkings took place.

This battle was one of the first occasions that very long range (VLR) aircraft were able to reach the Mid-Atlantic Gap. That was an Allied success in itself. In addition, the sorties were achieving a high level of HF/DF accuracy, as these excerpts from the Senior Officer's report show:

> 1850/19 - Aircraft told to investigate H/F D/F bearing 287° 10 miles.

> 1926/19 - Aircraft reported that he had attacked U-boat 280° 45 miles.

> 2150/19 - Aircraft told to investigate H/F D/F bearing 224° 5-10 mile.

> 2236/19 - Aircraft reported that he had investigated 224°, made two contacts which had disappeared and found a straggler bearing 215° 45 miles.

The last ship to be sunk was the *Canadian Star* on 18 March. She was on passage from New South Wales to Liverpool with 8000 tons of refrigerated food in her hold. Her crew of 69 were augmented by 22 passengers. Amongst these were Win Dobrée and her husband Bill.

Win had returned to her cabin at the end of the evening and had taken two aspirins to make sure that she would sleep. She lay down on her bunk, fully clothed, and closed her eyes. Before she had time to lapse into sleep there was a loud thud. Shortly afterwards the chief steward was at her door: 'Boat stations, please,' he said. Grabbing her coat and kitbag, she rushed to her husband's cabin. He had been the more successful in getting to sleep, so Win had difficulty in waking him and getting him into some clothes. On their way to the boat deck, Win noticed that she had dropped her lifebelt. They turned back to search for it. Then the lights went out. They fumbled in the dark bowels of the ship as the smell of cordite filled the menacing atmosphere.

Win had been fearful that they would be too late on deck for the boats. But their delay saved her life: the first boat, carrying only women, had gone off and capsized with all its occupants drowned. Once the remaining women were in the second boat, the half-full boat began to be lowered leaving desperate men standing on the deck. 'Hey, what about him? Can he come too?' Win shouted to the captain. Up came the boat. Once back in the water the men took to the oars and pulled in desperation to get it clear of the ship. Two-and-a-half hours later they reached a corvette. The Dobrées were lucky; 32 people lost their lives in the sinking of the *Canadian Star*.

The final tally of these two convoys was 22 out of 90 ships sunk, with a tonnage loss of 146,000. The merchant ships had been protected by 16 escorts (not all present all the time) from 38 U-boats (not all present all the time). Just one U-boat had been sunk. To the naval escort must be added the air presence. Planes from Newfoundland, Aldergrove, Iceland and Benbecula in the Outer Hebrides flew 46 sorties to protect the two convoys. On the negative side, Hedgehog had performed badly. It was used on five occasions and only once did all the projectiles fire. No more than four fired on the other occasions.

### Horton: 'I am really hopeful'

The battle of Convoys *HX-229* and *SC-122* led each side to draw its own conclusions. To both Dönitz and Hitler it was taken as a turning point in the Atlantic Battle. Hitler declared that 'the U-boat was the weapon to cut through the arteries of the enemy'. In conversation with Dönitz he said, 'There can be no question of easing up on the U-boat war.' He authorised Dönitz to increase production from 30 to 40 boats a month. But Hitler was deluded. The battle was to prove to be Dönitz's last great fling; U-boat losses were rising while tonnage sunk was falling. March saw the loss of 131 Allied merchant ships. In April only 57 were lost. In February and March Dönitz lost U-boats at the rate of 15 a month. That rate doubled in April and May. Soon Dönitz would be withdrawing U-boats from the no longer tenable North Atlantic.

Horton described the Atlantic Battle position in March in a letter to the retired Admiral Reginald Darke. The situation was 'pretty sombre up to date, because one hasn't had the means to do those very simple things for which numbers are essential'. He was in the process of putting escort carriers into support groups but, he said 'there has not been much foresight shown in the provision of all those dull things which are necessary if a flock of carriers are to be properly mothered and trained.' (Surely a comment on Percy Noble.) 'Air,' he added, 'is a tremendous factor ... the many promises that have been made [now] show signs of fulfilment ... after 3 ½ years of war'. At the end of the letter came the true Horton: 'although the last week has been one of the blackest on the sea, so far as the job is concerned, I am really hopeful'. Almost certainly he was one of very few naval commanders who could say that in the last week of March 1943.

# 28 Horton's offensive

## 'Attack and kill'

But hope was not enough. The following day, 24 March, Horton was ready to launch his offensive. This was not so much a big battle as a set of ideas based on his theme of 'attack and kill'.

The offensive had two strands, the main part being in the Atlantic with the subsidiary in the Bay of Biscay.

In the Atlantic Horton planned to use his air and sea forces to relentlessly hunt down and destroy the U-boats that were lurking near to the convoys. He forcefully forbade his commanders to go looking for U-boats in the wastes of the Atlantic Gap. It was no use, he said 'chasing a hornet all round the farm'. Instead they were to keep close to the convoys.

His more detailed instructions show that the spirit of Walker was now to prevail. As soon as an Escort Support Group arrived at a convoy the commander was to contact the senior officer at first daylight to obtain the latest information on enemy activity. The group was then to patrol around, but out of sight, of the convoy. On sighing a U-boat an escort support ship was to 'immediately report and attack, at the same time guiding warships and aircraft to the spot'. Once the other ships arrived, the senior officer was to take over and allocate tasks to his ships. Those not needed for the kill were to return to patrolling around the convoy.

Horton's message of urgency and aggressive action was revolutionary. Up to this point in the war, escort commanders had been under orders which included the phrase that they all knew by heart: 'The safe and timely arrival of the convoy at its destination is the primary object, and nothing releases the Escort Commander of his responsibility in this respect.' This had inhibited commanders from chasing U-boats. Only those careless of their reputations (such as Walker) had dared to stray from this decree. Now Horton was encouraging attack as the best form of defence. For him, success was to be measured in numbers of U-boats sunk rather than the number of convoys that evaded attack. He knew, however, that his tactics required the highest levels of skilful cooperation within the escort group, and between warships and planes.

A week or so after his offensive had begun, Horton wrote to his escort commanders to congratulate them on the work they had done in guarding the convoys through 'the most violent and tempestuous winter experienced for many years'. Then he ingenuously told them that 'it will only be necessary for each ship to reach the 100 per cent killing standard for the situation in the Atlantic to turn radically in our favour'. He was convinced that, with the new forces available to the Western Approaches Command, the escorts and the support groups could overwhelm the U-Boat Arm: 'Nothing will dishearten the Hun more than to realise that the Battle of the Atlantic has been lost and with it his last hope of defeating Britain,' he told them.

Two events at this time testify to Horton's astonishing coolness when faced with such terrifying responsibilities. On 19 March the last sinking in the *HX-229/SC-122* battle occurred. This was widely regarded as a sign that all was lost. Yet here is Horton, four days later, issuing orders that were to inspire and invigorate the thousands of officers and men who had been steadily losing the battle against the U-boats since the start of 1942. Like Churchill, Horton could combine courage with clarity of thinking, and then distil it into orders that enabled men to search deep into themselves to find the will to endure.

By March 1943 Horton's five Escort Support Groups were all operational, but resources were still difficult to come by so they were not yet as strong as he wished. Two of his groups were without destroyers, while only one group, Number 5, had an escort carrier. This deficiency was soon made up by the arrival of the carriers USS *Bogue* and HMSs *Dasher* and *Archer*.

True to his belief in training, Horton was determined to make sure that the air crews for his new carriers were ready for action from the day the ships came under his command. For this he recruited Vice Admiral Lumley Lyster. As the rear-admiral in charge of the carriers in the Mediterranean Fleet in 1940, Lyster had planned the Battle of Taranto (11-12 November) before taking up the command of the Home Fleet carriers. (Taranto, a stunning Allied victory over the Italian fleet, was the first battle in which both sides used aircraft to attack capital ships.) Horton gave Lyster one month to bring the air crew up to the standard needed for the difficult task of flying on and off carriers in mid-Atlantic. The hazards of small flight decks and the challenge of the tempestuous Atlantic weather were not to be allowed to interrupt his 'catch and kill' programme.

*A U-boat under air attack in the Bay of Biscay.*

At this time the navy had little experience of working carriers with convoys. Where should the carrier be? Would the carriers act independently or in a coordinated manner with the escort vessels? Horton could not risk his carriers on the ocean until the commanders and pilots had found answers to these questions. He turned to the tactical table, where the fleet air officers played out U-boat attacks. With their ideas gradually forming, they next operated their ships alongside HMS *Philante*. The results showed that, unless a carrier was at the centre of the convoy, it would have to have its own destroyers. Horton was alarmed at the thought that his escort commanders might be asked to take on the job of protecting a carrier. In a letter to the Admiralty he protested that 'it would confuse them to add the protection of a carrier as a call on their energies whilst developing purely defensive activities'. The decision was made that the carriers would have their own escorts, leaving them free to stand off from the convoys.

The arrival of planes working with the escorts from March 1943 onwards soon had an unwelcome impact on the U-boats. Of this period, Cremer remarked, 'far from finding themselves forced to submerge, the U-boats were being compelled to surface and were regularly finished off'. Meanwhile Dönitz was alarmed at the challenge of the increased air cover, which repeatedly prevented his boats from approaching convoys. An idea of this impact can be gained from entries in the War Log soon after Horton's offensive had begun:

> The fact that contact was lost with both sections in spite of the many boats is due to the very strong air activity by day on the 17th. Several boats were bombed and probably lagged further and further astern owing to constant air patrol. (War Log, 17 March)

> U-632 also tried to get there, but was several times forced to dive by aircraft and then continued on her outward passage. (War Log, 18 March)

> Strong air escort forced her [U-524] to remain at a great distance. Although she was 25 miles off, she was constantly approached by aircraft and forced to dive. She reported that she was able to shadow by location transmissions from air and surface escort forces, but could not approach the convoy. (War Log, 18 March)

At the same time that Horton was sending his Escort Support Groups into action, President Roosevelt badgered the United States Navy Department into putting more resources into defending convoys. The Department's response was to allocate 255 Liberators for patrols in the North Atlantic. The first 25 began work at the end of March. Initially these were flown by British air crews.

In Britain, Coastal Command was also expanding. Its eight anti-submarine and eleven anti-shipping squadrons gave it a total of 619 aircraft.

The U-boat men were petrified by the air attacks, mainly because there was next to no warning of them. The experience of *U-230* in March 1943 was typical of the terror that the Allied planes wreaked on their unsuspecting prey.

*U-230* was homeward-bound in the Bay of Biscay. Its Metox warning device was switched on. Darkness fell. That night the Metox receiver picked up three radar signals on three separate occasions. Each warning was followed by the arrival of a plane. Each forced a crash-dive, followed by bombs falling around the boat.

A fearful apprehension gripped Kapitänleutnant Paul Siegmann and his men as dawn broke on 26 March. At 10.12 am a lookout screamed 'Aircraft!' Fahnrich zur See Herbert Werner threw the Biscay Cross down the tower as his fellow seamen tumbled back into the boat. Werner, the last to descend, pulled the hatch closed. All this had taken 18 seconds. Ten seconds later the first bombs began to fall around the boat, one bomb tossing the boat's stern out of the water. Still puzzled as to why the Metox had given no warning of the Allied plane, Siegmann kept *U-230* below for half-an-hour. The boat's log tells the story of that day:

1225: Crash-dive before a two-engined aircraft. No radar impulses.

1250: *U-230* surfaced.

1332: Alarm. Aircraft. No radar detection. Four bombs exploded in close proximity, causing our rear planes to block in down position.

1405: We surfaced at high speed.

1422: Alarm. Four-engined Sunderland. Hard rudder manoeuvre. Four more bombs.

In the following night, *U-230* was compelled to crash-dive three times to avoid air attack and had 12 bombs dropped around it. The next day saw six more crash-dives, each followed by four bombs.

Perhaps news of this particularly intense series of attacks had reached Lorient, since when *U-230* finally crawled into harbour, having evaded yet further attacks, the men received a loud ovation and the Lorient band played as the boat slid into the inner harbour. 'Even our handful of veterans,' recalled Werner, 'found it a moving affair.'

While there was little that the U-boats could do to avoid attacks from the air, operational research reveals that their own lookout practices were partly to blame for the Allies' successful attacks. Using statistical methods, researchers were able to compare the number of actual sightings compared to the expected sightings. They found that, close to the Moroccan coast, a U-boat had only a six per cent chance of being sighted. At 400-600 miles from the coast, 33 per cent were sighted. Clearly, as the U-boats moved further from the coast, lookout vigilance declined.

## 10cm radar

It was, though, the 10cm radar in the planes that made the air attacks so precise. The production of a 10cm radar set had been a long struggle from the first demonstration of the magnetron in Randall's and Boot's laboratory to having a reliable device to put onto a production line for thousands of radar sets. Once available, the centimetric radar (also known as ASV III) was rapidly introduced to the search planes. The power of 10cm radar lay both in its capacity to detect smaller objects and in the fact that the Metox receivers in the U-boats could not detect the new signal. By 12 March 1943 Dönitz saw the devastating effects of this on his boats when every one of a pack of nine U-boats that attempted to reach a particular convoy was detected when it was still 10 to 15 miles from the merchant ships. Before they could get anywhere near the ships they were driven away by planes dropping depth charges. All the wolf pack tactics that Dönitz had developed over the previous three years were now threatened. He had no choice but to order his commanders to maintain contact 'at maximum range' and to keep out of the reach of the destroyers. If an escort approached they were to dive and make an underwater attack.

Despite its merits 10cm radar was no guarantee of success on the front line. It took time for pilots and other aircrew to master its use and then to deploy bombs and depth charges effectively. Flying Officer Gordon Lundon discovered how dangerous a U-boat could be when threatened from the air. On 4 March 1943 in the hours of darkness he was flying his Wellington bomber over the Bay of Biscay when his 10cm radar picked up the echo of a U-boat. Werner Schwaff, commander of *U-333*, was on the bridge. He and his watch were scanning the sea for the least sign of an enemy. Suddenly night turned to day as the boat was picked out by the Wellington's Leigh light. The men at the U-boat's Flak guns went into action, pumping incendiary ammunition in the direction of the light. Almost immediately the plane's left wing was on fire. But the bomber's aim was impeccable, with two of the four depth charges hitting the boat. One failed to detonate and the other bounced off to detonate in the sea. The attack had miscarried. Lundon and his crew failed to return to base. In this particular case 'the one that got away' was of little importance. Werner Schwaff, was a member of the Olympia Crew – the men who had joined the service in 1936, the year of the Berlin games. Despite this distinction, he was hardly a success, sinking just one ship of 5000 tons. And even that sinking of the Greek *Carras* was a shared enterprise since it had first been disabled by *U-666*. Schwaff was to die three months later in *U-440* with no further sinkings to his name. It is therefore ironic that this below-par commander should have outwitted a 10cm radar-guided attack.

Schwaff's uncharacteristic triumph did not set a trend. The U-boats were overwhelmed by the sudden arrival of death from the skies. By the end of April Dönitz ruled that it was now too dangerous for boats to pass through Biscay on the surface at night. They were to make the passage in daylight and rely on visual recognition of a potential air attack. Meanwhile urgent work began to find a means of detecting the mysterious new radar.

The use of aircraft against the U-boats in the Bay of Biscay had now reached its third and final phase. In the first phase (June-September 1942) the bombers, equipped with 1.5 m radar and Leigh lights, were able to spot 30 of the 71 boats that crossed the bay – a spotting rate of 43 per cent. In the second phase (October 1942 to January 1943) this rate plunged to 13 per cent as the U-boats benefited from their Metox radar detectors. And then came the third phase in which the bombers were equipped with 10cm radar. The U-boat Metox receivers were unable to detect this. During the day there was a small chance that they might see or hear a plane in time to dive. At night they had no means at all of foreseeing an aerial attack. Of the 101 boats that risked the passage in these conditions, 61 were detected. This sighting rate of sixty per cent gave the Allies domination of the Bay of Biscay.

An early victim of the failure of Metox to detect 10cm radar was *U-156*. This boat, which had an experienced crew, was on its fifth patrol of the war. It had already despatched 98,000 tons of Allied shipping under the command of U-boat ace Werner Hartenstein. This patrol had begun on 16 January but Hartenstein had failed to sink a single vessel. No doubt his men were weary when, on 8 March, the boat was caught in the 10cm radar of a PBY-5A Catalina from Squadron VP-53 based in Trinidad. Lieutenant E Dryden, dropped four 350 lb Mark 44 Torpex-filled depth charges that straddled the conning tower and broke the U-boat apart. There was then an explosion. The fate of the U-boat crew is not known – only 11 men were seen taking to the rafts. A subsequent search by USS *Barney* found nothing. It is doubtful whether the crew had any warning of this attack. With no warning from Metox, they had no reason to believe that their lives were in danger.

## Washington Convoy Conference

Just as the Allies were beginning to dominate the Atlantic, the Americans announced that they planned to withdraw vessels from the Atlantic for operations in the Pacific. This was a shock to their Allies, coming as it did less than two months after the Casablanca Conference at which the Americans had agreed that 'the defeat of the U-boat must remain a first charge on the resources of the United Nations'. A potential rift was opening up in the Allied front. A second conference followed in early March – the Washington Convoy Conference – at which 100 participants from the USA, Britain and Canada argued about priorities and strategy. Admiral Ernest King opened the conference on 1 March in a manner which suggested that he had already had second thoughts about the proposed move. While he warned that, 'You cannot consider anti-submarine warfare as divorced from the rest of the war effort,' and emphasised the importance of supplies to Russia, he nevertheless said that the main task for the conference was 'to find a way to escort convoys and get them safely to their destinations'. In the end, acrimony was avoided. The conference agreed to divide the Atlantic into two zones. Britain and Canada would provide escort cover in the North Atlantic, while the United States would cover the Central Atlantic. The latter included convoys to the Mediterranean, where so many American troops were fighting.

## The end of the small convoys

While Horton was squeezing every advantage possible out of the latest antisubmarine warfare technology, another change took place in the organisation of convoys which also proved to be a war-winning move. What might be called 'the mystery of Convoy *SC-118*' is a clue to a surprising discovery.

We have already met Convoy *SC-118* in the 'the nearing crisis' chapter. For the Allies it was both a success and a failure. It had fared badly in that eight merchant ships were sunk. That was a rate that was unacceptable by February

1943. But, of the eight sinkings, two were stragglers, that is, they were not in the area under escort protection. Of the six ships sunk within the convoy, five were torpedoed by *U-402* and one by *U-614*. But overall the battle was bad news for Dönitz – 18 of his 20 boats present had failed to sink or damage a single Allied ship in a large convoy that offered so many targets. Why had the Kriegsmarine done so badly?

The answer to the mystery lay in operational research. Everyone knew that a small convoy was safer than a large one. To this end, the Admiralty had kept convoys to the smallest sizes possible, given the shortage of escorts. But this self-evident doctrine was plain wrong. It was Professor Patrick Blackett who demonstrated its falsity. Blackett was at the University of Manchester when the war broke out. He had been a member of the Aeronautical Research Committee since 1935, but his most distinguished war-time work was in the new subject of operational research. (That is, researching an ongoing operation in order to improve it.) He observed that small convoys averaging 32 ships lost an average of 2.5% of vessels. Larger convoys averaging 54 ships suffered a loss of only 1.1%. How could this be so? he asked. He was able to establish that the strength of a convoy's protection was determined by just one parameter: the ratio of the number of destroyers to the *perimeter* of the convoy. If a convoy of 30 ships needed six destroyers, one of 60 ships needed only nine destroyers (not 12) to retain the same perimeter density. And, since larger convoys were no more likely to be found than smaller ones, it was clear that convoys should be as large as practicable.

It was many months before Blackett could convince the Admiralty of the rightness of his case, which he finally did in early 1943. Once larger convoys became the norm, there were fewer convoys. Fewer convoys meant that U-boats had less chance of stumbling on their prey, so they yielded a double bonus to the Allies. For Dönitz, the increase in convoy size was a disaster.

*The threat to the Atlantic bases*

As Dönitz reeled under Horton's onslaught, his boats suffered another set-back from the Luftwaffe. On 2 March he was informed that the channels leading into and out of the U-boat bases would no longer have air protection against Allied air raids. This had no direct impact on U-boat maintenance since that was done in the bomb-proof bunkers. The decision was, though, a double psychological blow for Dönitz; first was the simple fact of finding that his boats were unworthy of the Reich's protection; and second, as the Kriegsmarine withdrew surface craft from the Atlantic ports, an atmosphere of abandon and defeat set in. Cranes hung motionless, workshops were silent and the streets near traffic-free. Dönitz was now clinging to the periphery of the Reich.

But his boats were not yet beaten, as the next few weeks were to show.

*Black despair in the Admiralty*

Although there were initial successes from Horton's offensive in late March, these did not translate into the victory that the Allies so badly needed.

March sinkings were 630,000 tons. In the first ten days of the month, 41 ships were lost – a horrific enough figure. When 56 ships were sunk in the next ten days, catastrophe could surely not be far away. The mood in the Admiralty was one of black despair. Despite the priority which Churchill had given to the battle, despite the unimaginable ingenuity of the code-breakers, despite the near miraculous performance of the latest radar, and despite the indomitable courage of the escort crews, Germany was near to breaking the Allies. Had Horton been mistaken when he said he was 'really hopeful'?

One loss at this dark time was particularly poignant. On the day that the war broke out the newly-constructed destroyer *Jurua* was tied up at Vickers-Armstrongs in Barrow-in-Furness, waiting for delivery to the Brazilian Navy. Two days later the British Government purchased her and renamed her HMS *Harvester*. One of her earliest tasks was to take men off the beaches at Dunkirk.

She took off 272 men on 29 May 1940, but was withdrawn the next day, being too valuable to risk air attack. A change of mind led to her returning to the beaches on 30 May. In all she took off 2189 men. When her end came in March 1943, she went down fighting and her loss was redressed with extraordinary rapidity.

*Harvester* found *U-444* on the night of 10-11 March 1943 and attacked with depth charges, which forced the U-boat to the surface. Commander Arthur Tait followed standard practice for a warship nearly on top of a U-boat: he rammed his enemy. In doing so, one of *Harvester's* propellers jammed into the U-boat's hull. She limped off but was found and torpedoed by *U-432*. The U-boat submerged and the men celebrated their success with champagne and their stores of festive treats. They were still in this state when the French corvette *Aconit* arrived. Depth charges brought *U-432's* partying to an end. Forced to the surface, gunfire rid the boat of its captain and ramming put an end to the boat. Commander Tait and his 183 men who died that day had so deserved to live to see what was to happen just two weeks later.

## A new dawn

And then came April. Monthly sinkings plunged 50 per cent to 330,000 tons. In less than six weeks an indomitable U-Boat Arm had yielded to Horton's offensive. Horton, of course, would have given all the others involved – the planners, the seamen, the air crews, the scientists, the code-breakers – the credit they were due. But it was his drive and organisation that brought the pieces together and made them work in unison.

An Allied victory at last seemed possible.

# 29 Black May

## May 1943

It was mere coincidence that, just as Dönitz was following his last great battle, the British were about to provide the U-boat crews with some entertainment. Given what was to come, they were to be sorely in need of some light relief.

It all began with a man who would later make entertaining his life's work: Ian Fleming. Fleming was working in the Naval Intelligence Division at the Admiralty. In that capacity he had indulged in a wide variety of deception, espionage and entrapment operations. The fecundity of his brain seemed limitless. Most of his projects were small-scale, but his proposal for a radio station broadcasting to German submariners needed resources way beyond those of naval intelligence, so he called on Sefton Delmer. Delmer, Austrian-born and fluent in German, had a past that was uncomfortably close to the high ranks of the Nazi party. In 1931 he had been the first British journalist to interview Hitler. So obscure was his background that, before the war, the British thought he was spying for the Germans, and the Germans thought he was spying for the British. To add to the confusion, he had attended schools in Germany and London and graduated from Lincoln College, Oxford. By 1940 he was an announcer for the BBC's German Service. It was not long before he was working for the Political Warfare Executive: (a secret white and black propaganda unit run by the British Foreign Office). It was in that capacity that Fleming suggested to him the idea of 'Atlantiksender'. Churchill lent the proposal his strong support, arguing that the isolation of U-boat life made the submariners particularly susceptible to such a station, provided that it sounded genuine. With this backing, a remit for the station was soon agreed:

> To undermine the morale of the German armed forces in
> Western Europe – particularly of the U-boat crews operating
> in the Atlantic – by creating alarm in their minds regarding

conditions at home, by unsettling their faith in their arms and equipment and in their leaders, by rationalising bad discipline and performance of military duty, and wherever possible by encouraging actual desertion.

*Sefton Delmer, a journalist with a talent for black propaganda.*

Atlantiksender's first broadcast went out on 22 March 1943 and by November the station was using the 600 kW medium-wave transmitter, Aspidistra, hidden in an underground shelter in Ashdown Forest. Its three 360-feet aerials towered over the canopy of the ancient forest where once the Normans had hunted deer and, more recently, Christopher Robin had played Poohsticks. Broadcasting from 6.30 am to 8.00 am British Summer Time, the station offered a mix of news, music and entertainment. Even what the station called 'straight news' was presented as entertainment, with a mix of human interest stories. Atlantiksender fabricated a hook-up to an obscure German military radio station in the Balkans which provided news items, all concocted by the station, but always plausible. The station's sharpest weapon was its capacity to enter into the personal lives of the submariners. There were features that warned them about individual reckless commanders, reports of air raid damage in the home towns of the men, plus advice on how to apply for compassionate leave.

Atlantiksender's star announcer was Vicky, the 'sailor's sweetheart' who sent birthday greetings to her 'dear boys in blue', congratulated them on the birth of a son or daughter, and discussed the problems of their wives and families. Vicky could do this since the Admiralty had an astonishing set of press cuttings on the Kriegsmarine, going back well before the war. Births, marriages, promotions and other personal items were all filed ready to use to turn or undermine a seaman, and still updated as the war progressed. Vicky's sweet manner endeared many a seaman, yet the actress behind Vicky had lost half of her family in the Auschwitz gas chambers.

Cremer's own experience of the Allied intelligence behind Atlantiksender demonstrates the extent to which the British had penetrated the lives of the U-boat crews. As he was leaving his hotel on 2 June 1943 a friend greeted him with, 'You're sailing today, aren't you?' Cremer was astonished – boat departures were never made public and his friend was not in the Kriegsmarine. He asked, 'Who told you that?' to which his friend replied, 'The Atlantiksender spread it about last night: Cremer is sailing with *U-333* on 2 June.' He was also one of the few submariners to discover the full extent of the British intelligence on him when he saw his file card after the war. It detailed, he said, 'The most important dates in my life, my career, my weakness for sport, down to my favourite drink, rum'.

A wartime assessment of the station showed that it was one of the most popular radio stations not only with the submariners but also with Wehrmacht and Luftwaffe personnel. It was so influential that the German press took to issuing denials of its various stories. For example, the station's suggestion that the Chief of the Storm Troops was 'planning to form a Waffen-SA in opposition to the existing Waffen-SS' brought a sharp denial from Germany.

*Retreat to Berlin*

There was one further sign that the U-Boat Arm was in retreat when its headquarters moved yet again, this time to the Hotel am Steinplatz in Berlin. The symbolism of having to retreat first to Paris in March 1942 and then to Berlin in 1943 was unmistakable. Once, Dönitz and his officers had looked defiantly out on to the Atlantic. Then they loitered arrogantly in Bohemian Paris. Now they were pitiably cowering in bombed-out Berlin. There, Dönitz and his most trusted officers moved the U-boat flags on huge situation charts. With no fixed hours, officers came and went as the battles demanded. Night and day were one. At night, in the early days in Berlin, Dönitz and his officers often worked to the background drone of an occasional British Mosquito. Later, massive bombing formations thundered overhead. U-boat directing was suspended as the men and officers fled to their deep shelter.

*Black May*

The German submariners called May 1943 'Black May'. It was a month without a glimmer of hope. The utter desperation of the situation can be glimpsed in the Log Book of *U-230* on patrol as its radio operators logged deciphered calls from nearby U-boats:

> DESTROYER ATTACKED. SINKING. U-638. (5 May)
>
> ATTACKED BY DESTROYERS. DEPTH CHARGES.
> LEAVE BOAT. U-531. (5 May)
>
> ATTACKED BY CORVETTE. SINKING. U-438. (6 May)
>
> AIRCRAFT. BOMBS. RAMMED BY DESTROYER.
> SINKING. U-125. (5 May)

(The Log continues in this vein as sinking followed sinking, day after day.)

*U-638* had been depth-charged by HMS *Sunflower*; *U-531* was depth-charged by HMS *Sunflower*; *U-438* had been depth-charged by HMS *Pelican*; *U-125* had been rammed by HMS *Oribi* and sunk by gunfire from HMS *Snowflake*. In each case, there were no survivors.

The Allied air patrols were now inescapable in the Bay of Biscay. As recently as February the Allies had rejoiced at sighting 30 per cent of the U-boats passing through the Bay. Now, as centimetric radar was installed in the search planes, 80 per cent of boats were being tracked. The U-Boat Arm was baffled at the mysterious technology which they could not identify. Unable to conceive of an apparently undetectable radar, they plumped for infrared as the answer and began a search for paints that would not reflect back infrared rays.

Dönitz's response to the Allied successes was to press for more U-boats. He asked Albert Speer, Minister of Armaments and War Production, to take over U-boat construction since he was better placed to move production around as Allied air attacks pursued one U-boat boatyard after another. He told Hitler that, 'The U-Boat would be a failure if we did not sink more tonnage than the enemy could build' and submitted a plan for increased boat production. Nowhere in these moves did Dönitz make any reference to the reason why he was losing so many boats: air attack. Still blindly following the only strategy he knew – sinking tonnage – he put no effort into considering how Germany could respond to the air threat. Given the Allied superiority in the Bay of Biscay, more boats were just more targets for Allied planes. His weakness as a commander-in-chief was laid bare by this crisis; he responded as a U-boat commander.

(Dönitz may have been unaware of another reason for the poor performance of his boats at this time: the men knew how likely it was that they would not return from their next patrol. Increasingly they sought ways to delay departure, including searching their vessels for faults in order to prevent sailing.)

Dönitz, though, laid the blame for the sinkings on a new form of radar. Aware of how vulnerable his commanders felt as planes swept down on them without the least warning, he sought to reassure them. In a message of 3 May he told them how he sympathised with their 'difficult position' and assured them that '[I] shall continue to do everything within my powers as Commander-in-Chief to change this situation as rapidly as possible.' (What he meant by this is not clear. He repeatedly referred to the wonders of his new Walter U-boats, but he knew that these would not be ready within the next year or more.) Meanwhile he urged his men 'to continue your determined struggle' and told them that they would win because 'the enemy has weak spots everywhere'. His commanders might well have asked themselves how it was that they were not benefitting from these supposed 'weak spots'.

In the War Log, though, Dönitz was more realistic. 'We have to accept heavy losses, provided that the amount of enemy shipping sunk is proportionate.' In May, however, the ratio was one U-boat sunk to 10,000 gross tonnage of enemy shipping, whereas a short time ago it was one U-boat to 100,000 tons of shipping. U-boat losses in May had therefore reached 'an impossible height.'

Dönitz's realism was to the fore in early May when radar forced the abandonment of an attack on a convoy. He remarked, 'Radar location is thus robbing the submarine of her most important characteristic – ability to remain undetected.' In May the U-Boat Arm lost 42 boats, nearly tripling the April figure of fifteen. No amount of sympathetic or morale-boosting messages to his commanders could hide the truth: aircraft were now the principal cause of U-boat sinkings.

Although the Allies had surmounted the crisis of the battle, the U-boats were still able to inflict great harm but, from now on, usually at greater damage to themselves. Dönitz was to learn just how high a price he now had to pay when 43 of his U-boats descended on Convoy *ONS-5* in late April. There were

42 merchant ships in this Liverpool-Halifax convoy, many in ballast, which made station-keeping difficult in the rough seas. Captain Peter Gretton (later Vice Admiral Sir Peter Gretton) in HMS *Duncan* led the B7 Mid-Ocean Escort Force, although *Duncan* had to pull out on 4 May with a serious oil leak in her engine room.

On 28 April *U-650* found the convoy. By the evening four boats had arrived to begin what was to be a seven-day running battle. The weather at the start of the battle was horrendous. Air cover was impossible as the merchant ships struggled to stay with the convoy and the warships battled the storm. At one point on that day the convoy was reduced to 3-knots – almost stationary. Fortunately for the convoy, the U-boats were in difficulties too.

The scenes on 28-29 April were chaotic as the merchant ships attempted to sail on, while the U-boats were tossed violently in the boiling sea as they tried to position for attack. Gretton looked pityingly down on *Duncan's* deck, where the men, soaked by wave after wave of the angry sea crashing over them, fought to control the depth charges that were careering around the deck. In these near impossible conditions – one ship had its crow's nest filled by a wave – the U-boats attempted many attacks, while the warships' asdic led to chase after chase. The U-boats' first success came when the American freighter *McKeesport* was crippled by a torpedo and had to be abandoned. The storm, though, was inflicting greater damage on the convoy than the enemy as three ships left the scene on the 29 April, too mutilated to keep station. It was clear that a fearsome battle lay ahead. Horton despatched the 3$^{rd}$ Support Group from Newfoundland to join the battle.

The steady attrition of merchant ships and U-boats continued over the next few days. Then, during the night of 5-6 May fog brought relief. By 1.00 am visibility was down to 100 yards. The U-boats were blind; the escorts could see as clear as day with the aid of their 10cm radar. The exact sequence of what happened in the night is unclear, but it seems likely that HMS *Vidette* sank *U-*

*531* and *U-630*; HMS *Loosestrife* sank *U-192*; and HMS *Oribi* collided with *U-125*, which was then shelled by HMS *Snowflake* and later scuttled. As U-boat after U-boat succumbed to the escorts, Dönitz radioed his boats to report their positions. He noted in the War Log, 'this loss of six boats is very high and grave considering the short duration of the attack,' but he blamed the fog rather than the boats or his strategy.

The balance of the Battle of Convoy *ONS-5* was fearful reading for Dönitz. He had deployed 43 U-boats, lost six and had seven damaged. The sinkings of 63,000 tons were not enough to justify this attrition of his forces.

The Battle of Convoy *ONS-5* is widely regarded as the turning point in the Battle of the Atlantic.

Back in Derby House Horton was cautious in his response to the battles of the last few weeks. The Allies were in an overwhelmingly superior position. He feared, though, that Allied successes would only last until the Germans came up with their own technological response, be it a means of detecting 10-cm radar, or some other device. The moment called for an all-out offensive to drive the U-Boat Arm into a position from which it could not recover.

Horton's reaction was bold even by his standards. If the U-boats were so defenceless, it was time to cease avoiding them. He selected particular convoys to be routed *towards* the wolf packs. He ordered them to steam 'where the enemy concentration was known to be the strongest'. In a private letter to Pound he wrote: 'The shy tactics of the U-boat demand that the bait should be put right under its nose before it will take risks, and so give us a chance to make more kills.'

The intensity of Allied air attacks in the Bay of Biscay, combined with the steep rise in U-boat losses began to sap the morale of the submariners. Above them was a sky dominated by Allied planes. Ahead of them as their boats were towed out of their bunkers was a sea that had become a black hole into which U-boats disappeared. On the bases, men and officers brooded on the horrors that their next patrol would bring. Would their boat be, one day, yet another that failed to submit a radio report? Would their boat be one that would appear in the log as 'U... must be presumed lost'? The fear that this induced was heightened by the mystery of the losses. It was easy for the men to imagine that the Allies had some new weapon or infallible way of tracking U-boats. What they never understood was that the Allied success came as much from the hard slog of operational research, rigorous training, escort team work and as it did from radar and air support.

### 'The scissors snapped shut'

Until May 1943 those U-boats which successfully ran the gauntlet of the Bay of Biscay made for the relative safety of the Mid-Atlantic Gap – the one part of the ocean that was beyond the reach of land-based planes. This gap was closed in mid-May when the Canadian Air Force began operating planes based in Newfoundland. Cremer recalled, 'The scissors snapped shut to cut the U-boats' lifeline … Aircraft were humming everywhere, seeking to kill us.' With the closing of the gap the U-boat crews also lost those undisturbed areas off the convoy routes where they met supply ships and had time to sunbathe on deck and swim in the sea. These were brief but precious moments for men with skin sickly pale from weeks of underwater living and whose bodies were never clean in the oily stench of their U-boats. The sudden impossibility of enjoying even these fleeting moments of being at one with nature cruelly reminded them that the Allies were closing in.

### The search for an offensive

Dönitz's boats were now on the defensive. He was determined to reverse that. His first response was the 'U-Flak'.

Dönitz recognised that air attack was the primary cause of the sudden switch of the battle in favour of the Allies. If Göring would not bring the Allied planes down, he would. Dönitz rapidly brought forward the development of the 'U-Flak'. This was a modified Type VII U-boat with 20 mm and 37 mm quick-firing anti-aircraft guns mounted on its deck. The gunners were accommodated in the torpedo rooms of the boats, which sailed with five pre-loaded torpedo tubes. These U-Flaks escorted patrol U-boats across the Bay of Biscay. As soon as an Allied plane appeared, the patrol boats would submerge, leaving the U-Flaks to fight the bombers.

*U-Flak 1, one of seven anti-aircraft U-boats, none of which was able to withstand Allied air attacks.*

The U-Flaks were not a success. *U-Flak 1* (the converted *U-441*) brought down a Sunderland on its first sortie in May but had suffered enough damage to have to return to its base. Its second patrol, in mid-July, was a similar failure when three Beaufighters fell upon the boat. All its officers were killed, leaving the boat to return to base under the command of a doctor. *U-Flak 1* was then converted back for patrol duties. *U-Flak 2* (*U-256*) was equally unsuccessful.

In its brief sorties in October and November it damaged but failed to bring down two Allied planes.

The failure of the U-Flaks was in part due to the speed with which the Allies responded to this new threat. At first, U-Flaks picked off single planes. But the Allies responded by adapting Dönitz's wolf pack technique. When a plane spotted a U-Flak, it radioed its location, turned away and waited for other planes to arrive. Their subsequent mass attack was more than a lone U-Flak could sustain.

It was during this period that Dönitz discovered the weakness of the Type IX U-boat. This boat was 35 per cent heavier and 13 per cent longer than the Type VII and could carry 22 torpedoes. It was designed for endurance with a capacity to track convoys for long periods. In March and April Type IX boats proved to be three times more vulnerable to loss than Type VII. Dönitz attributed this to the greater technical complexity of the Type IX which made it more vulnerable to depth charge damage. He only quoted figures for this short period but if the Type IX was routinely three times more likely to be sunk than a Type VII, why did it take until mid-1943 to discover this, and why did Dönitz go on building them? By late 1944 he had 41 of the apparently inferior Type IXs in commission alongside 98 Type VIIs. If the Type IX was so poor, there should have been fewer of them in commission; but if it was superior to a Type VII, there should have been more of them. The failure to clarify this puzzle identifies it as strategic error number seven.

By mid-May Dönitz had little to offer his commanders other than fine words. He admitted: 'In his efforts to rob the submarines of their most valuable characteristic (invisibility) the enemy is several lengths ahead of us by virtue of his radar location.' He placed his faith in the capacity of his commanders to 'continue your determined struggle with the enemy and by pitting your ingenuity, ability and toughness against his tricks and technical developments, finally to finish him off'. Meanwhile he issued new orders designed to reduce the night-time sinking of surfaced U-boats by aircraft. From now on they were to submerge at night, and surface during the day just long enough to recharge their batteries. Night-time sinkings duly fell and, inevitably, day-time sinkings rose.

## Victory

Confirmation of the Allies' defeat of the U-boats came in the battle of Convoy *HX-239* in late May. There was a remarkable prelude to this battle, which did credit to the code-breakers on both sides. B-Dienst successfully learned the details of the convoy's passage, allowing Dönitz to direct a wolf pack to it. Bletchley Park read Dönitz's orders and re-routed the convoy. Then B-Dienst trumped this by reading the re-routing command, so enabling Dönitz to redirect his wolf pack to the new route.

On 23 May the U-boats once again massed in the path of a convoy. *HX-239's* 42 merchant ships were escorted by the B3 Escort Group and the 4th Escort Support Group, which included the carrier HMS *Archer*. Three days after leaving New York on 13 May, the convoy had been delayed by a day of thick fog, followed by heavy rain and the danger of icebergs. A storm then blew up, making it impossible for the planes on *Archer* to take to the skies. Despite the weather, the planes from the American carrier *Bogue* succeeded in sinking *U-569*. Then, on 23 May, the weather improved and more planes were quickly at work.

Soon afterwards Sub Lieutenant H Horrocks, the pilot of a Swordfish, had sighted *U-752* from 1500-feet at a distance of ten miles. He dived back into cloud and manoeuvred into an attack position. As he came out of the cloud the U-boat was to port, unaware of Horrocks. He careered down onto the boat, launching off four salvos of two rockets, each with a 25 lb warhead. He was at 800 yards when the first salvo fell 150 yards short of the boat. *U-752* had now made up for its earlier dilatory observations and promptly began to crash-dive. The second salvo then hit the water at 30 feet from the boat. Then came the third, this time 10 feet short. By now the U-boat was diving steeply, its stern sticking high out of the water. Horrocks' fourth salvo tore into the U-boat about twenty feet forward of its rudders. The boat surfaced and its men poured onto the decks to man the AA guns. Almost immediately a Martlet B arrived and blasted 600 rounds into the conning tower. The U-boat lay disabled as its crew scrambled out to drop into the sea. In his action Horrocks had been the first Allied service man to fire a rocket operationally – yet one more addition to the Allies' anti-U-boat weaponry.

For the next three days *Archer's* planes circled the convoy and not one U-boat exposed itself to the overwhelming force protecting the merchant vessels.

Convoy *HX-239* marks the end of the big convoy battles. When the Allies first began their major attrition of the U-boats in March, the successes were due to the new technology and the skill of the escort commanders. By May a new factor was yielding success: fear. The U-boat commanders were becoming timid. Dönitz had his own answer to this which came in a desperate signal to his commanders: 'If there is anyone who thinks that combating convoys is no longer possible, he is a weakling and no true U-boat captain. The battle of the Atlantic is getting harder but it is the determining element in the waging of the war.'

By the end of May it was clear that Dönitz's U-boat strategy had failed. He had set out to win a 'tonnage war'. At one time he had convinced himself that the Atlantic battle could be won if his boats could sink 700,000 tons of merchant shipping per month. Later he realised that the true figure was over 1 million tons per month. Yet in May 1943 sinkings were a mere 160,000 tons despite his having over 300 U-boats in commission, of which around 60 a day were at sea in the Atlantic. His response to this crisis was to demand more boats. He could not see that the arithmetic did not make sense. If 300 U-boats in commission sank 160,000 tons, how many boats would he need to sink 1 million tons? An unthinkable 1875 in the Atlantic alone. And even this would have been an under-estimate since tons sunk per boat per day had been on a downward slide for a long while.

It should have been obvious to both Hitler and Dönitz that building more boats and training more men, only for the Allies to send them to the bottom of the Atlantic, was a futile waste of resources. Unless the U-boats could be made more effective, their continued ventures into the Atlantic were no more than a gesture. The Allies were fortunate that neither man took a step back from the foolish decision to put more men and more boats to sea.

## Dönitz admits defeat

On 24 May Dönitz sat down to write a long entry in the War Log. The U-boat war in the Atlantic had now lasted 1350 days. He began with the recent U-boat losses:

> After 14 boats had been lost in the Atlantic in February, in March 13 and in April 12, the extent of the losses in the Atlantic in May has already reached the figure of 31 boats lost up to the 22nd May, and 2 further ones have probably been lost in the operation against HX 239 … in May in the Atlantic the sinking of about 10,000 GRT had to be paid for by [the] loss of a boat, while not long ago there was loss only with the sinking of about 100,000 GRT. The losses in May have, therefore, reached an impossible height.

Those last few words were Dönitz's admission that he had lost the Battle of the Atlantic. He then turned to how his boats were being lost: '60% were lost while proceeding and at waiting positions in the operational area'. Ultimately, he concluded, the high losses were due to 'the increased use of land-based aircraft and aircraft carriers, combined with the possibility of surprise now through the enemy radar location by day and night'.

Further on in his analysis he buried the sentence that was Horton's ultimate triumph: 'the situation in the North Atlantic now forces a temporary shifting of operations to areas less endangered by aircraft'. The U-Boat Arm was pulling out of the North Atlantic.

From now on Dönitz would live in a world of delusion which would encompass wildly optimistic morale-boosting messages to his commanders. The first of these – on 24 May – told them that 'we are fighting off successfully with the army and air force on all fronts' but 'You alone can, at the moment, make an offensive attack against the enemy and beat him.' He added: 'We will not allow ourselves to be forced into the defensive' but 'fight on with still more fortitude and decision in order to make ourselves even stronger for the decisive Battle of the North Atlantic, which will be carried out shortly with improved weapons, in the area most vulnerable for the enemy.'

When Dönitz met Hitler towards the end of May to review the U-boat war, much of the discussion concerned the undeniably poor performance of the boats. Hitler took little interest in how the situation might be redeemed, and readily agreed to Dönitz's request for more boats and more air support. But his interest was only fully aroused when Dönitz referred to the role his boats played in tying down Allied naval forces. Hitler burst into life, declaring, 'The enemy forces tied up by the U-boats are so extraordinarily large that even if we no longer have great successes, I cannot permit their releases.' It was an astonishing confession. The U-Boat Arm, once the Reich's most successful means of waging war, was now consigned to the humiliation of a holding operation. But Dönitz, who had come into the meeting with an order form for building thirty new U-boats a month, left the room with the '30' crossed out and replaced by '40'.

Although Dönitz confidently told Hitler that the U-boat war could be won with more boats and more air support, he told his adjutant, Commander Hansen-Nootbar, a different story. 'We'll get them in the end! But first we must have the new boats!' These were the Walter electric U-boats that could remain submerged indefinitely. It would be two years before the first boat was commissioned. Was Dönitz consciously deceiving his men or unconsciously deceiving himself over the continued viability of the Atlantic battle?

It was not just boats that Dönitz needed. He needed trained submariners too. This led to a bizarre attempt to rescue U-boat prisoners held in Canada. The men had been able to communicate their location by means of messages buried in apparently innocent letters to their families. (The hidden message lay, in coded form, in the first letter of each word.) It was Cremer – then working at the U-Boat Arm headquarters – who organised the rescue attempt. Commander Rudolf Franke in *U-262* was shadowing Convoy *HX-233* when he received the code word 'Elster'. This was the trigger to open a sealed envelope. Inside it he found instructions to go to a point on the western side of the Gulf of St Lawrence at the beginning of May. He was to await a signal from the shore at a certain time. It would indicate that the escaped submariners were awaiting rescue. Beyond these bare details, Franke was to use his initiative. When *U-262* reached the gulf, Franke found it frozen over. He first attempted to sail through the loose ice but it was too dense for his boat. He ordered a dive and began the hazardous task of taking a boat below ice. When he estimated that the boat was near enough to make contact with the shore Franke ordered the boat to surface. Several attempts were needed as the ice refused to break. Finally the boat broke through. As Franke surveyed his position from the conning tower he saw a dismal sight. The net-cutter was damaged, as was the AA gun; and from down below his men reported three torpedo bow caps jammed shut. All Franke could do was wait in his exposed position. After several nights of attempting a rendezvous there was no sign of any contact. Franke ordered a return to the open sea to await orders.

And so ended Black May. Barely two months after the Allies had gone through the nightmare of 700,000 tons sunk in March, apparently facing imminent defeat, the U-boat threat was tamed. Now the challenge for Horton was to keep it tamed. Dönitz was to prove to be a man who did not give up lightly.

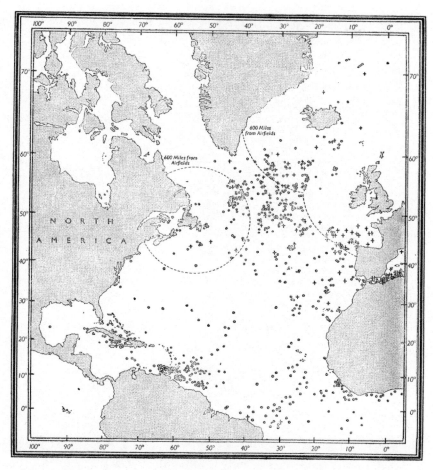

*Map 4. Sinkings August 1942-May 1943; o = Merchant ship; + = U-boat.*
*The arcs show the limit of air cover before the Mid-Atlantic gap was closed.*

291

# 30 Piling on the pressure

## May to June 1943

*'Now is the time to strike and strike hard'*

At the end of May Horton wrote to all the American, British and Canadian commanders who were working under him in the Atlantic to congratulate them on their 'hard work, hard training, and determination', their 'spectacular kills' and their 'many notable victories'. He summarised their achievements by noting that there had been 'a definite turn in our favour during the past two months'. 'The tide of the battle has been checked, if not turned and the enemy is showing signs of strain ... Now is the time to strike and strike hard.'

Two weeks later Horton was in reflective mood when writing to his friend Admiral Darke as he recalled the basis of the escorts' successes: 'The Support Groups inaugurated the change, when we got reinforcements from the Home Fleet in March – then came our own Support Groups and the escort carriers (very well trained too) – then new weapons and increased V.L.R. aircraft of Coastal Command. The combination was too much for the Hun ... he must be scratching his head and stern hard.'

Pleased as he was with what the Western Approaches Command had achieved, Horton anticipated an early return of the U-boats. There was to be neither pause nor diminution in his offensive. In so far as there was a moment to prepare for the next onslaught, Horton was determined to use it to keep up training standards.

The Admiralty had other ideas. With the U-boats at bay, they wanted to run more frequent convoys. This would have demanded yet more of the exhausted escorts and men. Horton was determined to block this proposal. He stormed off to London to insist that the Admiralty lay off making more demands on the escorts and so allow him to both provide the officers and men with sorely needed rest and vital refresher training. The meeting went badly until Horton issued an ultimatum: 'Buy your experience in training, and not when fighting the enemy', he roared, while thumping on the table and spitting out the words. The Admiralty backed down.

### Hunting in the Bay of Biscay

On the Allied side the escorts were now at the peak of their performance as technology, training and teamwork led to their domination of Biscay.

In May Commander Peter Gretton's Escort Group, working with air support, showed how confidently the Allies could now fight off U-boat attacks. Convoy *SC-130*, a slow convoy from Sydney, Nova Scotia, to Liverpool was met by Gretton's group on 15 May. Its 37 sluggish ships were in ten columns, surrounded by eight escorts. On 18 May Oberleutnant zur See Heinz Koch in *U-304* alerted Lorient to the presence of the convoy. Koch was on his first patrol. It was also to be his last, his only contribution to the war being his sighting report. During the night of 18-19 May more U-boats began to gather but Gretton's escorts frustrated their every attempt to approach the convoy. In the darkness before dawn Gretton turned the convoy through 90 degrees, hoping to lose the enemy. On the morning of 19 May, Liberator planes arrived from Iceland and began to patrol alongside the convoy. One plane sighted five U-boats, forcing them all to submerge. A Hudson joined in an attack on a U-boat, resulting in only minimal damage. Another boat – *U-273* – was sunk. Gretton's force was now joined by vessels from the 1st Support Group. Shortly afterwards *U-954* was sunk in a Hedgehog attack. The U-boat attacks continued throughout the day to no effect. By 20 May the U-boats were falling back but not before a Liberator had sunk *U-258*.

Once more the weakness of the new boat commanders was showing. *U-954* had been on its first patrol, under a commander of little distinction. Korvettenkapitän Odo Loewe had four patrols to his credit but had only sunk 17,500 tons in 30 months as a U-boat commander. This sinking had a particular grievous significance for Dönitz since his younger son, Peter, was on board. There were no survivors. *U-273* was another under-performing boat.

Oberleutnant zur See Hermann Rossmann was on his first patrol. Neither boat nor commander so much as damaged an Allied vessel. And finally, *U-258* was on its fourth patrol and had only sunk one 6000-ton vessel. Its commander, Kapitänleutnant Wilhelm von Mässenhausen, had the same record as his boat.

The final result of this massive attack on Convoy *SC-130* was three U-boats sunk and one damaged, with no loss to either the convoy or the escort. It was Dönitz who called off the attack, recognising the overwhelming superiority that the Allies now had. Horton would have been delighted had he been able to read the War Log's comment on his escorts:

> The amazing thing is that apparently at the time only 1 to 2 machines in all were escorting the convoy, according to intercept messages of aircraft operating. Each machine detected, however, during the whole day one boat more frequently than every quarter-hour, from which it must be concluded that the enemy's radar hardly missed a boat ...

> Several boats also reported efficient cooperation between aircraft and escorts, this being confirmed by 8 depth charge attacks in succession of which 4 were particularly heavy. 2 boats had to return owing to heavy damage.

In his memoirs Dönitz provided a tribute to the skill with which the Allies had outwitted his boats in the battles over convoys *SC-130* and *HX-239*: 'The convoy escorts worked in exemplary harmony with the specially trained "support groups." ... the continuous air cover ... most of them equipped with the new radar. There were also new and heavier depth charges and improved means of throwing them ... it became impossible to carry on the fight against the convoys.'

What was a calamity for Dönitz was a welcome fillip to Horton as he now concentrated his attacks on the Bay of Biscay where, amongst other technologies, HF/DF was yielding good results.

*An operator at an HF/DF set.*

Even without air cover, HF/DF was able to deliver devastating damage to the U-boat fleet, as when HMSs *Starling* and *Wild Goose* were working together on 1 June 1943. *Starling's* HF/DF set detected a U-boat at a range of about 25 miles on a bearing of 225 degrees. Walker radioed the report to the other ships in the group. Almost immediately *Wild Goose* picked up the same source on a bearing of 228 degrees. Two pencil lines on a chart were enough to locate the U-boat. *U-202* put up one of the most determined fights of the Atlantic battle. *Starling* began depth-charging the boat around 10.15 am. The boat's commander, Günter Poser, ordered a crash-dive to 400 feet, hoping to ride out the battle there. But Walker had developed his own technique for depth-charging deeply positioned U-boats. Three vessels in close line-abreast passed over the U-boat dumping their charges in a five second sequence. The fearful rumbling of the combined propellers overhead were unnerving for the men trapped in *U-202*. Poser, ordered the boat down ... and down ... and down. His engineers pleaded with him as the boat reached 750 feet. But Poser would not give up. Down the boat sank to 800 feet. The pleadings of the engineers were more desperate than ever. Still Poser was not satisfied. The boat sank to the staggering depth of 820 feet, where it was levelled and trimmed. Overhead Walker's group were still hovering and picking up asdic pings. Finally, just before midnight, *U-202* ran out of air and surfaced. At first Poser tried to avoid surrender despite the vicious gunfire that was raking his boat as it surfaced. Soon there were fifteen or so bodies on the deck. He gave the order to abandon ship and joined the 30 survivors.

By July there was little chance for a U-boat to fend off an air attack since the Allies had perfected working in numbers that overwhelmed the defences of any lone boat that dared to surface. One such attack took place around the end of July when a damaged boat surfaced to rendezvous with a torpedo boat. Almost immediately after surfacing, a Sunderland approached the boat from the stern at a range of 800 yards. The U-boat's AA opened fire and the Sunderland turned away. Two minutes later a second plane appeared. The two planes encircled the U-boat to run in together at 45° on its port and starboard sides. The starboard plane turned away from the heavy AA but dropped six bombs behind the boat. Meanwhile the second plane had dropped two bombs. Four gunners lay dead on the U-boat's deck. There was a brief respite of five minutes before a second pair of planes arrived. Another three gunners were put out of action, while the boat's motors all stopped. One plane left at this stage, leaving one last plane to run in for the third attack of the day. By now, all the trained gunners lay dead, while the inexpert attempts by the seamen to fire back at the plane brought no result. The crew's frantic attempt to save their boat ended as it began to sink. Their futile battle ended when the commander ordered 'Abandon ship' and the men – other than the stand-in gunners – took to the water. The commander claimed in his report that there was a fourth air attack in which the men in the water were machine-gunned. It is impossible to either verify or deny this since Dönitz does not tell us the precise date of the attack nor the identity of the U-boat.

Every U-boat that was sunk took the Allies a step nearer to the destruction of the Nazi tyranny. But some U-boats sinkings offered bigger steps than others. The milch cows were essential to keeping Dönitz's boats working for long periods on the high seas. Sinking these before they could take up station meant shorter and less productive patrols for the operational U-boats. Two of these boats were caught up in a rare incident on 30 July 1943. For only the second occasion in modern times, the combination of the flags '2','W', and 'N' were run up. 'General chase' had last been used at the Battle of the Falkland Islands on 8 December 1914 when Rear Admiral Sturdee's warships left Port Stanley in pursuit of Admiral von Spee's squadron. Now Walker was using it to free his escorts from his rules and operating procedures. The reason for this singular incident was that the two milch cows were being pinned down by a ferocious attack from a Halifax bomber, a United States Liberator and an Australian Sunderland. Only a free-for-all could work in such a mêlée.

The aircraft were the first to despatch a U-boat as Flight Lieutenant Dudley Marrows in his Sunderland depth-charged *U-461*, placing the charge immediately under the boat. He could hardly have had a better hit. The boat quickly disintegrated, leaving only 15 survivors.

The second milch cow, *U-462*, had also been hit by planes. With holes in its hull and men injured, the 39-year-old, Kapitänleutnant Bruno Vowe, who had never sunk or damaged a vessel in his eight patrols, hesitated. Should he dive with a damaged vessel, or attempt a surface escape under fire? He was saved from a decision when two large explosions tore open the foredeck. He ordered 'Abandon ship'.

With two milch cows sunk, there was still *U-504*, the milch cow escort vessel, at large. By the time that Walker's ships reached the boat it had submerged. Its seclusion was short-lived. HMS *Kite's* asdic located it within five minutes. It was time for one of Walker's creeping attacks, with *Kite* as the directing ship. *Woodpecker* and *Wild Goose* crept up until *Woodpecker* was directly over the boat. Twenty-two depth charges set to maximum depth brought the debris from the wrecked boat to the surface. There were no survivors.

In just over a year *U-504* had sunk fifteen vessels totally nearly 80,000 tons. It was unfortunate that the Allies had not sunk the boat seven months earlier when her then commander was Hans-Georg Poske. He sank 78,000 tons while in command of *U-504* before taking command of the U-boat training division, where he doubtless passed on his ship-sinking skills to many new commanders. Wilhelm Luis, the July 1943 commander of *U-504*, went down with his boat, never having sunk anything.

(As a footnote to this battle, the flags that Walker used are now on display in Bootle town hall.)

*The damaged milch cow U-462.*

While Horton was congratulating his escorts on their performance and preparing them for the return of the U-boats, Cremer was sunbathing on the deck of *U-333* as his boat pitched in the gentle swell of the Atlantic. The boat was secured to a sea anchor – a sail-cloth bag – to keep it head-on to the sea. In the seas nearby five other boats sat idle. There was nothing wrong with the boats, except that their supplies had run out. On *U-333* all the food had gone, leaving coffee as the sole refreshment. The cause of these shortages was the recent sinkings of milch cows; supplies at sea were now severely limited. The boats were, said Cremer, 'a prey to anything that might happen'.

## U-boat strategy crisis

At the U-Boat Arm headquarters in June, all was caution and uncertainty. Indeed, the mood might be described as one of paranoia. Dönitz had trained his men to act aggressively and fearlessly in the face of the Allies' highly professional escort vessels. Now he was encouraging them to cower in the presence of miasmas. In early June he warned about some of the new means that the Allies had for attacking U-boats. These included 'explosives fixed to lifeboats, cases, rafts, barrels etc.' Even a downed aircraft was to be feared: 'depth-charges which may roll out of the bomb racks'. These were the words of a man struggling to find an excuse for a fleet that dared not confront the planes and destroyers.

Additionally, the U-boats that had so boldly fought during the last three years were now ordered to travel in groups through the Bay of Biscay, proceeding on the surface so as to complete the passage in the shortest possible time. And, if Allied planes arrived, they were to fight them on the surface. The final words of this order neatly caught the defensive spirit in the changed atmosphere: 'Keep together at all costs.'

Two weeks later Dönitz had second thoughts about this order after the experience of a sortie of *U-68*, *U-155*, *U-159*, *U-415* and *U-634* in formation in mid-June. The group was spotted by four De Havilland Mosquito planes, which moved in to attack. Considering the scale of the Allied forces, the attack was a failure. Only *U-68* was hit, losing one man for the cost of one Mosquito hit. It survived to belly-flop land at its base. Despite the feebleness of the attack, Dönitz promptly declared that, 'This incident showed that it had become too dangerous to proceed all day on the surface' and ordered his boats to return to submerging in the day and surfacing at night only to recharge their batteries. This rapid switching of tactics is one more sign that Dönitz was no longer able to think clearly about the role of his boats.

Dönitz had been promised 40 new U-boats a month in mid-1943. The actual number was around 20 a month. When he complained to Hitler about the shortfall, Hitler said that he could not find the increased manpower that the Kriegsmarine wanted. He needed the men to defend the cities from bombing, to reinforce the armies in the east, and to defend Europe from invasion. Dönitz, Hitler told him, would have to learn to live 'from hand to mouth' for personnel like everyone else.

By July the situation in the Bay of Biscay had worsened. It was now so hazardous that Dönitz was looking at the prospects of using home ports and Norwegian bases. A closer study of this proposal was not encouraging. Of the 16 boats that had been sent out from these ports, five had been sunk trying to get past Iceland into the Atlantic and just two had reached their operational areas. Of these, *U-334* was promptly sunk by depth charges from HMSs *Jed* and *Pelican*, while *U-338* disappeared without trace. Another two were damaged while attempting to reach the Atlantic and were forced to return to base. The remaining three were sent off to refuel other boats. One had sunk by the time the report was prepared; one sank in November, never having sunk any target; and the third sank a ship in November and survived the war. So, to summarise: sixteen boats left port but only one ship was sunk by them. In Dönitz's search for a new strategy, neither Norway nor the home ports offered a solution.

*Horton's triumph*

As July drew to a close Dönitz knew that his boats were no match for the Allied planes. Without fighter cover in the Bay of Biscay their sorties were suicidal. He managed to persuade Göring to provide air cover from the Third Air-Fleet Command Operations Division during the first two weeks of July but it proved ineffective, with 20 U-boats having been lost in the Bay in the first 15 days of July. At an air conference on 19 July the Air Force declared that a close escort of the U-boats in the Bay would require 300 aircraft. No such planes were available. The best that the Air Force could offer was to continue to provide close support for incoming damaged U-boats. And this offer came with the warning that 'even for this task the available forces were too small, and getting steadily smaller'. On hearing the dismal Air Force report Dönitz ceded the Bay of Biscay to the Allies, ordering his boats to hug the north coast of Spain when going to and from the Atlantic.

For the thousands of Allied seamen and naval personnel who had for months and years stood tensed up on bridges, manhandled guns and depth charges as icy seas smashed over decks, or slept uneasily below as the U-boats prowled the sea, July 1943 was an eerie experience. There was not an enemy to be seen. There were no explosions in the night, nor flames from stricken ships on the horizon. Thirty-two convoys totalling 1367 vessels crossed the Atlantic without a single torpedo being fired. Horton had triumphed.

For how long was another matter.

# 31 Dönitz fights on

## August to December 1943

### Going through the motions

In his memoirs, Dönitz described the low mood that came over him as the Allied planes swept relentlessly across Biscay. He was deeply pessimistic as he confronted what he called an 'unequal struggle'. At first he contemplated abandoning the battle in order to free-up shipbuilding capacity for other purposes. Were he to carry on, he wrote 'U-boat losses would rise to an appalling height', sacrificing men to no purpose. He also considered pausing the battle until his new Walter U-boats were ready. He rejected this option on the grounds that the pause would demoralise his men. In the end, he wrote: 'I came to the bitter conclusion that we had no option but to fight on. The U-Boat Arm could not stand aside and watch the onslaught.'

Despite the battle now going so strongly against him, Dönitz had 437 boats in commission in mid-1943, of which 137 were operating in the Atlantic. They had sunk an impressive 230,000 tons in July but the August sinkings of 87,000 tons heralded the accelerating decline in the performance of the boats. In the early years of the war, a fleet of 137 operational boats would have had unimaginable consequences for the Allies. Now such a fleet was containable. It was also reducible from Allied action: Dönitz commissioned 22 boats in July but lost 33 to Allied action.

As Dönitz studied the figures in late August he was reluctant to see the Atlantic battle as lost. Knowing that he was losing his tonnage battle, he rationalised his weakened position. He argued that, despite the losses, the U-boat war had been justified because it had 'lead to [a] strong combination of the defence forces in the entire mid-Atlantic area and greatly taxed the strength of the enemy air forces'. While it was true that the battle had severely taxed the Allies, Dönitz's argument overlooked the fact that the Allied forces had survived in strength; the U-boat Arm, despite its size, was weakening by the day.

The shortage of milch cows had further reduced the effectiveness of the Atlantic boats. By October the position was critical as Dönitz ordered his commanders to make the protection of the milch cows their highest priority. When under air attack they were to surround a cow at 500 metres and continue to protect it until it had dived. Only once the milch cow had reached a safe depth were the protecting U-boats to dive.

With the U-Boat Arm repeatedly outflanked by the flood of new technology available to the Allies, Dönitz sought salvation in the lowest form of technology at his disposal: his men. In mid-September he (or perhaps Godt) issued detailed instructions for U-boat lookouts, such as:

> For aircraft lookouts, sun-glasses of normal strength should be unscrewed or raised so that the field of vision is greater. Use strong sun-glasses for looking into the sun. If the sun is low 1 aircraft lookout with sun-glasses on the side toward the sun, without sun-glasses on the side away from the sun.

These same instructions dealt with the minutiae of using Flak guns, the number of personnel on a U-boat bridge, and safe procedures for refuelling at sea. Although in name he was commander-in-chief, Dönitz could not stop thinking like a tactician or a U-boat commander. He saw his fleet through the narrow field of a periscope when he needed the panorama of a high peak above the battleground.

Another precaution against air attack was the U-Boat Arm order to switch off Metox 'as it is thought that enemy makes use of the receiver radiation to approach the U-boat from a great distance without himself using location gear'. This order followed extensive tests on the detectability of the Metox receiver's own radiation. The tests proved inconclusive but a captured British pilot had told his interrogators that Allied pilots homed in on this signal. The U-Boat arm naïvely accepted this deception.

Gloom was in the air by the autumn of 1943 when Herbert Werner landed at Brest. He noticed the empty berths, which in the spring had bustled with life. In the mess hall many seats were unoccupied and the conversation was subdued. 'The smell of death was everywhere,' he said.

With good news in short supply in October 1943, Dönitz used the award of the Knight's Cross with Oak Leaves, Swords and Diamonds to Wolfgang Lüth as a chance for some morale-boosting. (Lüth was the first Kriegsmarine officer to receive this distinction.) In a message to his commanders, Dönitz praised Lüth, saying, 'His dogged toughness, his lightning grasp and his determined spirit embody the exemplarily attitude and performance of the German U-boat men.'

*Kapitän zur See Wolfgang Lüth receiving the Knight's Cross with Oak Leaves, Swords and Diamonds from Hitler.*

By the end of the war Lüth would be second behind Kretschmer in tons sunk (225,000 compared to 273,000), having spent 600 days on patrol. He had joined the Reichsmarine in 1933, moved into U-boats in 1937 and learned his craft in the Spanish Civil War. Not yet a commander, he was serving in *U-38* on station in the Atlantic at the outbreak of war. His survival since that time, despite having fought against so many escorts, testifies to his skill as a boat commander. He was in every respect Dönitz's idea of a model commander – a type that was in increasingly short supply by late 1943. Lüth's end came in an odd way when he was a prisoner of war in 1945. He was shot by a German guard of a British-run prisoner of war camp when, returning drunk to the camp, he failed to correctly identify himself. Dönitz was so horrified at this that he requested permission from the British occupying force for a state funeral for Lüth. Permission was granted and on 16 May 1945 Lüth became the last person to have a Reich state funeral.

Another outstanding commander who was still demonstrating his skill and courage in late 1943 was Cremer. In mid-November he was commanding *U-333* when it attempted to sink the 7000-ton tanker *British Prestige,* but both his torpedoes missed their target. He submerged, reloaded his tubes and surfaced, ready to make a second attack on the tanker. He had barely put his eyes to his periscope when an aircraft flew over his boat. Cremer knew that *U-333* had been sighted by the plane but was unaware of the presence of the frigate HMS *Exe.* The warship immediately and unintentionally crashed into *U-333* before Cremer had even given the order to dive. He later described that moment:

> Suddenly everything went black and everything stopped, even the motors. In the whirl of the shock waves the rudderless boat was seized like a cork and thrust upwards. There was a cracking and a creaking noise, the world seemed to have come to an end, then crashes and thuds as the boat was thrown onto its side and everything loose came adrift. I managed to grab the steel strop on the periscope, then my legs were pulled from under me.

*U-333* was badly damaged but more was to come as depth charges blasted the boat from all sides. The periscope was shattered, as were many of the instruments when the boat began its uncontrollable dive. Men rushed up and down the boat with buckets, taking water from one end to another in an attempt to rebalance the boat. Once the boat was stabilised, Cremer's men feverishly repaired vital circuits to get the pumps and motors going again. As they worked, Cremer could still hear the destroyers prowling overhead.

By the time that the sea above them fell silent, the men were gasping for air. *U-333* surfaced. Ignoring the massive damage to the boat Cremer managed to get it back to base. On his return, Godt radioed a morale-boosting message to all U-boat commanders, praising Cremer for getting his boat home 'in spite of almost hopeless damage' and being 'hardly afloat'. With men like Cremer, willing to continue aggressive action when the battle seemed lost, Dönitz was still in a position to fight.

Godt, who was in charge of the day-to-day U-boat dispositions, shared Dönitz's predilection for using awards to raise morale in the boats. When Kapitänleutnant Rudolf Franke received the Knight's Cross in November 1943, Godt told the U-boat commanders that, in future, 'When considering decorations therefore I shall attach all the more weight to determination and perseverance in operations even if they do not lead to success.' Since Franke's total sinkings were three ships totalling only 13,000 tons and one Norwegian corvette of 900 tons, he was hardly a model commander. That Godt was reduced to giving high awards to such a mediocre officer suggests a sense of desperation.

### The acoustic torpedo

To the end, Dönitz put his faith in some wonder technology that would restore to his U-boats their supremacy of the early years of the war. In late 1943 his hopes lay in the acoustic torpedo. These were the centre of his counter-offensive of September 1943.

It was on 19 September 1943 that the 21 U-boats of the patrol line *Leuthen* to the south of Greenland, found two outward-bound convoys from Liverpool about 90 miles apart. Between them, Convoys *ONS-18* and *ON-202* comprised 65 ships with, initially, 14 escorts. Air cover was being provided by No. 120

Squadron from Iceland. Bletchley Park decrypts had suggested that U-boats were in the area, so Horton called up Support Group 9, which was patrolling to the south of the combined convoy. This massively supported convoy was about to fall victim to a new weapon.

*U-270* found *ONS-18* and opened the battle with a torpedo fired at the stern of the frigate HMS *Lagan* at 5.00 am on 20 September. *Lagan* was severely damaged with 30-feet of her stern missing. Additionally the force of the explosion had rained cans of food and depth charges down on her superstructure, causing considerable damage. Twenty-eight men and one officer were killed or missing. But this was no ordinary U-boat attack on a convoy. Until this point in the war, U-boats had sought out the merchant ships as their primary targets, in line with Dönitz's insistence that tonnage sunk was Germany's highest priority. So why had *U-270* picked out a destroyer and why had its commander, Paul-Friedrich Otto, aimed at the stern? (Most U-boat attacks were aimed midships to both destroy vital engines and to force the ship to break her back.)

The answer lay in a new weapon and a shift in tactics by Dönitz. The G7e acoustic torpedo had a guidance system which homed in on the noise of the propellers. This weapon had an advantage over the standard torpedoes in that it did not need precise aiming since it steered itself towards the sound of a ship's propellers. The wide aiming tolerance of the acoustic torpedo meant that even poor commanders could now sink ships. Otto himself demonstrated this. He had been a U-boat commander since September 1942 and this was his first – and last – hit in a total of 144 days at sea.

As soon as HMS *Lagan* was hit, the destroyer *Escapade* went after *U-270*, which had not had time to dive. HMS *Escapade* launched a battery of Hedgehog mortars but it misfired causing considerable damage to the destroyer and leaving *U-270* unharmed. The opening round of the battle had resulted in two destroyers being maimed within minutes. They had no choice but to retire from the fray. In the chaos that followed, *U-270* disappeared and played no further part in the attack on the two convoys.

*A G7e acoustic torpedo, designed to home in on a destroyer's propellers. The Allies soon found evasive techniques against what was a formidable threat to escort vessels.*

The actions continued sporadically until 22 November, during which time the convoy lost three escorts and six merchant ships. Amongst these was the particularly tragic loss of HMS *Itchen* to an acoustic torpedo from *U-666*. *Itchen* blew up instantly. She was carrying not only her 233 officers and men, but also survivors from HMCS *St. Croix*, sunk on 20 September. Just two men from *Itchen* and one from *St Croix* survived.

By the end of the battle, the U-boats reported having sunk 12 escorts and nine merchant ships, plus two ships damaged. This news was taken as a sign that the U-boat fleet was once more dominating the convoys. But the true figures were three U-boats sunk and three damaged for the price of three escorts and six merchant ships lost. The German successes were minimal considering that the 21 U-boats had 84 targets to choose from.

Horton's post-battle report to the Admiralty neatly summarised the two sides of the battle: 'This operation was notable in that it marked the renewal of attacks on North Atlantic convoys, and disclosed the use by U-boats of a new anti-escort weapon, the acoustic homing torpedo ("Gnat").' But, he added, 'The offensive action displayed throughout by the escorts of the combined convoys ... prevented the enemy from gaining the initiative and resulted in comparatively light losses in the convoy.' Whether Horton recognised it or not at the time, the battle of Convoys *ONS-18/ON-202* was the last large-scale U-boat attack of the war.

The acoustic torpedo was initially a fearsome weapon, made worse for the Allies by its targeted use against escort vessels. In December three warships – HMSs *Cuckmere*, *Tynedale* and *Holcombe* were hit within two days. *Cuckmere* survived but was found to be beyond repair; *Tynedale* broke her back with the loss of 73 men; and *Holcombe* sank in five minutes, with a loss of 84 men.

There were three principal counter-measures to the acoustic torpedo; two required no technical development. A vessel going very slowly made too little noise for the torpedo homing device to function. Alternatively, a fast vessel could easily outrun these torpedoes. The third option was to tow a noise-making device to act as a decoy. These were called 'foxers'. Usually it took several months for either side to produce a counter-measure to a new hostile device. But on this occasion, Allied intelligence knew by mid-1943 that an acoustic torpedo was under development and the first foxers were in production by the time the first acoustic torpedoes were used in action.

A study of known hits by acoustic torpedoes from September 1943 to the end of the war showed that, of the 32 warships hit, 22 had no counter-measures in use, while just seven were towing a foxer. In all, about 45 ships were sunk by acoustic torpedoes. The torpedoes had proved to be yet one more U-Boat Arm innovation that was countered before it could have any significant impact on the war.

## Naxos GSR receiver

Dönitz urgently needed a means of detecting 10cm radar. This breakthrough came on the night of 2-3 February 1943 when a Stirling bomber was out on a raid and crash-landed near Rotterdam. The plane was equipped with H2S (10cm) radar, which the Germans captured intact except for the cathode ray tube display. They realised the importance of the radar set but were baffled as to how it worked and, without the display system, had no way of seeing precisely what it did. Attempts to tease the secrets out of captured bomber crews initially failed. It was on 23 March that the Director General of Air Equipment, General Erhard Milch, was informed that prisoner interrogation had revealed that the missing displays were used to find targets by scanning the territory below the plane.

The Telefunken Company was set to work to unlock the secrets of this new radar. By a nice irony, their work was delayed when other captured H2S sets were destroyed at their factory by bombing raids – raids doubtless guided by H2S. Soon, though, Telefunken had established the nature of the H2S radar beam. The next step – to build an H2S detector – was achieved by September and the detectors began operational use in November. This first detector was designed for use in German fighters so that they could intercept Allied bombers. But there was an equally urgent need for an H2S detector for the U-boats.

The devices for U-boats – known as Naxos GSR receivers – were operating by September 1943. Once the receivers were in use, Allied operational researchers studied their effectiveness in preventing U-boat sightings. They concluded that the device enabled 25 per cent of boats that would have previously been detected to avoid detection. 44 per cent were detected when using the receiver but managed to dive before they were attacked; 31 per cent of boats gained nothing from their use of the receivers.

*The aerial of a Naxos receiver for detecting the 10cm radar signal from Allied bombers.*

The Naxos system was dependent on a cumbersome aerial that had to be retracted before submerging. When *U-625* was caught in a Leigh light on 2 January 1944 the boat's gunners went into immediate action, hitting the port engine and injuring the radio operator. The plane began to plunge towards the U-boat. When the order was given to dive, the gunners promptly slid down the conning tower ladder. But no one had thought of the two men taking down the Naxos aerial. The hatch closed; the boat dived; and the men drowned. Whether it was lookouts or the Naxos receiver that saved the boat that day, it was found by a Sunderland two months later and sunk. Naxos was not enough to save the U-boat fleet.

*Pound's death*

On 21 October, Admiral Pound, who had been in poor health for some time, died. His obvious successor was Horton. Somebody, somewhere, realised the potentially catastrophic consequences of taking Horton away from the Western Approaches Command; he was not offered the post. This was as he wanted it, telling a friend: 'Even if the post had been offered to me officially I should have refused – I have got Dönitz where I want him, and I intend to keep him there until the war is won!' The post went to the abrasive Admiral of the Fleet Andrew Cunningham.

*Stirling bombers. It was from one of these planes that the Germans captured 10cm radar equipment.*

*Targeting the rescue crews*

It was towards the end of 1943, when Dönitz was increasingly fearful that the U-boat war was irretrievably lost, that he re-issued a controversial order relating to rescue ships. The relevant passage, which was quoted by the prosecution at the Nuremburg Trials, ran:

> A so-called rescue ship is generally attached to every convoy, a special ship of up to 3000 gross registered tons, which is intended for the picking up of survivors after U-boat attacks. These ships are, for the most part, equipped with a shipborne aircraft and large motor-boats, are strongly armed with depth-charge throwers, and very manoeuvrable, so that they are often called U-Boat Traps by the commander. In view of the desired destruction of ships' crews, their sinking is of great value.

The timing of this re-issued order is significant. Dönitz had set out on a tonnage war; it had failed to defeat the Allies. At times, he prioritised tankers, but that strategy was also unsuccessful. Then he switched to sinking escort ships with acoustic torpedoes; that too failed. By late 1943 he was reduced to not just sinking ships but to encouraging his men to make sure that the seamen died with their ships.

Of course Dönitz was careful in his language. He had no intention of leaving a printed order to authorise murder. But, as the Nuremburg prosecutor pointed out, it was one thing to sink rescue ships in the confused mêlée of battle, but another thing to make them a priority target.

*Scharnhorst sunk*

The year 1943 was to finish with an irony that Dönitz – always a U-boat man – perhaps never noticed.

The war was going badly for the Nazi régime and the Allies were shipping supplies to the Soviet Union via the Arctic route in vast quantities. Because so much has been written about Convoy PQ-17, and because the Arctic route was particularly gruelling, the success of the Nazis in attacking these convoys is often overstated. In fact 93 per cent of the goods shipped by this route reached Russia, totalling four million tons. If all had gone to plan, Dönitz's U-boats would have been there in late 1943 to destroy the convoys. But his fleet was now too small to cover all war theatres and too vulnerable to Allied escort methods. So, in December 1943, the Grand Admiral fell back on sending out the *Scharnhorst* to attack the Arctic convoys. It was a humiliating come-down for a man who had so opposed Raeder's prestigious surface fleet. The details of the Battle of North Cape on 26 December 1943 need not concern us, but the outcome is highly relevant to the Battle of the Atlantic. The *Scharnhorst* left Norway on 25 December in search of Convoy *JW-55B*. Sailing with no escort, *Scharnhorst* met Force 1 at 9.00 am on 26 December. Force 1 included the three cruisers *Belfast*, *Norfolk* and *Sheffield*. After initially escaping from the force, *Scharnhorst* was found again at 4.48 pm when star shell from HMS *Belfast* revealed the unprotected vessel. She immediately came under the combined fire of HMSs *Duke of York*, *Jamaica* and *Belfast*. By 7.45 pm, *Scharnhorst* had capsized and sunk. Nearly 2000 men were drowned. The loss of the *Scharnhorst* was primarily due to two factors: first, going back to the Z-Plan, Raeder had built capital ships without any form of escort to protect them, only to allow them to face the much bigger forces of the Royal Navy; and second, as Dönitz rightly concluded, British radar was far superior to German radar. With the destruction of the *Scharnhorst* Germany had lost its main means of fighting in the seas around Norway and in the Arctic. Now the U-Boat Arm would be stretched even more thinly.

### An enfeebled U-Boat Arm

The year 1943 had been a rollercoaster year ride for both sides. Horton had taken the Allies from imminent defeat in the Battle of the Atlantic to being masters of the seas. The U-boats were now a menace rather than a threat. Many lower-ranking men and women also had their personal triumphs that year. In particular Walker had reason to feel smugly satisfied. There was fulsome praise from Horton when he recognised Walker's creeping attack as 'one of the main features' in his success. Horton continued, 'the attention of commanding officers is once again being drawn to its value'. This was high praise for a man who is said to have refused to attend the Tobermory course.

In December 1943 Dönitz had 129 boats at his Atlantic bases, down 25 since December 1942 – a reduction of 16 per cent. Superficially that is a small reduction but with the ever-growing Allied air strength and the search-power of 10cm radar and HF/DF, Dönitz needed an increase in boats if he was to maintain the tonnage sunk rate. And that he was far from doing. In December 1942 his boats sank 330,000 tons in the Atlantic; this had shrunk to 87,000 tons in December 1943.

Another problem for which Dönitz had no obvious solution was manning, particularly finding new commanders. Every U-boat sunk or captured meant the loss of a trained commander. As the aces disappeared they were replaced by hastily trained novices which, said Cremer 'gave them no idea of the actual conditions'. Nor did this training give the newcomers time to learn how to outwit the wide range of Allied defence tactics.

To add to Dönitz's multitudinous problems, the wider war was about to constrain his options. In November Hitler was considering how to fend off an Allied invasion of Europe. With no indication of 'where' and 'when' Hitler came to the conclusion that the Allies would invade via Northern Europe or, possibly, by landing in Denmark. It was time to put more of his forces on the defensive. And that meant more U-boats in the North Sea. He told Dönitz: 'A temporary diminution of submarine forces in the Atlantic must be accepted.'

Dönitz had little to comfort him. The year ended with him telling his commanders: 'The fifth Christmas at war finds us, both at the front and at home, firmly and more determinedly than ever behind our "Führer" in the battle for our future.'

# 32 In the shadow of D-Day

## January to June 1944

### U-boats at bay

On 4 January 1944 Russian units entered Poland. Two weeks later the British X Corps had begun to engage German forces at Monte Cassino in Italy. On 8 February the Allies agreed the details of Operation Overlord – the invasion of Normandy. The war in the west was now a land war with the Nazi forces losing ground day by day. The U-boat war had failed to fulfil Dönitz's ambition to cripple Allied operations by attacking the Atlantic supply lines and so pre-empt an invasion. But, as long as there was no invasion in Northern Europe, Dönitz continued to believe that he would yet prevail.

Having been forced out of the mid-Atlantic, Dönitz concentrated his boats in the Bay of Biscay in the hope of attacking south-bound and Mediterranean-bound convoys. For once, his boats were supported by long-range planes. He had great hopes of this new strategy, but Walker's Escort Group of *Starling*, *Wild Goose*, *Woodpecker*, *Magpie* and *Wren* had other ideas. Walker was despatched to the area in support of various convoys over a 20-day period.

When Walker's group arrived in Biscay, its first task was to support the 81 ships of Convoy *SL-147*. On the scene were the two escort carriers, HMS *Nairana* (on her first patrol) and HMS *Activity*. He deployed his own ships to form an outer screen at six miles from the convoy. The carriers were to stand further out during the day, coming inside the convoy at night when they would not be able to operate their aircraft. On the day that Walker's group arrived, U-boat radio traffic indicated that about ten boats were nearby. By the following day this had increased to around 15 boats. Dönitz was taking the convoy seriously.

At dawn on 9 February the sea was heavy and visibility was poor from dense mist. As men moved around the decks of the ships, every sound was eerily muffled in the deadened atmosphere. The weather and sea conditions were strange; throughout the three-week running battle asdic proved unreliable and even plain misleading. Men's eyes and ears were to take its place.

*The escort carrier HMS Nairana which could carry up to 20 planes.*

Able Seaman J G Wall in *Wild Goose* was the first sailor to make up for the deficiencies of asdic when he spotted a U-boat trimmed down to the top half of its conning tower. He estimated that it was one-and-a-half miles ahead of the ship. As soon as Walker heard the report, he ordered the convoy to change course, leaving *Wild Goose* to chase the U-boat. The boat promptly dived but as *Wild Goose* neared its position it re-surfaced. Once more it was Wall who saw its periscope rising out of the sea. *Wild Goose* was too far away to use her depth charges so Commander David Wemyss ordered the guns into action. The boat submerged. By now *Woodpecker* had arrived. Walker directed

*Woodpecker* in a creeping attack. Twenty-six depth charges later the sea rose up from a massive explosion in the depths. Walker ordered a star shell display. In the blaze of light the seamen gazed down on the strewn debris from the U-boat. *Starling* let down a boat to collect a coat and other items to testify to the successful sinking.

That night the convoy escaped attack from *U-264*. It was potentially a major threat since it had been fitted with a snorkel in December. Spotting it would be near to impossible at the best of times; with asdic proving so troublesome, *U-264* was in a strong position to attack. Her commander, Hartwig Looks, was one of the Olympia Crew and had sunk 17,000 tons of shipping. But luck was not with Looks that night. He moved into an attack position ahead of the convoy and dived. Suddenly his hydrophones stopped working. He surfaced and found that he had lost sight of the convoy.

Early on 9 February the U-boats were busy signalling – almost certainly responding to imperative calls from Dönitz to report their positions. The escorts' HF/DF sets showed the boats to be 10 miles ahead of the convoy – a perfect attack position. But before the U-boats could move into action, *Magpie* and *Kite* had been despatched to tackle one of the boats. Their search proved simple: *Kite* was careering through the heavy sea when up popped the U-boat at 800 yards. The boat crash-dived and Lieutenant Commander Segram reduced speed for fear of encountering a gnat. He dropped a depth charge to act as a decoy and was rewarded by a gigantic double explosion as an unseen gnat and the charge detonated in unison.

Meanwhile *Wild Goose* had made contact with a U-boat. Commander Wemyss ordered 7 knots to avoid gnat detection. Then, in a show of snowflake, he saw a boat preparing to dive. Before he could take any evasive action, a tower of water rose in the sea, where a gnat had outrun its course and harmlessly exploded. By now it was clear that the acoustic torpedoes were a major threat to the escort, although the commanders were skilfully anticipating them and taking evasive action. But sinking the U-boats was better than evasive action. Walker directed *Wild Goose* in a creeping attack, but without success. The night's work ended with a third expended Gnat harmlessly detonating.

*A camouflaged snorkel. The benefits of the device were far out-weighed by the slow speed of a snorkel-using U-boat.*

Walker's *Starling* was the target of an attack at 9.00 am the next day. Yet again it was a lookout who saw the torpedo speeding towards the ship. The situation seemed hopeless – there was no way that *Starling* could race her way to safety. It was Walker's quick brain that brought salvation. He yelled 'Hard a'port' and called for depth charges at shallow depth. The rule book would have called this a suicidal move since *Starling* would be caught by her own charges. The ship swung to port as terrified seamen lay flat on the deck. Five yards off *Starling's* quarter deck her own depth charges went off just as they caught the torpedo. A mountain of water rose to engulf *Starling*, as the reserve depth charges rolled off the deck into the sea. The knife switches below jumped and every bottle in the wardroom was a mass of shards. But *Starling* had survived.

The ship shook off its drenching. The knife switches were re-set. And the officers and men once more thanked the heavens for having Walker as their commander. Within minutes Walker was directing *Wild Goose* in a creeping attack; 150 depth charges, and three hours later, the wreckage of *U-734* rose to the surface. One more U-boat that had never sunk a thing was gone, along with Hans-Jörg Blauert, who had achieved nothing in his year as a U-boat commander.

Walker had been lucky in depth-charging a Gnat so close to his ship. Lieutenant Commander W F Segram, in *Kite*, was less lucky when he tried the same trick. From the deck of *Starling*, *Kite* disappeared as the sea seemed to rise up to swallow her. She reappeared, all in one piece, as the water fell back. But it was soon clear that she had sprung enough leaks to be relegated to the side-lines.

This still left a nearby U-boat to be despatched. Twenty-six depth charges from *Magpie* failed to find the boat. Walker decided that a new approach was needed. He sent *Magpie* on a creeping attack with Hedgehog while *Starling* was dropping depth charges. Their reward was a simultaneous double explosion. For insurance, Walker added ten depth charges to ensure that neither vessel would succumb to a Gnat. Soon the remains of *U-238* confirmed the effectiveness of Walker's latest ingenuity.

The U-boats had now had enough of Walker's methods. Convoy *SL-147* was left to continue its passage. On the following day Walker's group was supporting Convoy *HX-277*, which provided another opportunity for *Wild Goose* and *Magpie* to work together as they destroyed a U-boat with their depth charges. Then it was on to supporting Convoy *ON-224* on 19 February.

*U-264*, which had lost Convoy *SL-147*, was now hovering around Convoy *ON-224*. Walker and his group found Looks to be a very determined commander. Hour after hour they pounded his boat with depth charges. But Walker was equally determined. Gradually the damage inside *U-264* became more and more serious. The lights had ceased working and the engines had parted from their mountings, while one propeller was jammed. Looks might have attempted to creep away had the snorkel not malfunctioned. But the men and the boat had reached their limit. *U-264* surfaced into a rough sea and gunfire at 5.00 pm. Looks was the last to leave after setting the scuttling charges. The firing ceased as *Starling*, *Wild Goose* and *Woodpecker* pulled the whole crew out of the water.

Soon after the sinking of *U-264*, *Kite* developed engine problems and was ordered back to Liverpool. Then a gnat finally found a target as the stern was ripped off *Woodpecker*.

Walker's group had sunk six U-boats and captured the crew of one of them. Not a single merchant ship was lost in the area during those 20 days. The price was just *Woodpecker*, which lost her stern and foundered when being towed to port in a gale.

This success provided Horton with a grand opportunity for morale-raising back home. When Walker's Escort Group steamed up the Mersey in February 1944 the harbour sides were lined with cheering crowds and a band played *A-hunting We Will Go*. The complements from various warships, including *King George V* were lined up, along the quay, along with Wrens, merchant sailors and dockyard workers. When Walker landed he was met and congratulated by Horton, the Lord Mayor, and A V Alexander, the First Lord of the Admiralty.

*Wild Goose's triumphal entry to Liverpool in February 1944.*

There was little room for congratulations in the U-Boat Arm, but there was, though, a new piece of technology on the way. On 10 January *U-267* slipped out of St Nazaire for work in the Bay of Biscay. It was there for the first deployment of Thetis 2c decoys – a new deception device. Thetis consisted of a buoy on which was mounted a wooden mast, topped with a metal dipole. On an Allied radar screen this device would have looked like a U-boat. Dönitz looked forward to Allied planes and warships chasing after these miasmas in a sea otherwise empty of Kriegsmarine activity. The decoys were dropped in the Atlantic from January to August, as far west as 31 degrees. They never seem to have bothered the Allies much, but they were a hassle to the U-boats: storing and handling a five-metre device was not easy. By August the U-Boat Arm decided that U-boat space was needed for 'more important things'.

*U-267's* role in deploying the ineffective Thetis gives us a chance to look at the boat itself, which proved to be of doubtful value to the U-Boat Arm or

322

the German war effort. It was remarkable for both its longevity and its futile performance. It had been commissioned on 11 June 1942, had undertaken seven war patrols, and would be the last boat to leave St Nazaire on 23 September 1944, from where it went to Stavanger. It effectively survived the war when its commander, Bernhard Knieper, choose to scuttle it on 5 May 1945. During its unproductive life it was depth-charged three times. On the first two occasions the damage was slight; the third attack caused more serious damage but the boat was back in service two months later. Yet, in all that time *U-267* never sank or damaged an Allied ship. It was symbolic of how ineffective many of Dönitz's boats and commanders were.

With his diminishing number of operational U-boats, Dönitz could not afford patrols that failed to find convoys. He became increasingly dependent on search planes to locate convoys and guide his boats to them. Yet the fiasco of mid-February showed how far short he was of this requirement. Two Junkers 88s, seventeen Junkers 290s, three Focke-Wulf 200s and two BV 222 flying boats were sent out to reconnoitre between 13 and 18 February. The loss of three Junkers 290s to an Allied escort carrier was rewarded with a positive convoy sighting. But that intensive reconnaissance mission had left the Luftwaffe without men and planes to shadow the convoy and guide the U-boats to it. The convoy sailed on unmolested. So short-manned was the Luftwaffe at this stage, that they told Godt that he would have to accept a 14-day rest period before each two- to three-day reconnaissance mission.

Back in London there was a degree of relief as the nightmare of the U-boat war began to recede in early 1944 and the much anticipated invasion of Europe raised hopes of an early end to the war. It was in this optimistic atmosphere that A V Alexander, First Lord of the Admiralty, sought Parliament's approval for the Royal Navy's 1944-45 expenditure. He opened his speech in the House of Commons on 7 March with a report on the turnaround in the Battle of the Atlantic, noting that in 1941 the Allies had lost one ship out of every 181 that sailed. By 1942 this was down to one in every 233; and in 1943 losses had fallen to one in every 344. He attributed this success to 'the growth and efficiency of Coastal Command' and 'the skill and the leadership of the senior officers of our escort groups'. And, perhaps anticipating the memoirs and histories that would flood the bookshops after the war, he singled out (a rarity in such a debate) three commanders for special praise: Captain F J Walker, CB, DSO; Commander P W Gretton, DSO; and Commander A A Tait, DSO, who had died in March 1943 when HMS *Harvester* was sunk by *U-432*.

While Alexander could pause to offer congratulations and report victories, Godt and Dönitz fretted over the decreasing level of air support and their rapidly diminishing boat numbers. By March 1944 the 130 operational boats that had been in the Atlantic at 1 January were down to 109. New commissions were failing to keep pace with the combination of losses and boat withdrawals to the Mediterranean and the Arctic. Of the 11 newly commissioned boats in January, six went to Northern Waters; in February eight out of eighteen new boats went there in anticipation of an Allied landing in Norway.

What Dönitz needed was a step-change in his armoury.

That step-change was, he hoped, the snorkel. (We have seen how *U-264* was an early recipient of this.) The snorkel was a device to allow a U-boat to emit its diesel exhaust to the atmosphere and take in fresh air while submerged. It consisted of a telescopic mast with a set of valves at its top to exchange gases. A critical part of the design was its floating valve, which closed the air intake when the boat submerged or the waves washed over it. Dönitz was ecstatic at the prospect of his boats roaming the seas out of sight of the Allied ships and planes, telling Hitler in January that, 'we shall slash Britain's supply with a new submarine weapon'.

However, like so many Kriegsmarine innovations, the snorkel was rushed into service in a primitive state. There were the simple mechanical problems like failures in the raising and lowering mechanism. There were breakdowns in the ventilation systems that could leave seamen gasping for air as their boats filled with diesel exhaust. These issues could have been fixed with a longer development period, but there were more fundamental issues of principle that Dönitz had failed to think through.

As long as a boat was using its snorkel, it was stuck at its low submerged speed. A snorkel-fitted boat traversed around 50 to 60 miles a day and could be outrun by even the slowest cargo ships in the Atlantic. Dönitz was trading mobility (the essence of warfare by 1944) for security. The snorkel might save his boats from air attack; it would not lead them to convoys moving at six or seven knots. Worse, a snorkel-submerged boat could neither use its radio to transmit nor its hydrophones, nor could it dispose of waste. (Boats could still receive U-Boat Arm radio signals from the long wave 15 kHz to 25 kHz Goliath transmitter.)

Living with a snorkel was not a pleasant experience. The U-boat ace Günter Hessler (who was incidentally Dönitz's son-in-law) recalled: 'The atmosphere, which was always pretty foul in a snorkel boat, was further polluted by the stench of decaying waste food and other refuse. The odour was so repulsive that dockyard workers recoiled from the open hatch of a returning snort boat.' Later the U-Boat Arm recommended bundling up refuse and stuffing it in a torpedo tube. Once full, the waste could be ejected by firing it as if it were a torpedo. Even so, the men were implored to 'Use as few fresh provisions as possible so that there will be little evil-smelling waste.' In essence, the snorkel was a defensive device. That Dönitz placed so much reliance on it tells us a good deal about his state of mind in early 1944.

While the snorkel had no impact on the continuing Allied ascendency, Dönitz clung to his greatest hope: the Walter U-boat. Professor Hellmuth Walter, a leading German engineer, had first suggested in 1933 that a U-boat could be powered by a hydrogen peroxide-based ($H_2O_2$) fuel that supplied its own oxygen, so not needing to take in air from the atmosphere. In the following year he produced a design for a 300-ton submarine that had an underwater speed of 30 knots. But it was not until 1939 that the Kriegsmarine commissioned a U-boat based on this design. The prototype that took to the water in 1940 managed an impressive 23 knots submerged. The first war-ready boat (*U-792*) was delivered in September 1943, more or less as a one-off.

The leap from the diesel U-boat to the Walter boat was potentially as important as the Allied leap from 1.5 m radar to 10-cm radar. But the Allies had the materials and manpower to manufacture radar sets by the tens of thousands in time to make a difference. Dönitz had no access to the men and materials needed to turn out Walter boats. And the production sites were high-priority targets for Allied planes. They scored a particularly significant hit when they bombed the Siemens-Schuckert Works in February 1944, where the electric motors for the boats were produced. And, with a design so far ahead of traditional U-boats, there was no potential for substitute component supplies. As a result there were just ten completed Walter boats at the end of the war, not one of them having been in action.

By March 1944 the intensive Allied air attacks in the Bay of Biscay and the increasing presence of Allied craft in the Biscay coastal waters, finally forced Dönitz to end escorting U-boats in their initial passage to sea. Having lost the Battle of the Atlantic, Dönitz now had to fight a last-ditch battle to protect the coast from sea and air attack.

D-Day, though, was calling.

*D-day*

By April 1944 all German forces in the west lived in anticipation of the inevitable Allied invasion. Here was an opportunity for Dönitz's boats to prove themselves to be indispensable. An invasion meant thousands of vessels – more targets than history had ever seen in one place before. Still with no idea of where the landing beaches would be, he made plans for seven groups of boats to be spread from the Channel port of Dieppe in the east to Bordeaux on the Atlantic coast in the south.

But his orders spoke more of bravado than confidence. While he wrote that, 'Every man and weapon destroyed *before* reaching the beaches lessens the enemy's chances of ultimate success,' he also said that, 'Every boat that inflicts losses on the enemy while he is landing has fulfilled its primary function even though it perishes in so doing.' When the detailed order came, Werner recalls 'deadly silence gripped the room'. The order ran:

ATTACK AND SINK INVASION FLEET WITH THE
FINAL OBJECTIVE OF DESTROYING ENEMY SHIPS BY
RAMMING

It was to be a kamikaze attack. Not surprisingly, all leave – even in port – was banned. Men went ashore under escort for a frenzy of activities – bus rides, hikes, games – to take their minds off the Reich's final demand: their lives.

*D-Day landings, unimpeded by Dönitz's 70 boats that were at sea.*

Just six days before the landings, Dönitz had 70 U-boats ready to repel the invasion fleet. If he lacked any warning of what was to come, he only needed to note that six boats had been sunk on their way from Norway to the Channel. Nor were Dönitz's boats to lack a welcome when they moved in for the attack.

Even as he was making his D-Day dispositions, five Escort Support Groups were on patrol at the western end of the Channel. Overhead, British, Canadian, Australian and American planes monitored activity in the French ports.

When the first Allied warships were detected sailing towards the Normandy beaches in the early hours of 6 June, Dönitz realised how few of his boats were anywhere near the landing areas. Thirty-six of them were lying in wait along the Atlantic coast off Brest, St Nazaire, La Pallice and Lorient. Hurried orders sent them north. Meanwhile, on the previous day, *U-704* had been sunk by a Liberator off the Brittany coast with the loss of all hands. It was an early warning of what was waiting to greet Dönitz's boats. Two were sunk as they approached the Channel from the west and four were badly damaged by aircraft. Of those boats that succeeded in attacking the invasion fleet, their performance was no more than a gnat's bite on the elephant of the mighty force. During the initial landings, the boats sank seven escorts, three landing ships, and 13 freighters, totalling 59,000 tons. They had 6939 targets to choose from. Nothing could have more vividly demonstrated the irrelevance of the U-boats in the face of the stupendous size of the forces that the Allies had assembled.

During the first two weeks after the D-Day landings Dönitz anxiously awaited news from his boats, especially those that he had sent to attempt a passage up the River Seine. At the same time he was also using boats to deliver war materials to Cherbourg, where the situation was 'very grave, deep penetration into fortress, which can no longer hold out until transport boats arrive'. The U-Boat Arm was ordered to support the land forces 'by every available means'. As the land war began to eclipse that of the Atlantic, a mere five U-boats returned from D-Day. Dönitz was compelled to bow to events.

# 33 After D-Day

## July to December 1944

### Masters of the seas

On 3 August 1944 a seemingly endless flotilla of ships appeared at the mouth of the Mersey. They spread so far and in such numbers that no onlooker could count them nor see the limit of their extent. This was the major part of the 159 ships of Convoy *HX-300*, the largest convoy of the war. It had sailed from Halifax, Nova Scotia, on 17 July and had crossed the Atlantic unmolested. Its statistics were staggering. The ships carried over one million tons of cargo, including 220,000 tons of foodstuffs and 310,000 tons of petroleum products. Also aboard were over 10,000 vehicles. Most of these ships were to unload at British ports. Others were destined for Iceland. Fifty-nine ships were onward-bound to the Soviet Union. It was just two months since the Allies had demonstrated that they ruled the Channel as the invasion fleet defied the U-boats. Convoy *HX-300* showed that the Atlantic was now theirs as well.

### The end of the Atlantic bases

This mastery was evident to Vice Admiral Schirlitz, naval commander of the Atlantic Coast, when he noted in mid-July that there was not one German surface vessel to be seen on the Atlantic coast at La Rochelle: 'The enemy in this sea area feels himself totally safe', he said. Schirlitz's sea contact with the Reich was cut. Behind him the massing Allied armies prepared to cut off the Atlantic ports from contact with the German forces to the east.

Life on the beleaguered bases grew harder by the day. The repair yards faced increasing difficulties as the Allies strengthened their hold on western France. Supplies by rail and sea had now stopped. Totally dependent on air freight, the yards at Brest – which had full order books – continued to work on repairs to nine U-boats and 35 small vessels. Labour, though, was critically short. By 15 July, 250 of the 6000 French workers had already melted away.

Those who still wished to work were often thwarted by a lack of public transport. And, on top of all those problems, sabotage of the plant and the rail lines was increasing.

From Dönitz's viewpoint the war had left him behind. The Channel seethed with Allied warships, the air above was patrolled by Allied planes and the Wehrmacht was fully engaged with the massive invasion force. His boats could only go through the motions of attacking the invasion force in the months after the D-Day landings. By early July he had a mere 13 boats in what was called the Western Group. Some typical entries from the War Log tell all:

1 July

Reports of Successes: None.

2 July

Air reconnaissance: None.

> The U-boat situation in operations area Seine Bay is still not clear, as boats have not reported. Also there have been no U-boat sightings in this area for the past week. There is therefore the possibility that there have been very heavy losses, especially as a broadcast from the Calais propaganda transmitter speaks of the sinking of 10 boats in the Channel area. (So far this station's reports of U-boat losses have always been accurate).

The end for the bases could not be far off. In early August the 2nd Minesweeping Flotilla began evacuating German workers from Lorient, while U-boats carried out evacuations from the other Atlantic bases. Those U-boats making their return passage to the bases faced heavy Allied opposition as they entered the Bay of Biscay. Seven out of the 15 boats were sunk. Meanwhile the last 13 boats at Brest were ready to leave. Still in their berths, the RAF arrived on 5 August and dropped four Tallboy bombs on the Brest bunkers. These bunkers lacked the latest form of reinforcement so the Tallboys burst into the berthing area below. Despite this attack, all but two of the boats were later able to sail. Although the Tallboy damage to the boats was modest, the bombing had a devastating effect on the French workers. They fled in panic. The Germans had no will to force them to return. For these workers the agony of their war was over.

The Atlantic bases were now worthless. Lacking workers and supplies, threatened by land, sea and air, they were no longer a safe haven for the U-boats. On 26 August Dönitz ordered the remaining boats to sail for Norway. The end had come so suddenly that many of the crews were still on home leave. Scratch crews faced the terrifying prospect of taking the boats through perilous waters, thick with Allied craft. Many never reached Norway.

All that the Germans could now do was to deny the harbour facilities to the Allies. Mines were strewn in the entrances, block ships were sunk and there were even attempts to blow up the bunkers with torpedo warheads. But the bunkers were the one thing the U-boat service got right. They resisted all attempts at destruction. At Bordeaux much of the demolition was thwarted by a non-commissioned officer who blew up the explosives store.

The capture of the Atlantic ports would prove a monumental task for the Allied armies – Saint-Nazaire did not surrender until after the official end of the war. At La Rochelle, Vice Admiral Schirlitz, with no Atlantic coast left to command, lead 22,000 soldiers in defending the city against the Allied siege until their capitulation on 7 May 1945.

By September the U-Boat Arm was severely weakened and could only manage 15 sinkings in all sectors. Attempts to continue attacking convoys around Newfoundland, the Caribbean and the Gold Coast were abandoned. So too were the continuing operations in the Channel. It was taking seven to nine weeks to reach from Norway as the snorkel-equipped boats spent long periods submerged. With the end of their attacks against the invasion force, all operations were now squeezed into the northern British coastal waters and off Reykjavik. But even these sorties were perilous. In August, 12 out of 23 boats were lost on their first patrol. Not only was the operational area decreasing, but so was the number of available bases. Allied bombing of German ports and harbours now rendered these unsafe for U-boat servicing. (There were no bomb-proof bunkers in German ports.) All boats from now on were based in Norwegian ports.

While the U-boats would continue to find occasional opportunities for sinking small vessels in coastal waters, where the snorkel proved an effective aid to avoiding detection, the overall picture was one of a broken service. In the last six months of 1944, U-boat convoy sinkings averaged only 43,000 tons a month. Against Dönitz's first estimate that he needed to sink 700,000 tons a month, and his later realisation that the figure was more like 1 million tons a month, the performance of his boast was derisory.

*The battleship Tirpitz, sunk by RAF bombers in November 1944. Her prodigious fuel consumption never compensated for her minor role in the war.*

To add to the desperate position in which the U-Boat Arm now was, the great battleship *Tirpitz* was bombed as she lay in Ofotfjord in Norway on 12 November and capsized. In a subsequent explosion around 1000 men lost their lives. This was the last of Raeder's great vessels that were intended to annihilate the convoys. The ship had played a negligible part in the war but its few brief sorties had consumed vast quantities of fuel oil.

# 34 Dönitz dreams on

## January to May 1945

*Dönitz in denial*

In the last five months of the European war, Dönitz's boats sank 330,000 tons of merchant shipping: 66,000 tons per month. This was at a cost of 171 U-boats sunk by the Allies. Gone were the times when Dönitz could report his boats as sinking hundreds of tons per boat per day. In January his operational boats managed 30 tons per day. February was better at 70 tons per day.

It is hard to reconcile these feeble figures with the delusional reports that Dönitz gave to Hitler at this time. While he was awaiting the return of four boats from British coastal waters in January he admitted that they might not return and made the case for further 'intensive operations' but argued that 'shipping losses so near their coast must be very unpleasant to the British'. He told Hitler that he would have 60 more boats ready to sail by the end of February 'unless further serious damage was done to yards in the near future'. It sounded as if he thought the U-boat war was about to return to full-scale operations.

Dönitz's delusions continued in February when he reported to Hitler that he had lost seven boats in recent operations but they had each sunk an average of 4.4 vessels. Assuming that he had around 20 boats in operational areas during January, such a rate of sinking would equal 80 vessels in the month. The true figure was around 20.

Even these over-estimated daily tonnage sunk rates were low compared to the glory days of 1942. Dönitz's answer to this was to announce that he would shorten the turn-round time of the boats in harbour. This, he said, would be achieved by an increase in skilled dockyard workers. Where and how he was to find these workers when every corner of the Reich was desperate for labour was not made clear.

334

Meanwhile Dönitz was explaining why he was *not* extending the U-boat operational areas at this time. The problem was the Type VIIC boat – the commonest U-boat in his fleet. Its slow submerged speed made it useless for reaching remote operational areas underwater. (Surface passage was now an impossibility.) Only the arrival of the Walter boats could re-open the attacks on the Atlantic convoys.

## Walter U-boats

In the closing months of the European war it seemed more than likely that Germany would be defeated with the technology that she had. The Allies could out-produce Germany in men, tanks, guns, planes ... Only some technological advance could reverse the daily attrition of German resources. The V-1 unmanned planes, the V-2 rockets, and the Walter U-boats were all potentially able to change the course of the war. In the case of the rockets and planes, they failed because there were so few of them. In all they dropped 2500 tons of explosive material on London in the last nine months of the war. American planes dropped 3000 tons of explosive on Berlin in *one day* on 18 March 1945.

As to the Walter boats, they never reached the stage of significant deployment in war. They were delayed by two factors. First, their design was complex and problematic. While Germany was losing ground and resources day by day, only easily produced, reliable technology made much sense. The cutting-edge Walter boats were too experimental for the ominous position of the German war. The second factor that delayed production was astute Allied bombing. To protect production, Speer had a mass of distributed sites far apart, each producing one section of a pre-fabricated boat. Since these massive sections needed railways and canals for delivery to the final assembly sites, railways and canals became high-priority bombing targets. (This method of delivery also severely restricted the size and shape of the hull so as to ensure that it could be transported to the assembly area.) However, despite these problems the first Walter boat was commissioned in February 1945.

Within days of that commissioning, U-boat production was being discussed at Yalta in early February, where the Allied commanders were in conference. The First Sea Lord, Admiral Andrew Cunningham, spoke of the need to capture the U-boat assembly sites in Kiel, Hamburg and Danzig. He asked Stalin whether Danzig was yet within artillery range of the advancing Soviet forces. Stalin replied that his forces had not yet taken Danzig but forecast that it would soon be in Russian hands. It was taken on 30 March.

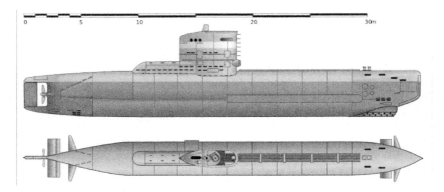

*A modern drawing of a Walter U-boat by Heriberto Arribas Abato.*

Even as Dönitz was urging Hitler to allocate more resources to the Walter boats, he was engaged in a massive building operation of conventional boats. By 23 February he had 237 boats undergoing trials or in training and another 114 under construction. He knew (because he himself had argued the case) that the future belonged to the Walter boats, but he remained obsessed with producing what he acknowledged to be an obsolete machine. The very next day reality broke in as five of the Walter boats were destroyed by Allied bombing of the A G Weser yard in Bremen. Irrespective of which type of boat Dönitz built, few had any prospect of entering service given the six-month training period needed for new crews.

Despite the Allied bombing and the technical complications, the first six Walter boats became operational in April. Between them they sank or damaged

14,500 tons of Allied shipping. But this Type XXIII boat was too late. In the first two weeks of April, 24 Type XXIIIs were destroyed by Allied bombing and 12 were damaged. These raids truly marked the end of the Battle of the Atlantic.

Nor were the Allies completely unprepared had Dönitz ever succeeded in producing a mass of Walter boats. According to Horton, his staff had been working on methods to defeat the new boats and had been modifying British submarines to make them faster. His escort commanders were already being trained in methods for hunting down the un-huntable (as Dönitz thought) boats. It was almost as if Horton was relishing the new challenge.

### Last days of the U-boats

Dönitz's surreal view of his position enabled him to not see or to ignore what was going on around him. While he was moving from one delusional idea to another for re-invigorating the U-boat war, the Reich had other priorities. On 13 January 1945 Soviet Union troops began their East Prussian Offensive. Rescuing the fleeing German population became a priority for the Kriegsmarine. Every available ship and U-boat was sent into the Baltic to take off the trapped population.

The relentless Soviet advance reached Danzig (now Gdansk) on 28 March and the U-boat construction sites there fell into Russian hands. 136 had been built here, many in the famous Hala U-Bootow (U-boat hall). All the half-built boats and the stock of materials and components were lost to the U-Boat Arm.

### A new Chancellor

On 30 April 1945 Hitler received the news that Soviet forces were only a few blocks away from his Berlin bunker. He had already told his military leaders that he would shoot himself rather than be captured. On 29 April he had married his mistress, Eva Braun. As the Soviet guns boomed on the surface, deep in the bunker Hitler put a pistol to his head and pulled the trigger. By his side, Eva Braun bit into a cyanide pill.

Under the terms of Hitler's will, Dönitz became Chancellor of the Reich. With Berlin in the hands of the Allies, he and his ministers fled to Flensburg-Mürwik near the Danish border to set up a new government.

On 1 May Dönitz spoke to the German people, announcing the formation of his government. After praising Hitler who 'had recognised the frightful danger of Bolshevism and dedicated his existence to this struggle', he declared that, 'It is my first task to save Germany from destruction by the advancing Bolshevist enemy.' Dönitz intended to continue the war.

Sometime around 6 May Dönitz wrote an address that he intended to give to his officials. Whether he ever gave it is not known, but since it includes his last words on the U-boats during wartime, what he said is of considerable interest. He told his staff that Germany had to accept 'total capitulation' even though it was 'especially bitter' since the British would get hold of the U-boats. He had wanted to destroy the boats but General Eisenhower had demanded immediate unconditional surrender. If Dönitz did not accept this, Eisenhower would return all German troops and civilians fleeing the east back to the Russians. As Dönitz saw it he was making a great *personal* sacrifice in not destroying the U-boats in order to save the German people from the Soviet Union troops.

As well as losing his U-boats at the end of the war, Dönitz had lost his two sons during the war. The younger, Peter, was a submariner. He had been a watch officer on *U-954* when it was attacked by a Liberator bomber on 19 May 1943. There were no survivors. On Peter's death, his elder brother, Klaus, was removed from naval combat duty to train to be doctor. Although forbidden to take up a combat role, he celebrated his twenty-fourth birthday by going out with the *S-141* E-boat for an attack on Selsey. The French destroyer *La Combattante* and the British frigate HMS *Rowley* intercepted *S-141* and the other E-boats alongside it. *Combattante* opened fire on *S-141*, destroying the lightly-built wooden boat. Six crew members were pulled from the water, but Klaus had perished.

*U-boats surrendering to the Harwich force.*

### U-Boat surrenders

The first U-boat to surrender was *U-249* commanded by Oberleutnant zur See Uwe Kock on 10 May. He had been in command of the boat for ten months but had been out on patrol for a mere 48 days, during which time he had sunk nothing. The boat had seen 18 months of service with no sinkings. Some boats that turned themselves in were a greater relief to the Allies. *U-532* not only came with a fearful record – 47,000 tons sunk – but was carrying a cargo that Germany sorely needed. Its hull was stuffed with 110 tons of tin, 601 tons of rubber, eight tons of wolfram (a mineral rich in tungsten, vital for hardened warheads) and five tons of molybdenum ore (used in many items of military hardware). It was blockade-running cargo boats like these that had sustained Germany's armaments industry for the six years of the war.

By the last day of May, 49 boats had surrendered at sea. The final tally was 156 surrenders, leaving around 220 boats that had been scuttled by their crews. The Allies retained some of the boats for various purposes, but 116 were scuttled in Operation Deadlight between November 1945 and February 1946 somewhere out in the Atlantic – a fitting resting place for the boats that had so nearly brought Britain to the point of surrender. By that time the boats were in a poor state: 56 of them sank of their own accord while being towed out to the scuttling zone.

The U-boat crews which survived had been lucky. Of all the branches of the German forces, the U-boats had the highest mortality rate at 75 per cent. 793 U-boats had been sunk, and 28,000 men had died at sea.

*Three guilty men in captivity. Albert Speer (Reich Minister of Armaments and War Production), Karl Dönitz (Grand Admiral and Commander-in-Chief), and Alfred Jodl (General and Chief of the Operations Staff for the Armed Forces High Command).*

# 35 Why the Allies won

*Introduction*

The Battle of the Atlantic lasted for 2075 days. During that time 3500 Allied merchant vessels were sunk, taking with them 36,000 merchant seamen. 175 escort vessels were sunk, along with 36,200 naval personnel. Victory had extorted a fearful price. But how had that victory been won?

The Battle of the Atlantic was, effectively, won in the spring of 1943. Nothing that the U-Boat Arm did after that date came anywhere near to re-establishing a war-winning rate of sinking of Allied shipping. Hence it is possible to ask why the Allies won this battle without having to consider the wider issue of why they won the war as a whole. (This topic is brilliantly explored in Richard Overy's book *Why The Allies Won*.)

There are four core elements to a battle of the scale and duration of the Battle of the Atlantic: preparation, resources, strategy and leadership. Since Germany initiated the battle by putting its U-boats to sea in August 1939, I shall analyse the battle in terms of German provocation followed by Allied response for each of these aspects of the battle.

*German preparation*

One of the questions that we have to settle is the 'too early' aspect of the war. (This applies to both sides.) Although Hitler was ambivalent about whether he wanted war with Britain, he nevertheless built up bomber and fighter air fleets with the capacity to mount a major attack on Britain. But with only 21 operational ocean-going U-boats, he was taking a huge risk in provoking Britain into declaring war in September 1939. Hitler's action only made sense if he was certain (and who can be in war?) that his air force would drive Britain into an early surrender. From the German viewpoint, then, the accusation that Hitler accepted war 'too early' in relation to his U-boat fleet stands. But – and this is the crucial question – would things have been any different if he had held off war for another year? The answer appears to be

'No'. Once at war, Hitler let the operational U-boat fleet *shrink* in the first year of war. In September 1939, Germany had 57 U-boats of which 45 were deployed on operations (but only 21 in the Atlantic). Twelve months later the fleet had grown slightly to 69 boats but the total on all operations was down to 23. So, even if Hitler had managed to delay the war for another year, the evidence is that he would still have entered it with a ridiculously small U-boat fleet. He simply did not see the U-boats as a critical part of Germany's armoury.

If Hitler did not understand the weakness of Germany's naval position, Raeder did. When he heard that Britain and France had declared war on Germany the news came 'like a bombshell'. He knew that the Kriegsmarine was not ready. In despair he wrote on 1 September 1939: 'Today the war against England-France broke out, which the Führer had previously assured us we would not have to confront until 1944'. We can have no better witness than Raeder to the unpreparedness of the German Navy. So, in one sense we might ask 'How did it take the Allies so long to extinguish the U-boat menace?' (See below.)

In conclusion we can say without any prevarication that Germany in September 1939 was in no way prepared for a *naval* war with Britain. (And, of course, at that date, Hitler would have had to include the French Navy in his considerations.) But it also seems likely that Hitler's lack of understanding of naval warfare would have left his U-Boat Arm equally ill-prepared at a later date.

## Allied preparation

After the First World War a wave of anti-war feeling gripped Britain. As late as June 1935 the Peace Pledge Union organised a Peace Ballot in which 11 million people voted. Its results showed an overwhelming desire to end, through international agreements, war and preparation for war. In this atmosphere Prime Minister Stanley Baldwin's government, which had taken office that month, had no wish to embark on large-scale rearmament. Once Britain belatedly began to rearm, what money there was went to defending the colonies and trade routes in the Far East and defending the homeland from invasion. The emphasis was on preparation for a *defensive* war, not an *attacking* one.

The most obvious threat to Britain was the Luftwaffe, which was expanding rapidly in the late 1930s. In response, Britain prioritised the production of front-line planes and the development of radar. Key to this defence strategy was the chain of radar stations to enable Britain's small air force of around 1500 front-line planes to engage German planes before they could reach their targets. As a result Battle of Britain that raged in the British skies in the summer of 1940 held back the enemy. By a terrifyingly tight margin, Britain had survived. Survived, because the British Government had made the defence of the skies their highest priority in preparing for war. But what about defending the merchant ships?

The escort situation was altogether different. One of the (too few) technical triumphs of the First World War was asdic. Its success closed off Admiralty thinking to further means of detecting submarines. So confident were they as to the power of asdic that they took Winston Churchill and others to sea to demonstrate their wonder technology. Mounted under unrealistically favourable conditions, the demonstrations convinced politicians that the navy had the U-boat problem under control. Churchill's sanguine assessment in 1939 was a view that many shared: 'The submarine should be quite controllable in the outer seas and certainly in the Mediterranean', he wrote. In the early weeks of the war, this confidence seemed well-founded as Churchill, by now First Lord of the Admiralty, reported to the House of Commons on 26 September 1939 the *declining* rate of merchant sinkings from 65,000 tons in the first week, to 46,000 tons in the second week, and only 21,000 tons in the third week. He concluded by telling the House of Commons: 'I am entitled to say that so far as they go these figures do not need to cause any undue despondency or alarm.' He – and the Admiralty – could not have been more wrong. As the war intensified, the U-boat commanders simply took to attacking when surfaced, undetectable by asdic. Hence the performance of the escorts in the early years of the war contributed little to the final Atlantic victory.

### German resources

The next factor to consider is resources. As far as the Battle of the Atlantic was concerned, there would hardly be a day when Dönitz was not bemoaning a lack of boats or shipyard workers. As Cremer neatly summarised it: 'They built faster than we could sink.' In the early years of the war, Hitler was so confident of, first, putting Britain out of the war, and then conquering the Soviet Union, that he attached little priority to the construction of U-boats. Before the invasion of the Soviet Union, when resources were still plentiful, the U-boat construction programme was just 49 boats for the year. The following year – when Hitler was to stretch resources beyond their limits – the planned output was 221 boats. By February 1942 cutbacks in the U-boat construction programme began, as 154 boats were struck from the 1942 and 1943 targets. Hitler's failure to recognise the importance of the Atlantic battle in the early years of the war was a serious error. Until early 1943 the Allies were struggling with too few escort vessels, lack of air cover and poor U-boat detection equipment. These were the years when even moderately well-commanded boats could sink merchant vessels. By the time that Germany attempted to make U-boat production a priority for resources and manpower, it was too late. And 10cm radar and air cover were lying in wait to, at least, force the boats to submerge, but often to send them to the bottom.

Manning the boats also proved problematic. In the early years of the war many of the U-boat commanders and men were experienced sailors. They were supported by a thorough training programme and enjoyed good facilities for rest and recreation between patrols. Once the war in the east had begun to consume ever-more resources, manning the U-boats grew to be a problem. The service – traditionally largely volunteers – became more reliant on conscripts. Training periods were truncated and the men served under worsening conditions. And it is worth noting that manning had perhaps been a problem from quite early on in the war. Of the 1171 boats that went to sea, only 674 sank anything. It is clear that a lack of targets is not a sufficient explanation for this poor performance. Over and over again, one or two boats in a wolf pack attack would be responsible for almost all the sinkings. The other boats, within firing distance of ready targets failed to score any hits. The most obvious explanation of this is inadequate commanders.

While there is little evidence of any significant drop in morale in the U-boat service, even in the last weeks of the war, it is safe to assume that the rapid decline in tons sunk per boat per day from 1943 onwards was in part due to the quality of the crews. Many escort commanders reported a marked decline in aggressive attacks after March 1943. Meanwhile the Allied escorts continued to be supported by exceptional standards of training, a steady supply of ever more sophisticated technology and commanders at the height of their powers.

Germany was self-sufficient only in potash and coal. 33 other crucial raw materials had to be largely imported. 70 per cent of her copper was imported, 80 to 90 per cent of her rubber, and 99 per cent of her aluminium. But Germany's lack of oil was her greatest weakness in waging war. In 1937, 42 per cent of her oil came from Mexico and the West Indies, while 23 per cent came from the United States – sources that would cease to be available on the outbreak of war. Romania, supplying 12 per cent, was seen as a critical supply in war, but Hitler was to rely principally on the production of synthetic oil from coal and lignite. (Four tons of coal produced one ton of oil. Lignite's yield was half that of coal.) Although the programme was remarkably successful, it never succeeded in Hitler's ambition of making Germany self-sufficient in oil. On mobilisation the annual synthetic oil output was 5.7 million tons, or half Germany's consumption at that time. Germany never overcame the oil problem. After the war, British Intelligence interrogated the leading Nazis on the effects of the bombing campaign on German war production. There was a strong consensus that the attacks on the synthetic oil plants had been the decisive factor in their defeat. Göring remarked that, 'without fuel, nobody can conduct a war'.

The impact of oil shortages on the U-boat fleet was modest in the early stages of the war. True, every time that Raeder sent his capital ships to sea there was a scurrying round to gather enough fuel, which possibly restricted U-boat operations. But later in the war, U-boats were kept in harbour (or idle at sea) for want of fuel. Even so, it is doubtful that this had any impact on the war since, by 1944, the U-boats were a spent force, whether they went to sea or not.

One factor that did not particularly contribute to Germany losing the Atlantic battle was the U-boat construction yards. Right up to the very last months they were turning out new U-boats. 283 were produced in 1944 and 98 in 1945. These figures highlight just how hard fought the Battle of the Atlantic was. Additionally, the Walter boats would probably have been a very serious threat to Allied search technology although Horton claimed that this problem was being researched. Only Allied bombing of the yards and associated works in the closing months of the war prevented a potentially fearful recrudescence of the battle.

*Allied resources*

Until America joined the war, Britain had no choice but to fight a purely defensive war while building up her war supplies. Resources became a serious issue after the fall of France and Britain 'stood alone'. The ten destroyers lost at Norway, combined with six lost and the 19 damaged at Dunkirk, *and* the loss of the French Navy overturned all estimates of Britain's escort resources. As a result, early convoys sailed with as few as two escort vessels. After the Battle of Britain, the escort shortage ensured that this was Britain's most vulnerable period during the war. The merchant fleet only escaped annihilation because Germany had so few operational ocean-going U-boats. As the number of U-boats grew, so did the size of the Allied forces against them. In the case of the Canadian Navy it had six destroyers and 4000 officers and men in 1939. It ended the war with 939 warships and 94,000 officers and men. At the peak of the anti-U-boat campaign there would be up to 700 merchant ships at sea protected by 100 warships. While there were periods when the battle seemed perilously close to being lost in late 1942 and early 1943, ultimately the Allies disposed of forces that overwhelmed the U-boats. But this illustrates an important aspect of the battle. From the moment that the United Stated joined the war, the Allies grew in material strength every day. Meanwhile, the increase in the number of U-boats was unable to keep pace with the growth of the Allied escort system. While in 1940 the U-boats sank 900 tons per day at sea, by late 1942 this had fallen to 149 tons per day. In the final analysis, Allied resources had overwhelmed German resources.

Notwithstanding the important role of the sheer quantity of escort vessels, technology was the Allies greatest strength in the U-boat war. While, as I have noted earlier, the British Admiralty was initially complacent about the U-boat threat, placing too much faith in asdic, their experience in the First World War had left them disposed to search for new methods and ideas. They had seen how the sinkings of 880,000 tons of shipping in April 1917 were stemmed by the introduction of convoys and the use of asdic, which quickly halved the monthly tonnage sunk. This attitude of mind was crucial to winning the U-boat war. Dönitz placed greater faith in 'more of the same' as he demanded increased U-boat construction, while spending much less time on technological developments. The Allies placed their faith in finding *new* means to fight more effectively. Thus Allied radar, HF/DF, Leigh lights, improved depth charges, and so on, made every escort vessel and plane more effective, while the U-boats' individual performances steadily sank.

Along with the high priority that the Allies gave to new technology, there was its counterpart: operational research. Operational research was essential if resources were not to be wasted. Air Marshal Sir Arthur Harris notoriously placed little value on operational research, so enabling him to waste resources on his carpet-bombing. His bombing reduced German output by at most 2.5 per cent and just one German civilian died for every two bombers lost (Overy 2013, p. 299). The resilience of German civilians is amply demonstrated in the letters of Tilli Wolff-Mönckeberg *On The Other Side*, written while living through the Allied bombing of Hamburg. The Germans could 'take it' just as defiantly and courageously as the British did in the Blitz. The Admiralty, on the other hand, used operational research to squeeze the maximum number of U-boat sinkings out of their inadequate escort resources. The outstanding example here is the discovery that large convoys were a better use of resources than smaller ones.

### German strategy and organisation

We have seen how slow the growth of the U-Boat Arm was in the Second World War. In part this was the result of Hitler's belief that (first) Britain would collapse within weeks, and (later) Russia would collapse within months. The war would be over before there could be any significant increase in the U-boat fleet. But that is only a part of the story. Overriding all other reasons is the fundamental fact that (despite fine phrases to the contrary) Hitler never made the U-boat war a priority. He understood land war. He was neither interested in, nor knowledgeable about, sea war.

Alongside the failure to prioritise the U-boat war was Hitler's and Raeder's big-ship obsession. These vessels consumed vast resources to little effect. The fleet was too small to take on the Royal Navy; its bases were hemmed in by

British-controlled waters; and every Reichsmark spent on a warship was a Reichsmark less for U-boats and the E-boats. (The E-boats were ultra-light-weight wooden torpedo boats, used in shallow waters where U-boats could not operate. They were phenomenally effective.) Not one of the capital ships had any influence on the war other than occasionally tying down Allied forces to hunt for them once they dared to go to sea. They were a vanity project, and one that distracted both Raeder and Hitler from making better use of the U-Boat Arm.

When the Allied interrogators interviewed Godt and his team after the war, they were surprised to find how small the U-boat headquarters was, and that it had no research unit working alongside it. This fits the impression that one gets from reading the War Log. At the height of the battle, everything is neatly recorded, but with little evidence of analysis. The interviewers also concluded that 'in the main the U-boat officer lacks one vital attribute, imagination'. This is inevitably a subjective assessment, but it fits Dönitz's belief that he could win the war with 'more of the same'.

## Allied strategy and organisation

Allied strategy in the Battle of the Atlantic was in very sharp contrast to German strategy. More than any other reason for the Allies overcoming the U-boats is that Churchill declared their defeat to be *the* priority, which he then backed up with resources. (Even if he wavered over planes for Coastal Command in 1942.) Looking more closely at the strategy that followed, what stands out is its integrated nature: fundamental research (e.g. radar), operational research (e.g. depth charges versus Hedgehog, large convoys), training, code-breaking and air support all worked together, with regular flows of information between them.

A roll-call of the names of the men guiding the battle at the strategic level says a lot about the brainpower that Britain assigned to the battle. At Bletchley Park there were Alan Turing, Gordon Welchman and Dilly Knox, (amongst other brilliant minds). Working on radar there was Robert Watson-Watt and his lesser-known but equally important colleague, Edward Bowen, who masterminded the development of airborne radar. In operational research there was Patrick Blackett. At sea there were men like Frederic Walker, questioning received wisdom and experimenting with novel attack methods. And, tying it all together from November 1942, was Max Horton, driving men to do what they thought to be impossible; supporting them to the limit of his own prodigious endurance. What all these men shared was a belief that the navy could always do better. Every innovation from the first fuzzy radar images onwards could be bettered. It was a triumph of dedication and teamwork.

## German leadership and command structure

One of the most significant weaknesses on the German side was the command structure. It was Hitler's habit to meet his ministers and senior commanders individually. In consequence the Kriegsmarine had no knowledge of what Hitler had agreed with the Luftwaffe. When Dönitz obtained Hitler's agreement to an allocation of planes for air support, he had no way of knowing whether Hitler had informed Göring to this effect. Instead of fostering cooperation between the three services, Hitler played one against the other. The U-boat War Log is littered with Dönitz's complaints about lack of air cover and Göring's refusal to cooperate with the U-boats on patrol, despite, on many occasions, his having obtained Hitler's promise to rectify this deficiency.

In the case of the Kriegsmarine, there was also the lack of unity of purpose between Raeder and Dönitz. At one level Dönitz was no doubt pleased that Raeder left him alone. But when Dönitz saw oil that he wanted for his U-boats being pumped into *Hipper* or *Scharnhorst*, the lack of a common strategy left him powerless to intervene.

## Allied leadership and command structure

The Allied command structure was the exact opposite of the German one. A nice illustration of the quality of that structure occurred on 23 December

1941. The Americans had been at war since 8 December, following the Japanese attack on Pearl Harbor on 7 December. Their senior commanders were running from crisis to crisis as they met with the British at the First Washington Conference. The American side included the irascible Admiral Ernest King and the combative General George Marshall, both of whom jealously protected their domains from the other's encroachment. Both were famed for being very short-tempered. As the American delegation sat down at the conference table, they had discussed nothing, brought no agenda, and seemed more intent on rivalry than cooperation. They looked in amazement at the British delegation that faced them: Churchill, Pound, Lord Beaverbrook (war production), Field Marshal Sir John Dill, and Air Chief Marshal Sir Charles Portal. 'They knew their stuff', commented one American. The British team came prepared, in agreement, and focused on winning the war.

This cohesion was second nature to the British delegation, dating back to 1902 when Prime Minister Arthur Balfour established the Committee of Imperial Defence. In peace and in war, the heads of the services and the senior civil servants from the ministries met in these meetings to plan and resource the defence of Britain. During the Second World War the chiefs of staff met together every day under the chairmanship of either Churchill or his deputy, Clement Attlee. While many of their debates were sharply worded, the chiefs of staff were united in their belief in inter-service cooperation.

But we can't leave the subject of leadership in the Battle of the Atlantic without singling out one man: Max Horton. 'No one played a more critical part in the Battle of the Atlantic than Admiral Horton.' wrote his colleague Air Marshal Sir John Slessor after the war. Had the Kriegsmarine had a man of Horton's vision, single-mindedness, drive and acumen, the Battle of the Atlantic might have been a different story.

*Conclusion*

As the above analysis shows, the winning of the Battle of the Atlantic for the Allies, and its loss by Germany, had multiple causes. A few, though, stand out.

On the German side the ones that contributed most to their losing the battle are: failing to prioritise the battle; failing to innovate; and the shortage of oil.

On the Allied side, winning was principally due to: making the battle the highest priority; effective coordination; a heavy emphasis on training; technical innovations; code-breaking; and Horton's leadership.

Why is the Allied list longer? Because the Allies tackled the battle from all possible angles, while Dönitz remained fixated on the idea that he only needed more U-boats to defeat the Allies.

While Dönitz would have rejected any suggestion that his strategy was mistaken, he would not have disputed much of the rest of this analysis. In particular he blamed the lost battle on Hitler's failure 'to throw into the Battle of the Atlantic all the forces at their command immediately the war began and they had failed to provide in good time the means we required with which to fight the battle, namely, an adequate number of U-boats'. He also singled out the lack of skilled workmen which led to the U-boats taking longer and longer to be repaired. 'Fewer and fewer boats were at sea ... and less enemy tonnage sunk,' he concluded.

# Postscript

**Edward Bowen** (1911-1991): After the war Bowen went to Australia, where he became Chief of the Division of Radiophysics at the Radiophysics Laboratory, and did important work on developing radio telescopes. His memoir, *Radar Days*, is the best account of the development of radar in the pre-war and war years.

**Peter-Erich Cremer** (1911-1992): Cremer returned to civilian life and wrote two war memoirs: *U-333: The story of a U-boat Ace*; *U-Boat Commander: A Periscope View of the Battle of the Atlantic.*

**Karl Dönitz** (1891-1980): Dönitz was one of the defendants at the Nuremberg Trials. He was found guilty on the charge of planning, initiating and waging wars of aggression and other crimes against peace; and on the charge of war crimes. He was sentenced to ten years' imprisonment but released on the grounds of ill-health in 1956. His memoirs, *Ten Years and Twenty Days* were published in 1958. During the rest of his life he continued to defend his actions in the war and never expressed any remorse.

**Eberhard Godt** (1900-1995): Godt was taken prisoner in 1945 and appeared as a witness at the Nuremberg Trials. Later he was one of the authors of a history of the Kriegsmarine's operations.

**Max Horton** (1883-1951): Horton retired from the navy in August 1945. He continued to take an interest in naval affairs but was careful to avoid trying to influence the new generation of naval officers. He died without leaving what would have been a spirited memoir. According to his biographer he was given a state funeral in Liverpool but I can find no trace of this, although King George VI sent a personal a representative to the funeral. (The last admiral to receive a state funeral was Nelson in 1806. Admiral Lord Fisher and Admiral Lord Beresford received ceremonial funerals in 1920 and 1919 respectively.)

**Erich Raeder** (1876-1960): Raeder was one of the defendants at the Nuremberg Trials. He was found guilty on three counts: participation in a common plan or conspiracy for the accomplishment of a crime against peace; planning, initiating and waging wars of aggression and other crimes against peace; and war crimes. He was sentenced to life imprisonment but was released on grounds of ill-health in 1955, aged 79. He wrote his autobiography – *Grand Admiral* – with the help of ghost writers.

**Otto Kretschmer** (1912-1998): Kretschmer was taken prisoner in 1943 and sent to a prisoner of war camp in Canada, where he remained until 1947. He later served in the West Germany Navy and in NATO as a staff officer.

**Sir Percy Noble** (1980-1955): Noble served as Head of the British Naval Delegation to Washington DC from 1942-1945, at which point he retired from the navy.

**Sir Gilbert Stephenson** (1877-1972): Stephenson stayed at Tobermory to the end of the war. After the war he became Honorary Commodore of the Sea Cadet Corps. He left no memoir but Richard Baker's biography of Stephenson draws on post-war interviews with the admiral. (Richard Baker RNVR achieved fame as a television news reader.)

**Frederic John Walker** (1896-1944): Walker took part in the defence of the D-Day landing sites over an intense two-week period. On his return to Liverpool, he felt unwell and died of thrombosis within days of landing. His funeral in Liverpool was attended by over 1000 people.

**Alan Turing** (1912-1954): Turing worked on developing computers at National Physical Laboratory after the war and later went to the University of Cambridge in 1947 and the University of Manchester in 1948. He committed suicide in 1954 following a conviction for homosexuality in 1952. He received a posthumous pardon from the Queen in 2013.

**Robert Watson-Watt** (1892-1973): Watson-Watt was knighted for his work in radar. He became a consulting engineer and in 1952 moved to Canada, where he wrote *Three Steps to Victory*, his interesting but incoherently rambling memoirs, punctuated with many pithy comments.

# Postscript

**Rodger Winn** (1903-1972): Winn returned to the Bar after the war and was later a Lord Justice of Appeal.

# Glossary

**AA**: Anti-aircraft. Any action taken to damage or destroy aircraft.

**Acoustic torpedo**: A torpedo which can detect the sound of a ship's propellers and navigate itself towards the sound source.

**Admiralty**: The central administration of the Royal Navy**Error! Bookmark not defined.**, based in Admiralty House, London. Its political head was the First Lord; its professional head was the First Sea Lord.

**Anti-Submarine Training School**: The Royal Navy's training establishment for training the officers and men of escort ships. Founded in 1940 and based at Tobermory in Scotland.

**ASW**: Anti-submarine warfare.

**Aldis lamp**: A shuttered light for sending Morse code signals between ships or between planes and ships.

**Atlantic bases**: The U-boat bases at Brest, Lorient, and La Pallice (near La Rochelle). Occupied in mid-1940. Abandoned in mid-1944.

**Atlantiksender**: A fake radio station set up by British Intelligence in 1943 to undermine the morale of U-boat crews.

**Asdic** (US: sonar): The use of an underwater sound wave sent out from a search ship. A returning echo indicated the presence of some underwater object.

**ASV radar**: Airborne Surface Vessel radar as used by maritime patrol aircraft to locate vessels on the surface. See also Radar.

**Axis (powers)**: Germany, Italy and Japan.

**B-Dienst**: The German Naval Intelligence Service.

**Black May**: The name that the U-boat service gave to May 1943.

**Bletchley Park**: A country house in Bedfordshire, used as the base for the Government Code and Cypher School. It now houses a museum recording the work of the wartime codebreakers.

**Blockade runner**: A ship or submarine taking cargo or passengers through blockaded waters. Blockade running U-boats were used by Germany to bring in critical supplies such as rubber.

**Buttercup**: An escort manoeuvre to turn an attack by a U-boat into an attack *on* the U-boat.

**Capital ships**: The largest ships in a fleet. There is no firm definition of the term, but cruisers, carriers and battleships are always classed as capital ships.

**Coastal Command**: A branch of the Royal Air Force, tasked with protecting convoy vessels from both U-boats and Luftwaffe attacks.

**Compass platform**: The bridge in a ship from which the ship is commanded. (Large ships had multiple bridges.)

**Conning position**: Any place in a ship from which it can be steered.

**Convoy**: A group of ships travelling together.

**Convoy commodore**: A naval officer in charge of the merchant ships in a convoy. He took up station in one of the convoy ships. Usually a formerly retired officer. His role was distinct from that of the escort commander.

**Corvette**: A small warship, generally designed for coastal work, but often used on the high seas in the Battle of the Atlantic.

**Denmark Strait**: The sea passage between Greenland and Iceland.

**Depth charge**: An underwater bomb, usually with a fuse set to detonate at a given depth. The setting was adjusted immediately before the charge was launched.

**Derby House**: See Western Approaches Command.

**Destroyer**: A fast, well-armed, long-endurance vessel capable of protecting larger warships.

**Dipole**: An aerial consisting of two metal wires or rods. These may be straight or folded. The combined length is half the wavelength that the aerial is tuned to.

**Distress call**: An SOS call sent on the international distress frequency of 500 KHz (600 m). This frequency is no longer in use for distress calls.

**E-boat**: A high-speed lightweight wooden boat carrying torpedoes. They were used very effectively to attack coastal convoys in the North Sea.

**Enigma**: A coding machine manufactured by the German company Scherbius and Ritter. It was originally designed for commercial purposes when it first went on sale in the 1920s. The German armed forces later developed their own versions of this machine.

**Escort**: A warship or ships accompanying merchant shipping to protect it from attack.

**Escort carrier**: An aircraft carrier used to accompany convoys.

**Escort commander**: The officer in command of the naval vessels protecting a merchant fleet convoy.

**Escort group**: A group of warships that regularly worked together when escorting convoys. Such a group would have trained as a group.

**Escort support group**: A group of warships available for despatch to assist escorts which had encountered a heavy U-boat presence.

**Fahnrich zur See**: Midshipman.

**Fathom**: A depth of 6 feet (1.8 metres).

**First Happy Time**: The U-boat Arm's name for the period from the fall of France to around October 1940 when the large number of escort vessels held in reserve to forestall an invasion of Britain left the Atlantic lightly escorted. During this time, few U-boats were sunk.

**First Lord of the Admiralty**: The political head of the British Admiralty, who was always a member of the Cabinet. During World War II, this was Winston

Churchill (to May 1940) and A V Alexander, the Labour MP, from May 1940 to the end of the European war.

**First Sea Lord**: The professional head of the Royal Navy. During the Second World War, the post was held by Sir Dudley Pound from 12 June 1939 to 15 October 1943; and Admiral of the Fleet Andrew Cunningham from 15 October 1943 to 24 May 1946.

**Flak**: German shorthand for anti-aircraft weaponry.

**Flak U-boat**: A U-boat modified for carrying anti-aircraft guns.

**Foxer**: A noise-making device, towed by a destroyer to decoy acoustic torpedoes.

**Fregatten Kapitän**: British equivalent: commander.

**Freighter**: Alternative name for a merchant or cargo vessel.

**Gnat**: See acoustic torpedo.

**Government Code and Cypher School**: See Bletchley Park.

**Gross tonnage (GRT)**: A measure of the volume of a ship.

**Gun director station**: A post in a warship from which an officer can direct (aim) one or more guns elsewhere in the vessel.

**H2S**: Ground-scanning radar, used in planes to identify land-based targets.

**Hague Conventions**: The agreements reached at two conventions in the Hague in 1899 and 1907. They set out the laws of war and introduced the concept of a 'war crime'.

**Hedgehog**: A mortar-throwing device, mounted in the prow of an escort vessel.

**HF/DF**: A radio-based direction-finding system that only required one receiving set. It could be used by escort vessels to locate U-boats from their radio signals back to their bases.

**Hydrophone**: A U-boat underwater listening device for detecting the sound of a ship's propellers or engines

**Iceland-Faeroe passage**: The sea passage between the North Sea and the Atlantic, running between the Faeroe Islands and Iceland.

**Kampfgeschwader 40 (KG 40)**: A German bomber wing, mostly engaged in maritime patrolling.

**Kapitän zur See**: Captain.

**Kriegsmarine**: German Navy 1935-1945. Predecessors: Imperial German Navy 1871-1918 and Reichsmarine 1919-1935.

**Knot**: A speed of one nautical mile per hour, which equals 1.15 mph.

**Leigh light**: A powerful searchlight fitted under the wings of Allied planes to help locate U-boats at night.

**Lorient**: French Atlantic port where the U-Boat Arm had its headquarters from mid-1940 until the St Nazaire raid in March 1942, at which time the headquarters moved to Paris.

**Luftwaffe**: The German Air Force 1933-1946.

**Magnetic mine**: A mine activated by the magnetism of a ship passing over it.

**Magnetron**: A device for generating high-powered microwaves. It was critical to the development of 10cm radar.

**Megahertz**: An electronic signal which oscillates one million times a second. 1 MHz has a wavelength of 300 m. A 200 MHz signal has a wavelength of 1.5 metres, as used in ASV Mk I radar.

**Merchant ship**: A ship that transports cargo or goods for payment.

**Metox**: A device installed in U-boats to detect 1.5 m radar.

**Mid-Atlantic Gap**: The section of the Atlantic that was beyond the reach of bombers. The gap was closed in May 1943 with the introduction of very long-range planes.

**Milch cows**: U-boats modified to act as supply vessels to other U-boats patrolling at sea.

**Mine**: In a naval context, a bomb left in a sea way with the intention of destroying passing ships. Mines could be floating, tethered at a specific depth, or placed on the sea bed.

**MZ (magnetic) firing mechanism**: A torpedo detonator which detected the target ship's magnetism. It was complicated to use since its settings depended on the strength of the Earth's magnetism in the attack zone and the size of the target vessel.

**Naxos GSR receivers**: A device installed in U-boats to detect 10cm radar. It was not particularly effective.

**Nuremberg Trials**: A series of trials held by the victorious powers at Nuremberg between 20 November 1945 and 1 October 1946.

**Oberleutnant** (Luftwaffe): Wing Commander.

**Oberleutnant zur See**: Sub lieutenant (Royal Navy); Lieutenant - junior grade (US Navy).

**Ocean boarding vessels**: Requisitioned merchant ships, armed and used for intercepting foreign ships on the high seas.

**Olympia Crew**: The men who joined the U-boat service in 1936.

**Operation Berlin**: A raiding operation by *Scharnhorst* and *Gneisenau*, January–March 1941.

**Operation Drumbeat**: The U-boat operations on the American east coast in early 1942.

**Operational Intelligence Centre**: A unit which interpreted intercepted German, Italian and Japanese radio communications. Based in the Admiralty.

**Operational research**: Research into an on-going operation, designed to improve that operation.

**Pan-American Safety Zone**: That area of the eastern Atlantic where United States forces escorted convoys bound for Europe when America had not yet entered the war.

**Pineapple**: An escort manoeuvre designed to locate U-boats thought to be lying ahead of a convoy.

**Pressure hull**: The inner of the two hulls of a submarine, designed to retain its shape up to the maximum specified safe depth for the boat.

**Radar**: Principal types used in locating U-boats: ASV Mk I. Wavelength 1.5 m; ASV Mk II. Wavelength 1.5 m; ASV Mk III. Wavelength 10cm; ASV Mk.VI. Same as ASV Mk III except that it had an additional attenuator device that reduced the signal strength as soon as a U-boat was detected. This made it less likely that the U-boat would detect the radar signal.

**Raspberry**: A manoeuvre to locate and attack a U-boat immediately after it has struck a merchant ship.

**Repeater**: An indicator which shows the reading of a device elsewhere in a ship. Compass and rudder repeaters are examples of this.

**RNR**: Royal Naval Reserve: the volunteer reserve force of the Royal Navy.

**Scapa Flow**: The principal anchorage of the Royal Navy's Home Fleet. Situated in the Orkneys.

**Second Happy Time**: The U-boat Arm's name for the period January to April/May 1942 when they were working off the east cost of America.

**Sloop**: A warship between the size of a corvette and a frigate.

**Snorkel**: A device to allow a U-boat to emit diesel exhaust to the atmosphere and take in fresh air while submerged.

**Special Operations Executive** (SOE): A unit set up in July 1940 for carrying out minor raids, sabotage attacks and reconnaissance.

**Special service ship**: Heavily armed merchant ships designed to lure U-boats to attack them.

**Square** (re U-boats): The U-boat radio signals did not use standard map references. Instead the Atlantic Ocean was split into thousands of squares, each identified by a set of code letters.

**Squid**: A three-barrelled mortar. Successor to Hedgehog.

**Star shell**: Shells filled with magnesium to light up a target on land or at sea.

**Step-aside**: An escort manoeuvre to avoid an acoustic torpedo.

**Submarine Tracking Room**: An intelligence unit at the Admiralty which collated intelligence related to U-boat activity, with the aim of knowing where the U-boats were operating.

**Support Group**: See Escort Support Group.

**Surface raider**: A warship on a mission to capture or sink enemy shipping.

**Swordfish**: A biplane torpedo bomber.

**Tallboy**: A 5-ton bomb developed by Barnes Wallis for use on structures that could not be penetrated by the other bombs available at that time. Tallboys inflicted considerable damage on V-2 rocket production and on *Tirpitz*, but failed to do much damage to the U-boat pens.

**Thetis 2c**: A free-floating decoy device designed to appear to Allied radar as a U-boat.

**Torpedo**: A self-propelled underwater missile with an explosive warhead.

**Tramp steamer**: A merchant ship that has no fixed route, picking up goods wherever its services are needed.

**Type 271 radar**. A 10-cm radar system for use in warships.

**Type IX U-boat**. 35 per cent heavier and 13 per cent longer than the Type VII.

**Type VII U-boat**: The commonest U-boat in the Second World War.

**U-boat**: In the context of this book, any German submarine.

**U-Flak**: See Flak U-boat.

**Ultra**: Intelligence derived from Enigma decrypts.

**United Nations**: The Allies.

**V-1 unmanned plane**: Also known as a 'flying bomb', these planes were launched from the Continent on a flight path to London. They fell to earth when their engines cut out, dropping a 1870 lb bomb.

**V-2 rocket**: A guided rocket launched from the Continent on a flight path to London, carrying a 2200 lb warhead. Their navigation system was crudely calibrated, enabling British counter-intelligence to feedback false information on where the rockets were landing.

**Very light**: A distress flare fired from a Very pistol.

**VLR aircraft**: Aircraft with a long flight endurance, enabling them to operate in the Mid-Atlantic Gap.

**Walter U-boat**: A U-boat powered by a hydrogen peroxide ($H_2O_2$) based fuel that supplied its own oxygen, so not needing to take in air from the atmosphere.

**Wehrmacht**: The German army 1935 to 1946.

**Western Approaches**: The area of the Atlantic Sea to the west of the United Kingdom, extending to 30 degrees west.

**Western Approaches Command**: The command unit for protecting convoys in the Atlantic. Based in Plymouth 1939 to early 1941. Thereafter based at Derby House in Liverpool.

**Western Approaches Tactical Unit** (WATU): A unit which trained escort officers in the tactics of locating and destroying U-boats.

**Wolf pack**: A group of U-boats, working together under the direction of the U-Boat Arm headquarters.

**Z-Plan**: Late 1930s plan for the construction of the ships of the Kriegsmarine.

# Kriegsmarine capital ships

**Battleships**

*Bismarck*. Completed 1941. Sunk 1941.

*Tirpitz*. Completed 1941. Sunk 1944.

**Battlecruisers**

*Scharnhorst*. Completed 1939. Sunk 1943.

*Gneisenau*. Completed 1938. Decommissioned 1942.

**Pre-dreadnought battleships**

*Hannover*. Completed 1905. Scrapped c 1944.

*Schleswig-Holstein*. Completed 1906. Sunk 1944.

*Schlesien*. Completed 1906. Mined 1945.

**Heavy cruisers**

*Deutschland* (renamed *Lützow*). Commissioned 1933. Survived the war.

*Admiral Scheer*. Laid down 1931. Commissioned 1933.

*Admiral Graf Spee*. Commissioned 1936. Scuttled 1939.

*Admiral Hipper*. Commissioned 1939. Scuttled 1945.

*Blücher*. Commissioned 1939. Sunk 1940.

*Prinz Eugen*. Commissioned 1940. Survived the war.

**Light cruisers**

*Emden*. Commissioned 1925. Scuttled 1945.

*Königsberg*. Commissioned 1929. Sunk 1940.

*Karlsruhe*. Commissioned 1929. Sunk 1940.

*Köln*. Commissioned 1930. Sunk 1945.

*Leipzig*. Completed 1931. Survived the war.

*Nürnberg*. Commissioned 1935. Survived the war.

# The seven strategic errors

1 The Kriegsmarine had too few U-boats at the start of the war – and especially too few ocean-going boats – to have any significant effect on Allied merchant shipping.

2 The U-boats concentrated on sinking merchant ships, deliberately avoiding taking on escort vessels. This gave the Allies time to build up their totally inadequate escort forces.

3 The Kriegsmarine wasted vast sums of money on building a surface fleet that was too small to be a threat to the Allied navies. Had those resources been put into U-boats before war broke out, the threat to the Allied merchant ships would have been immense.

4 The Kriegsmarine surface fleet was squandered in the invasions of Denmark and Norway, with a loss of 57 vessels, leaving it in a severely weakened state.

5 Dönitz's strategy was essentially 'more of the same'. He and the Kriegsmarine placed little importance on developing new technology.

6 Hitler and Göring failed to recognise how important air support was to the U-Boat Arm, leaving Dönitz to fight an unequal battle once the Allies took to the skies on a huge scale from 1943 onwards. In the second half of the war, air power was the deciding in every theatre.

7 The Kriegsmarine failed to resolve the Type VII versus Type IX U-boat mystery. If the Type IX was as vulnerable to sinking as Dönitz claimed, why did he go on building so many of them, rather than concentrating on Type VIIs?

# Works cited

Anon. 1945. *Foreign Relations Of The United States: Diplomatic Papers, Conferences At Malta And Yalta*. Online at: https://history.state.gov/historicaldocuments/frus1945Malta

Anon. 2007. *German Invasion Plans for the British Isles 1940*. Bodleian Library.

Anon. nd. *History of U-boat policy*. Online copy: http://www.uboatarchive.net/U-boatPolicy.htm

Anon. 1946. *The Battle Of The Atlantic – The Official Account Of The Fight Against The U-Boats 1939-1945*. HMSO.

Bailey, C H. 1998. *The Battle of the Atlantic: The Corvettes and Their Crews: An Oral History*. Sutton Publishing.

Baker, R. 2015. The *Terror of Tobermory*. Birlinn Ltd.

Bekker, C. 1974. *Hitler's Naval War*. Macdonald and Jane's.

Bell, P M H. 1986. *The Origins of the Second World War in Europe*. Longman.

Bird, K W. 2006. *Erich Raeder: Admiral of the Third Reich*. Naval Institute Press.

Bowen, E G. 1987. *Radar Days*. Adam Hilger.

Brodhurst, R. 2000. *Churchill's Anchor: A Biography of Admiral of the Fleet Sir Dudley Pound*. Pen & Sword.

Buell T B. 2012. *Master of Seapower: A Biography of Fleet Admiral Ernest J. King*. Naval Institute Press.

Burn, Alan. 1996. *The Fighting Commodores: Convoy Commanders in the Second World War*. Pen & Sword.

Caulfield, M. 1959. *Tomorrow Never Came*. W W Norton.

Chalmers, W S. 1954. *Max Horton and the Western Approaches*. Hodder and Stoughton.

Churchill, W S. 1949-1954 *The Second World War*. 6 Vols. Cassell.

Colville, J. 1986. *The Fringes of Power*, Vol 1: 1939-1941. Sceptre.

Cremer, P. 1984. *U-boat Commande*r. US Naval Institute Press.

Dönitz, Admiral K. 1961. *Memoirs of the Nazi Twilight*. Belmont Books.

Dönitz, Admiral K. 1946. *The Conduct Of The War At Sea*. On line at: http://www.karl-doenitz.com.

# Works cited

Fleming, P. 1957. *Operation Sea Lion*. Simon and Schuster.

Gilbert, M. 1983. *Winston S Churchill: Finest Hour 1939-1941*. William Heinemann Ltd.

Gilbert, M. 1986. *Winston S Churchill: Road to Victory 1941-1945*. William Heinemann Ltd.

Granville, W and Kerr, J L. 1957. *The RNVR: A Record of Achievement*. Harrap.

Gretton, P. 1971. *Convoy Escort Commander*. Corgi.

*Hansard* 1803–2005: http://hansard.millbanksystems.com/.

Haslop, D. Britain, 2013. *Germany and the Battle of the Atlantic: A Comparative Study*. Bloomsbury Studies in Military History.

Hawkins, I (Ed). 2003. *Destroyer: An Anthology of First-Hand Accounts of the War at Sea, 1939-1945*. Conway Maritime Press.

Hellwinkell, L. 2014. *Hitler's Gateway to the Atlantic: German Naval Bases in France 1940-1945*. Seaforth Publishing.

Hinsley, F H.1993. *British Intelligence in The Second World War*. (Abridged) HMSO.

Hollis, Sir Leslie.1956. *One Marine's Tale*. Andre Deutsch.

Ismay, H. 1960. *The Memoirs of General Lord Ismay*. Viking Press.

Jones, R V. 1979. *Most Secret War*. Cornet Books.

Kennedy, L. 1942. *Sub Lieutenant*. Batsford Books

Kershaw, I. 2000. *Hitler 1936-1945: Nemesis*. Allen Lane The Penguin Press.

Kingsley, F A (Ed). 1995. *The Development of Radar Equipments for the Royal Navy, 1935-45*. Palgrave.

Lavery, B. 2006. *Churchill's Navy*. Conway.

Llewellyn-Jones, M. 2014. *The Royal Navy and Anti-submarine Warfare, 1917-49*. Routledge.

Lovell, B. 1991. *Echoes of War: The Story of H2S Radar*. CRC Press.

Macintyre. D. 1961. *The Battle of the Atlantic*. Batsford.

Müllenheim-Rechberg, B von. 1982. *Battleship Bismarck: A Survivor's Story*. Grafton.

# Works cited

*Naval Review*, Vol. XXVIII. No. 3.

*Nuremberg Trial transcripts*. Online at http://avalon.law.yale.edu.

OEG Report No 51 ASW in World War II. Hyper War website.

Overy, R. 2014. *The Bombing War: Europe 1939-1945*. Allen Lane.

Overy, R. 1995. *Why the Allies Won*. Jonathan Cape.

Owen, J and Walters, G. 2005. *The Voice of War*. Penguin Books.

Padfield, P. 1993. *Dönitz: The Last Führer*. Victor Gollancz.

Raeder, E. 2001. *Grand Admiral*. Da Capo Press.

Robertson, T. 1969. *Walker RN*. Macmillan.

Robertson, T. 2011. *The Golden Horseshoe: The Wartime Career of Otto Kretschmer, U-Boat Ace*. Naval Institute Press.

Roskill, S. 2004. *Churchill and the Admirals*. Pen and Sword.

Roskill, S. Various. *The War at* Sea. Multi-volume. HMSO.

Rowen, R. *Grey and Black Propaganda against Nazi Germany*. National Archives FO 898/51.

Sebag-Montefiore, H. 2008. *Enigma: The Battle For The Code*. The Folio Society.

Showell, J P M. 2000. *Enigma U-boats: Breaking the Code*. Ian Allan.

Smith, M. 2001. *The Secrets of Station X*. Biteback Publishing.

Sternhell, C and Thorndike, A. *OEG Report No 51 ASW in World War II*. Online at: http://navgunschl2.sakura.ne.jp/tenji/oeg_asw/OEG_No51_E.pdf.

Till, G (Ed). 1994. *Seapower: Theory and Practice*. Taylor & Francis.

Trevor-Roper, H. 2004. *Hitler's War Directives 1939-1945*. Birlinn.

Veronico, N A. 2015. *Hidden Warships: Finding World War II's Abandoned, Sunk, and Preserved Warships*. Zenith Press.

*War Log* (War Diary and War Standing Orders of Commander-in-Chief, Submarines). Uboatarchive.net.

Werner, H A. 1969. *Iron Coffins*. Arthur Barker Ltd.

West, N. 2010. *Historical Dictionary of Naval Intelligence*. Scarecrow Press.

## Works cited

Williams, M. 1979. *Captain Gilbert Roberts RN and the Anti-U-Boat School*. Cassell.

Wolff-Mönckeberg, M. *On the Other Side: Letters to my Children from Germany 1940-46*. Persephone Books.

*Women in War Newsletter* (Autumn/Winter 2016).

WW2 People's War (BBC): http://www.bbc.co.uk/history/ww2peopleswar/

# References

CCA: Churchill College Archives.

Churchill WW2: Winston Churchill *The Second World War*.

History (U): History of U-Boat Policy 1939-1945.

TNA: The National Archives.


**Preliminaries**

'I don't think' CCA FISR 8/39 (FP 4941).

Convoy *SC-7*

'a lightly-armed' Macintyre 1961, p. 41. '22:05 – Sighted two' Escort commander's report. '09:55 – Sighted tug' Escort commander's report.

**Permission to build**

'much pleasure' *British Documents on Foreign Affairs* Series 5, Vol 46. 'Today is the' Bekker 1974, p. 26. 'If we are' HC Deb 22 July 1935 Vol 304 cc1499-562. 'The scale of' Bird 2006, p. 9. 'the fear of' Bird 2006, p. 1. 'a smart, industrious' Haslop 2013. 'in no way' Bird 2006, p. 137. 'For my political' Bekker 1974, p. 34. 'The bomber will' HC Deb 10 Nov 1932 Vol 270 cc525-641. 'is an easy' *Manchester Guardian* 4 March 1935.

War fever

'in accordance with' Robertson 2011, p. 24. 'in spite of' *War Log*, 17 Aug 1939.

**Day of decision**

'I am speaking to' *The Times*, 4 Sept 1939. 'Hostilities with Britain' Bekker 1974, p. 18. 'Winston is back' Churchill 1948, p. 320. 'What now?' Bekker 1974, p. 22. 'On this day' Bekker 1974, pp. 22-3. 'Damnation! So it's' Bekker 1974, p. 25. 'Open hostilities against' *War Log*, 3 Sept 1939. 'My immediate move' Bekker 1974, p. 18-9.

**An innocent victim**

'*Athenia* torpedoed 56.42' Caulfield 1959, p. 67. 'The orders so' *War Log*, 4 Sept 1939. 'By order of' Bekker 1974, p. 20.

**Early skirmishes**

'a clean-cut fellow' Uboat.net. 'merchant ships and' Trevor-Roper 2004, p. 48. 'over-optimism' HC Deb 26 Sept 1939 Vol 351 cc1239-46. 'very large number' HC Deb 26 Sept 1939 Vol 351 cc1239-46. 'The ideal Unit' Churchill 1948, p. 341. 'Convoy in square' *War Log*, 15 Sept 1939. 'the branch in' *War Log*, 8 Sept 1939. 'decisive damage on' *War Log*, 28 Sept 1939.

**The folly of the search units**

'At that time' uboataces.com. 'by word of' *The War Illustrated*, Vol 1, No. 4, pp. 115-116. 'standing at the' ww2memories.wordpress.com. '*Courageous* destroyed. *U-29*' uboataces.com. 'I have bad' Churchill 1948, p. 340. 'whether this ship' HC Deb

# References

20 Sept 1939 Vol 351 cc957-8. 'the only thing' Churchill 1949, p. 529. 'a marvellous system' Gilbert 1976, p. 948. 'The submarine should' Churchill 1948, p. 325.

**Testing the waters**

'merchant ships in' *History (U)*. p. 4. 'I'm pretty sure' Dönitz 1961, p. 13. 'were assuming serious' Gilbert 1983, p. 95. 'some special reason' Dönitz 1961, p 20. 'to eliminate the' *War Log*, 14 Nov 1939.

Reclaiming the oceans

'even if inferior' Bird 2006, p. 141. 'She's a damned' Bekker 1974, p. 38. Do not use' *Naval Review*, Vol. XXVIII. No. 3. '[I felt] baulked' Owen & Walters 2005, pp. 27-9. 'as we knew' *The War Illustrated*, Vol 1, No. 17. 'able to stand' Churchill 1948, p. 416. 'fight your way' Churchill 1948, p. 414. 'Late in the' *Naval Review*, Vol XXVIII. No. 3. 'I am happy' Churchill 1948, p. 414. 'Battleships are supposed' Bekker 1974, p. 52. 'In this sombre' *Naval Review*, Vol XXVIII. No. 3.

**The promise of radar**

No citations.

**Gold from the Thames mud**

'a grave menace' Gilbert 1983 Finest Hour, p. 82. 'It was enough' Bekker 1974, pp. 65-6. 'thrilled' WSC WW2 (i) 1948, p. 396-398. 'You should discontinue 'http://www.chem.ucl.ac.uk/resources/history/people/goodeve_cf/cfg_bio.html#admir alty 'Urgent. Please summon' ibid.

**Was that it?**

'too conservative' *History (U)*, p. 5. 'the greatest difficulty' *War Log*, 21 Jan 1940. 'Until I hear' *War Log*, 8 Jan 1940. 'Our faithful asdic' Gilbert 1983, p. 136. 'at full pitch' *Manchester Guardian*, 29 Jan 1940. 'by the quickest' Sebag-Montefiore 2001, p. 102. 'in the single' Churchill 1948, p. 448. 'missed the bus' Churchill 1948, p. 461.

**A new war**

'breaks all rules' Bird 2006, p. 145. 'unequivocal strategic mistake' Bird 2006, pp. 146-7. 'The spell was' Bekker 1974, p. 182. 'a matter of' Gilbert 1983, p. 551. 'sales to a' Gilbert 1983, p. 605. '[could] bring Britain' Bekker 1974, p. 172. 'readily transversed' *German Invasion Plans*. 'air superiority' Fleming 1957, p. 219. 'hazardous' Fleming 1957, pp. 244-5.

**'The Terror of Tobermory'**

'a refresher course' Baker, p 97. 'very old' http://www.bbc.co.uk/history/ww2peopleswar/stories/46/a2792946.shtml 'it was murder' Bailey 1998, p. 12. 'I had a' Baker 1999, p. 98. 'In many cases' Baker 1999, p. 130. 'a real tyrant' http://www.harry-tates.org.uk/veteranstales3.htm 'The extreme conscientiousness' Baker 1999, p. 128. '*Western Isles* methods' Baker 1999, p. 148.

**The rise of the wolf packs**

'U-47 made contact' *War Log*, 20 Sept 1940. 'Vessel of some' Kretschmer's U-Boat Log. 'early intelligence of' *War Log*, 22 Sept 1940. 'Field Marshal Göring' Bekker 1974, p. 194. 'wipe out the' Bell 1986, p. 194. 'At the present rate' Bekker 1974, p. 192. 'your heroic achievement' Robertson 2011, p. 202. 'unfair ... All my' Robertson

2011, p. 108. 'in such weather' Cremer 1984, pp. 38-41. 'reasonably successful' *History (U)*. pp. 8-9. '50 or 60 of' Churchill 1949, p. 356.

**The return of the surface raiders**

'the achievements of' Bekker 1974, pp. 201-2. 'operational surprise and' Bird 2006, p. 175. 'for valour in' https://en.wikipedia.org/wiki/Edward_Fegen 'The main target' Bird 2006, p. 176. 'If we go' Robertson 2011, p. 98. 'on equal terms' Bekker 1974, p. 210. 'Break away!' Bekker 1974, p. 211. 'the annihilation of' Bekker 1974, p. 215. 'constant' *History (U)*, p. 7.

**Dönitz at bay**

'so decisive to' Trevor-Roper 2004, p. 103. 'with almost impossible' Dönitz *The Conduct Of The War At Sea*. 'We cannot go' Churchill 1949, p. 531. 'a carefully planned' Hornell's Report www.warsailors.com. 'Against such attacks' Hornell's Report www.warsailors.com. 'The next four' Directive by the Minister of Defence, March 6, 1941. 'These numbers were' Dönitz 1961, p. 36. 'to get whatever' *The Independent*, 3 Jan 2016. 'pressing home the' *The London Gazette*, 13th March, 1942.

**Three aces down**

No citations.

**Operation Rheinübung**

'gaining local and' Bird 2006, p. 177-8. 'piecemeal' Bird 2006, p. 179. 'There is a powerful' Bekker 1974, p. 218. 'in furtherance of' Bekker 1974, p. 219. 'There have been' Bekker 1974, p. 219. 'only with great' Müllenheim-Rechberg 1982, p. 33. 'two large warships' Müllenheim-Rechberg 1982, p. 77. 'one of the' *The Independent*, 22 July 1993. 'The *Hood* – it's' Müllenheim-Rechberg 1982, p. 107. 'The sight I' Müllenheim-Rechberg 1982, p. 109. . 'Have we got' Gilbert 1983, p. 1094. 'we were met' https://www.defensemedianetwork.com/stories/the-american-who-helped-sink-the-bismarck/ 'EMERGENCY ALL U-BOATS' Werner, p. 33. 'The sinking of' Müllenheim-Rechberg 1982, p. 222. 'BISMARCK VICTIM OF' Werner, p. 34. 'unavoidable' Bird 2006, p. 181. 'to contradict the' Bekker 1974, p. 229. 'his instructions to' Bird 2006, p. 183.

**Calm before the storm**

'Once we have' HC Deb 09 April 1941 Vol 370 cc1587-605. 'can be taken. *War Log*, 30 July 1941. 'U-Boats needed the' *History (U)*, p. 10. 'after the end' *War Log*, 6 Jan 1942. 'the safe arrival' Gilbert 1983, pp. 1131-2. 'In spite of' Miller Centre website. 'the situation was' Hinsley 1993, p. 126. 'Am not able' Sebag-Montefiore 2001, p. 171. 'U-boats are the' Robertson 1958, p. 26. 'daring, skill and determination' http://www.old-merseytimes.co.uk/johnnywalker.html. 'Once submerged' Robertson 1958, pp. 26-7. 'Torpedoes passing astern' Robertson 1958, pp. 32-7. '*U-574* hung for' Robertson 1958, p. 43. 'a complete lack' Dönitz 1961, p. 38. 'the measure was' Dönitz 1961, pp. 39-40. Some remedy must' *War Log*, 8 Nov 1941. 'longer intensive training' *History (U)*, p. 13.

**The Second Happy Time**

'came five years' Bird 2006, pp. 170-1. 'created a state' https://en.wikipedia.org/wiki/German_declaration_of_war_against_the_United_States . 'strike a heavy' *History (U)*, p. 17. 'It is a' Roskill *The War At Sea II*, p. 95. 'a complete success' Dönitz 1961, p. 54. 'deeply concerned at' Churchill 1951, pp. 103-4. 'clumsy' *War Log*, 8 Feb 1942. 'perhaps the most'

# References

https://en.wikipedia.org/wiki/Ernest_King#World_War_II. 'It should be' Macintyre 1961, p. 141. 'twenty-four of our' Churchill 1951, p. 102. 'it was better' *History (U)*, p. 23. 'enjoy' Cremer 1984, p. 80. 'Find out what' Williams, 1979, p. 85. 'Well, you can' Williams 1979, p. 86.

## Dönitz triumphant

'[the Bay] has become' *War Log*, 11 June 1942. 'Outward and inward-bound' *War Log*, 21 Aug 1942. 'unfavourable air situation' *War Log*, 3 Sept 1942. 'U-boat losses are' Cremer 1984, p. 82. 'ever increasing difficulties' *War Log*, 21 Aug 1942. 'The bottleneck of' Nuremburg evidence against Dönitz: http://avalon.law.yale.edu/imt/chap16_part14.asp. 'attempts to rescue' *War Log*, 17 Sept 1942. 'Be hard. Think' Padfield 1993, p. 255. 'Even if it' Padfield 1993, p. 255. 'Operations against convoys' Dönitz 1961, pp. 71-2. 'inch-thick iron stanchions' Bailey 1998, p. 60. 'might be fatal' *History (U)*, p. 33. 'They all lacked' Werner, p. 191.

## Developments in anti-submarine warfare

'safeguard our vital' Brodhurst 2000, p. 267. 'an immediate increase' Brodhurst 2000, p. 269. 'merely an obstacle' Brodhurst 2000, pp. 269-70. 'we have lost' Brodhurst 2000, p. 271. 'The number of' Roskill *The War At Sea II*, p. 210. 'Squadron Leader Ensor' www.tracesofwar.com. 'my three day' Cremer 1984, p. 89.

## Dönitz's nemesis

'Prospects of success' *War Log*, 8 Nov 1942. 'any precautionary concentration' Dönitz 1961, p 75. 'Thank God we' Chalmers 1954, p 144. 'There was no' Haslop 2013. 'a technician who' Chalmers 1954, p. 194. 'an outstanding submarine' Dönitz 1961, p. 88. 'could see no' Chalmers 1954, p. 217. 'uncongenial' Chalmers 1954, p. 155. 'And what do' Williams 1979, p. 117. 'I will look' Chalmers 1954, p. 218. 'rise above all' Roskill *The War At Sea II*, p. 216. 'a very serious' Chalmers, p. 160. 'The only way' Chalmers 1954, p. 160. 'many examples of' Chalmers 1954, p. 162. 'the glamour of' Chalmers 1954, p. 167.

## Raeder's despair

'luck was entirely' Dönitz 1961, p. 90. 'The defeat of' Churchill 1951, p. 619. 'a needless drain' Bekker, p. 292. 'Very quietly, then' Raeder p. 372. 'especially suitable' Padfield 1993, p. 263. 'decisive impact' Bird 2006, p. 127. 'primarily to the' Bird 2006, p. 201. 'All has to' Padfield 1993, p. 267. 'defend Norway against' Dönitz 1961, p. 128. 'The tonnage war' *War Log*, 19 Dec 1942.

## Entering the critical phase

'It literally rained' http://archives.lorient.fr/comptoir-des-historiques/1939-1945 'potentially annihilating superiority' Padfield 1993, p. 265. 'For the towing' Gretton 1964, pp. 136-7.

## Can it get worse?

'the U-boat was' Kershaw 2000, p. 585. 'pretty sombre up' Chalmers 1954, p. 188.

## Horton's offensive

'chasing a hornet' Chalmers 1954, pp. 189-90. 'immediately report and' Chalmers 1954, pp. 189-90. 'The safe and' Chalmers 1954, p. 167. 'the most violent' Chalmers 1954, p. 193. 'it would confuse' Chalmers 1954, p. 186. 'far from finding' Cremer 1984, p. 133. 'Aircraft!' Werner, p. 105. 'Even our handful' Werner, p. 106. 'at maximum range' Dönitz 1961, p. 97. 'the defeat of' Chalmers 1954, p. 187. You cannot consider' Buell 2012.

**Black May**

'To undermine the' TNA FO 898/51. 'You're sailing' Cremer 1984, p. 138. 'The most important' Cremer 1984, p. 126. 'planning to form' NA FO 898/51. 'DESTROYER ATTACKED' Werner, p. 117. 'The U-Boat would' *History (U)*, p. 38. 'difficult position' *War Log*, 3 May 1943. 'We have to' Chalmers 1943, p. 199. 'enemy radar' *War Log*, 6 May 1943. 'this loss of' *War Log*, 26 Apr 1943. 'where the enemy concentration' Chalmers, 1954, p. 192. 'The scissors snapped' Cremer 1984, pp. 132 and 140. 'If there is' Brodhurst 2000, p. 275. 'After 14 boats' *War Log*, 24 May 1943. 'we are fighting' *War Log*, 24 May 1943. 'The enemy forces' Padfield 1993, p. 306. 'We'll get them' Padfield 1993, p. 310.

**Piling on the pressure**

'hard work, hard' Chalmers 1954, pp. 199-200. 'The Support Groups' Chalmers 1954, p. 200. 'Buy your experience' Chalmers 1954, pp. 206-7. 'The amazing thing' *War Log*, 18 May 1943. 'The convoy escorts' Dönitz 1961, p. 101. 'a prey to' Cremer 1984, p. 147. 'explosives fixed to' *War Log*, 5 June 1943. 'Keep together at' *War Log*, 6 June 1943. 'This incident showed' *War Log*, 14 June 1943. 'from hand to mouth' *History (U)*, p. 39. 'even for this' *History (U)*, p. 39-40.

**Dönitz fights on**

'unequal struggle' Dönitz 1961, p. 158. 'lead to [a]' *War Log*, 23 Aug 1943. 'For aircraft lookouts' *War Log*, 16 Sept 1939. 'as it is' *War Log*, 14 Aug 1943. 'The smell of' Werner, p. 172. 'His dogged toughness' *War Log*, 24 Oct 1943. 'Suddenly everything went' Cremer 1984, pp. 155-60. 'in spite of' *War Log*, 12 Dec 1943. 'When considering decorations' *War Log*, 13 Nov 1943. 'This operation was' https://www.warsailors.com/convoys. 'Even if the' Chalmers 1954, p. 211. 'A so-called rescue' Nuremburg evidence against Dönitz. 'one of the' Robertson 1958, p. 138. 'gave them no' Cremer 1984, p. 160. 'A temporary diminution' Trevor-Roper 2004, pp. 218-24. 'The fifth Christmas' *War Log*, 24 Dec 1943.

**In the shadow of D-Day**

'the growth and' HC Deb 07 March 1944 Vol 397 cc1880-957. 'we shall slash' Chalmers 1954, pp. 211-2. 'The atmosphere, which' https://weaponsandwarfare.com. 'Use as few' *War Log*, 22 July 1944. 'Every man and' Dönitz 1961, p. 171. 'ATTACK AND SINK' Werner, p. 213. 'very grave, deep' *War Log*, 22 June 1944.

**After D-Day**

'The enemy in' Hellwinkell 2014, p. 140.

**Dönitz dreams on**

'intensive operations' *History (U)*, p. 49. 'had recognized the' http://www.jewishvirtuallibrary.org/ 'total capitulation' http://www.ibiblio.org/hyperwar/

**Why the Allies won**

'like a bombshell' Bird 2006, p. 137. 'The submarine should' Churchill 1948, p. 325. 'I am entitled' HC Deb 26 Sept 1939 Vol 351 cc1239-46. 'They built faster' Cremer 1984, p. 81. 'without fuel, nobody' Overy 2013, p. 400. 'in the main' Padfield 1993,

p. 281. 'They knew their' Buell 2012. 'No one played' Roskill *The War At Sea II*, p. 376. 'to throw into' Dönitz 1961, p. 107.

**Postscript**

No citations.

# Index

Index

Casey, D A, 254

Chair, Somerset de, 53

Chamberlain, Neville, 27, 28, 29, 43, 88, 98

Channel Dash, 204–5

Chatfield, Adm of the Flt Ernle, 54

Cherwell, Lord, 234

Churchill, Winston, 38, 41, 144, 145, 163, 231, 234, 239, 264, 273, 351, 359

Appeal to Roosevelt, 104, 128

As Minister of Defence, 121

Asdic, 54, 93, 343–44

Establishes Western Tactical Unit, 200

Exposed to *U-56*, 91

Fails to support Coastal Cmd, 219, 234

First Lord of the Admiralty, 28–29, 28–29

French Navy appeal, 102

*Graf Spee* sinking, 71, 74

His war strategy, 349, 351

HMS *Courageous* sinking, 52, 53

Magnetic mines, 82, 84, 85

Merchant losses, 43–44, 61, 139, 195

Scapa Flow visit, 44

Search units, 45

Supports Atlantiksender, 275

U-boat forecast, 41

War progress, 93, 98, 171

Warns of U-boat danger, 17

Western Approaches Cmd move, 141

Clemenceau, Georges, 14

Coastal Command, 142, 144, 165, 180, 218, 220, 234, 267, 292, 324, 349, 357

Code-breaking

1941 successes, 175–76

Germans successes, 225–26

Weather ships capture 1941, 146–49

Comber, William, 66

Committee of Imperial Defence, 351

Convoys

Air support, 218–21

First departures, 41–42

*HG-53*, 143

*HG-73*, 176

*HG-76*, 179, 182, 183

*HX-1*, 41

*HX-106*, 137, 138

*HX-112*, 153

*HX-133*, 175

*HX-239*, 286–87, 294

*HX-277*, 321

*HX-300*, 329

*HX-47*, 43

*HX-72*, 114–18, 114, 118, 119

*HX-84*, 131

*JW-51B*, 242

Large convoys, 271–72

*OA-1*, 41

*OB-1*, 41

*OB-290*, 143

*OB-293*, 153

*OG-69*, 172

*OG-71*, 176

*ON-224*, 321

*ON-92*, 208–10

*ONS-154*, 237–38

*ONS-165*, 254

*ONS-18* and *ON-202* attack, 306–9

*ONS-5*, 280–81

*PQ-17*, 242, 313

*S-130*, 293–94

*SC-104*, 254

*SC-118*, 252–54, 271

*SC-122/HX-229* attack, 256–61

*SC-130*, 293, 294

*SC-26*, 171–72

*SC-42*, 176, 171–72, 187, 188

*SC-67*, 202

*SC-7*, 6, 188

*SL-118*, 224

*SL-147*, 316, 320, 321

*TM-1*, 240–41

*WS-5A*, 133

Copland, Chief Officer, 35, 37, 38

Cornelius, Professor, 61

Index

# Index

# T

# U

Index

Printed in Great Britain
by Amazon

48692700R00224